William B Whitecar

Four Years Aboard the Whaleship

Embracing cruises in the Pacific, Atlantic, Indian, and Antarctic oceans, in the years

1855, '6, '7, '8, '9

William B Whitecar

Four Years Aboard the Whaleship
Embracing cruises in the Pacific, Atlantic, Indian, and Antarctic oceans, in the years 1855, '6, '7, '8, '9

ISBN/EAN: 9783337316303

Printed in Europe, USA, Canada, Australia, Japan

Cover: Foto ©Andreas Hilbeck / pixelio.de

More available books at **www.hansebooks.com**

PHILADELPHIA:
J. B. LIPPINCOTT & CO.
LONDON: TRÜBNER & CO.
1860.

R,

Y EFFORTS

PROPER CHANNEL,

[gated by

THE AUTHOR.

(v)

PREFACE.

HAVING been one of the crew of an American whaleship, I cruised on the ocean for the four years of my life that have just elapsed. During this long period it frequently occurred to me, and excited my wonder, how little knowledge of the whaling-service in its practical features was possessed by the people ashore, excepting a small portion of those residing in cities whose maritime trade is represented almost exclusively by whaleships.

My convictions as to the utility of an exposition of one's daily experience in this service — of the good, bad, and indifferent fortune, as well as the perils of a pursuit which engages so many of our American youth — were so forcible, that

I was led, at the moment of embarking on my voyage, to keep a log-book or journal, in which, at the expiration of each nautical day, I noted the different employments of the crew, manner of sailing the vessel, incidents arising in the capturing of whales, general personal treatment, amount and quality of provisions, and the phases of the weather in different latitudes.

Thus a description of life at sea alone came within my original intention; but as I progressed, and became more interested in my self-imposed task, (which, by the way, enabled me to occupy pleasantly what would otherwise have been weary and unprofitable hours,) it seemed to me, that my journal would not be complete, unless I should also describe the seaman's bearing when ashore, at liberty, and unrestrained by discipline; and, as such a description involved adventures in various localities of the globe, I at first was unconsciously betrayed into a still farther enlargement of my task: namely, to incorporate the most striking (or, rather, those in which I was most interested) features and characteristics of the countries and people we visited.

PREFACE. ix

My object, however, was merely to complete a narrative which might be read to my relatives and friends, in the family circle, by the homestead fireside: fancying, indeed, that it would really interest and amuse those, whose knowledge of such incidents in a whaleman's cruise, both on the sea and land, was limited.

Publishing a book was not, therefore, within the object aimed at; but through the advice of many kind (possibly, too partial) friends, I have been induced to submit the manuscript to my generous and enterprising publishers, who, despite its imperfections, have determined to present it to the public.

Such being the ground upon which I have now come forward as an author, I trust that due allowance will be made for the literary imperfections of my book, when I further state, that the entire matter comprised in my journal was written at sea, on a sailor's chest, amongst seamen, by night and by day, amid storm and calm, in localities situate between the latitudes 41° 30' north and 45° south, and longitudes 71° west and

170° east—embracing a wide field for observation: and comprehends bird's eye views in Australia, New Zealand, and other British possessions in the Pacific, Atlantic, and Indian oceans, also in the Malay, Mascarenha, Azore, and Abrolhas' islands.

Throughout the recital, I have confined myself entirely to facts, without drawing on my imagination for coloring; but I have been forced, from a fear of being too voluminous in this, my first effort, to omit much that came under my observation during the voyage, which at some future period I may find time to lay before the public.

Before taking leave of the subject, I would, if it were in my power, press upon the notice of the Federal government the necessity of cherishing and encouraging this important branch of our commerce.

If good seamen are to be formed anywhere, it is in the whaling-service of this country. Here it is, on a three or four years' voyage, that a man becomes acquainted with the minutiæ of a seaman's duty; and from the great proportion of the time spent at sea in vessels cruising for whales, the crew become perfectly familiar with, and wholly at home upon, the sea.

The class of men, too, who sail from home in our whaling-vessels, being generally well-informed men, and having home-connections, understand and appreciate our free institutions; but it is too often the case that, in the absence of any special inducement to remain true to their engagement, a large proportion of the original crew desert from the vessel. To obviate this, the government should attach a bounty to the earnings of every sailor who remains in this service, in the same vessel, for three years or more; and by this means foster a class of citizens accustomed to danger and emergencies, not only in their everyday occupation of battling with the elements, but by their familiarization with peril in their conflicts with the Leviathen of the deep — citizens, who would at all times be prepared to take charge of our Navy, and defend the nation's honor and privileges against the world!

With these brief prefatory observations, I respectfully throw myself upon the generosity of the reading community, and plead my novitiate in the world of letters to secure me from too rigid a criticism.

WILLIAM B. WHITECAR, JR.

PHILADELPHIA, July 26th, 1859.

FOUR YEARS

ABOARD THE

WHALESHIP.

CHAPTER I.

IN June, 1855, having decided upon embarking on a whaling voyage, I took the steamboat from Philadelphia to Tacony, thence by railway to New York, where, after a delay of a few hours, I boarded the steamer Metropolis, and after a fine run of twelve hours, landed in Fall River; there I entered the cars, and at five o'clock of the morning of June 20, I took up my quarters in the city of New Bedford.

I immediately instituted inquiries as to the preliminaries attendant on the preparation for such a voyage. I soon acquired this information, and was consigned to the tender mercies of one of that class known by seafaring men as Land-sharks, a description of whom I shall attempt hereafter.

This person treated me with much urbanity, desiring me to leave my hotel to reside at a boarding-house of his selection, stating to me at the same time that numbers of whalemen, outward and homeward bound, were located there. My suspicions were slightly aroused regarding the accommodations of this boarding-house, by the earnestness with which he urged my locating in it; but no other inducement was requisite for me to coincide with his wishes than the one he last named; I being desirous, before going afloat, to mingle and converse with the initiated, to learn, if possible, something concerning the profession in which I was about to embark. So, without more ado, I proceeded to this domicile, which was located on South Water Street. It was kept by a widow lady, who, for the moderate sum of four dollars per week, for each, furnished just such edibles as you do not get at the Girard, in Philadelphia, or the Metropolitan, in New York. The meat was, in nine cases out of ten, salted; she wishing, in the abundance of her forethought, to render the salt junk, which she knew would form the principal article of our diet when at sea, agreeable to our palates; or, on the other hand, desiring to give us a predisposition to scurvy ere yet we were aboard ship. These motives were variously assigned by we tyros as the cause for the over-proportion of the saline in our food; as for those who had been at sea before, they appeared to relish the old lady's corned pork and beef, and if we made any remark to them in reference to its profusion, they would answer us pertinently, "You will eat worse grub than that, old fellow, before you have done with whaling;" and these prophetic words ofttimes recurred to my memory months, ay, years, afterward. Do not think, kind reader, that I was rendered fastidious by former indulgence; far from it. I had made up my mind to a change of diet, but not to so great a one; for in the four weeks that I remained in this house, we never had but one meal of fresh meat — it was fried beefsteak; and even that the cook and a supernumerary, who had been engaged to assist him, with the aid of a jug of New England rum, managed to burn to a cinder, so that we were compelled to resort to our old provender.

As soon as my companion and myself had become members of this household, we, with our assiduous friend the Shark, proceeded to the agent's, with whom he wished us to engage, and after being approved by the Captain, and having made inquiries as to the character of the vessel and her commander, we enrolled our names upon the articles of the Barque Pacific, of New Bedford, Captain John W. Sherman, bound to the South Atlantic and Indian Oceans, to cruise for sperm and right whales. The vessel was of three hundred and eighty tons burthen, capable of carrying three thousand barrels of oil, and fitted out for forty months; she was then undergoing thorough repairs, having but two months previously returned from a voyage of thirty months' duration, in which she had been very successful; and this, with several previous very remunerative voyages, had given her the name of a lucky ship, which insured her a good crew; seamen, as a class, being superstitious, are always eager to sail in a ship with which some favorable omen is, or has been, connected, auguring from such data her subsequent success.

As she would not be ready for sea for about three weeks after I had joined her, I had plenty of leisure time to look around me. The principal objects in my eyes were, of course, the wharves and shipping; and, indeed, the scene there presented was one of interest to any observer; bustle and activity was everywhere apparent; ships loading, discharging, repairing, &c., in every direction. Here one might be seen hove on her beam-ends, receiving a new copper jacket; another totally dismantled, preparatory to receiving new spars; on another the riggers were aloft at work, with their merry song; below, still another might be seen weather-beaten and shabby, her copper covered with moss and barnacles, she having returned but a few hours before from a long voyage, and the casks being hoisted from her hold contain part of her cargo of oil, gleaned, during her four years of cruising, from the monsters of the Pacific, Atlantic, Indian, Arctic, and Antarctic Oceans. Alongside this weather-worn ship, and in strong contrast with her whole appearance, lies a smart, trim-looking vessel, such a one as makes Jack Tar's heart bound to look at; her hull is perfect in model, her spars all rake jauntily aft, her yards are squared by the lifts and braces, whilst the fresh appearance of her paint gives her a coquettish look and bespeaks her ready for sea. They are now putting aboard of her the remnant of her provisions not yet stowed; and as we pass up the gangway we come in contact with a sailor's chest being conveyed aboard under the Argus eyes of its hardy owner, who forms one of her crew.

On the wharves hundreds of coopers are employed coopering oil casks. Their continual strokes of hammer upon driver, united with the heavy rolling of the oil trucks, creating a Babel-like confusion from which a stranger is glad to escape.

NEW BEDFORD. 17

Whichever way we cast an eye we see oil casks or whalebone, harpoons or lances, or some one or other of the various et ceteras belonging to the whaleman's pursuit; in fact, the yield of the whale supports New Bedford, and is the nucleus around which clusters all the manufactures of the city; and its vitality as a community must ever depend upon the number of vessels it sends out in pursuit of the whale. After gazing again and again at these objects, to me so interesting, I diverted myself by walking through the town, with no other object but to kill time—hours seeming days, and days months, that intervened between this time and the day fixed for our departure; in fact, I had become so infatuated with the idea of going to sea, that I viewed everything through a glass whose tint was blue—blue water always dancing and rippling before my mind's eye. In my perambulations through this city of whalemen I found that it was laid out with something like care—the streets, like those of Philadelphia, at right angles; many of the houses neat and well built, and, with the exception of a part of one street near the river, wear a quiet and respectable aspect. One street is an exception to the rule, it being occupied by houses of ill-fame, where many a dollar, earned by exposure to the storm on a long voyage, has been filched from the hardy mariner by the harpies who occupy its tenements; and after what I had always read and heard of the puritanical exactness of our New England brethren, I confess that I was astonished that such a sink was permitted by the citizens of the Bay State to remain in existence for the unsophisticated seaman to be entrapped by. A liquor law had been

2*   B

passed by the legislature of the State of Massachusetts, and whilst I was in New Bedford was professedly in operation — but only professedly, as numbers of houses existed wherein liquor was sold, which, from their public location, must have been known to the authorities.

At my boarding-house, arrivals were continually occurring of young men, from various parts of the Union, to embark on board whale-ships. I viewed with regret the extreme youth of many of them. There is a systematized mode of procedure carried on in our larger Atlantic and Lake cities, for the purpose of recruiting this service. Shipping agents engage young men, taking advantage of their inexperience or necessities, paint whaling and its appurtenances in vivid colors, induce them to sign their names, and then convey them to New Bedford; and when they come to review their outfit bills, they will find a charge of from ten to fourteen dollars for the agent's services. Among the arrivals at our house was one from Western Pennsylvania, who talked sailor, walked sailor, and dressed sailor, rolling when he walked so as almost to take in a pocketful of sand on each side, and wore an immense kedge anchor on his neckerchief; he was looked at by the inexperienced as a prodigy, but by old sailors with a contemptuous expression, always accompanied by the remark, "Too much salt water there." This individual was afterward the most miserable poltroon in our ship, and despite his vauntings of personal qualifications as a seaman, lashed himself with a yard arm gasket to the main topgallant rigging whilst engaged in furling the main topgallant sail. Such is generally the case—men who talk loudly of their ability ashore are apt to be inefficient at sea.

And now, after remaining until wearied out, our ship is ready to sail to-morrow. As is customary on the day before sailing, each man proceeds to his outfitter and procures his clothing; the owners usually allow to the foremast hands an advance of seventy-five dollars, for which the foremast hand gives the outfitter an order, and receives his clothing. The Shark, or outfitter, charges double the price of good, for worthless articles, which must be taken at his prices, as there is no redress. By the time the foremast hands' board-bill and pocket-money are deducted from his advance, the wardrobe he is able to procure is slender and insufficient, so that in the course of a few months he will be compelled to resort to the slop-chest, where, if the ship has been successful, he will be eagerly welcomed — the more so, as the Captain is often interested in the profits of the slop-chest; if unsuccessful, and he has a liberal Captain, his necessities will be supplied; if, on the other hand, he should be parsimonious, scowling looks will be all the relief he gets, and he will be forced to beg from his shipmates, who will not allow him to suffer, although the prudent are cautious, as in a three years' voyage every man must be careful of his effects, as they constitute his capital.

Having procured our outfits about three o'clock in the afternoon of Monday, July 23d, we went aboard, desiring to pass one night on the vessel before she sailed. Soon after we hauled out into the stream, and were towed by a steamboat down to Clarke's Point, where we let go our larboard anchor. During the afternoon others of the crew arrived, amongst them a fine-looking old tar who knew the ropes, and had a three gallon jug of New England rum stowed away in his chest, which, as soon as carried into the forecastle, he produced and passed around time after time, until all those who would imbibe were more than half seas over, making night hideous with their discordant clang. At noon the next day the Captain and others came aboard in the pilot boat. The sails were loosed, windlass manned, anchor hove up to the inspiriting chant. We are bound to the Western Ocean, and soon the old Pacific was aweigh and off to sea again, leaving the land of her flag far in the distance.

All was bustle and confusion aboard the ship, we having no less than fourteen green hands, and the few foremast hands who had before followed the sea were so overcome by the ardent that they were useless; so that the officers were obliged in almost every case to execute their own orders. We were blessed with a head wind, and were obliged to beat out of the bay, and, with the consequent hurry and excitement attendant on tacking ship, little leisure was left to us for reflection; but as the sun sank low in the horizon, and the blue hills of the land of my birth, and love, and veneration — the home of me and mine—were gradually becoming more and more indistinct—as I looked around me on the expanse of water, extending on every side, I felt alone; and then, and not till then, did I feel the momentous character of what I had undertaken; then I bethought me of the thousand little comforts of home, the many kindnesses I had received from relatives and friends, and I leaned my head on the bulwarks, and felt as if I knew what desolation and heart-sickness were for the first time. This state of affairs could not last long, so I rallied and attempted to look brave and careless; but the effort was vain, for if any person had taken the trouble to look at my lugubrious countenance, they could have seen, that under an attempted careless exterior I carried an aching breast; but all hands were too fully occupied by their personal feelings to notice me, and so it passed unremarked.

Towards evening, that most annoying and distressing of all petty maladies — viz., sea-sickness, made its appearance amongst our green hands; having experienced it before, I escaped with but little annoyance; not so with some other poor fellows, and amongst those I noticed the person I mentioned before, who claimed so intimate an acquaintance with the sea, utterly prostrated; a few hours previous he was the blithest of the party, and was singing with great zest —

> "A life on the ocean wave,
> And a home on the rolling deep."

but now, alas! he was tuneless, and almost breathless; but I imagined that had he been able to sing, the burden of his lay would have been —

> "The sea, the sea, the horrid sea."

This individual, from a circumstance which I have before alluded to, had received the appellation of Kedge Anchor, or Cage Anchor, or it was sometimes abbreviated to Cage; and as he will figure repeatedly as I proceed, I may as well at the outset give him the cognomen by which he was known during his stay aboard with us. His sickness, and ludicrous exclamations of "I wish I was on the steam-wagon again" (he had formerly been brakeman on the New York and Erie Railroad), and pathetic entreaties to be allowed to die in peace, when desired to do anything, excited the mirth of all, no sympathy being tendered to him except in one instance, when one of the seamen offered him a pint of salt water, assuring him it was a cordial; a mouthful was sufficient to undeceive him, he spat out the nauseating draught, and the queer expression he wore on his phiz, and no less queer entreaty to take the darned thing away, were so humorous as to shock his auditors into merriment, and secured him against farther molestation.

The reason that so many green hands are shipped in vessels engaged in this trade, is, that they are to be engaged for a trifling proportion of the vessel's earnings, and the great difficulty of procuring those who have before been to sea, to go before the mast a second time; no man whomsoever, if he can make any pretensions to mediocrity, being obliged a second time to go before the mast; he is always qualified for the post of boat-steerer, and can attain it without any trouble; and those who are not disgusted with their first voyage and have a particle of energy or ambition in their composition, invariably do so; and from boatsteerer gradually ascend to be captains. Whaling is, in fact, a progressive service, and although the probation comprises the best part of a man's life, yet the pinnacle of their fame is an honorable one; and as the boys who are educated in New Bedford are brought up with the idea that to be a whaling skipper is the *ne plus ultra* of all stations in life, so they consider it as the acme of all their ambitious hopes.

At dusk the captain called the ship's company aft, and addressed them to the effect, that we were all together bound on a long voyage, in all probability to last for years, and he considered it as necessary that we should at the outset fully understand each other. He then went on to say that all hands should receive a sufficient supply of such provision as was in the ship, so long as it was not wasted. He stated that none of the crew forward should be misused or imposed upon by the officers. He then told us, that if there were any rascals in the crew he should detect them; and concluded by stating that as long as we used him well, he should return the compliment, and vice versa. This was plane sailing, and all understood him. Immediately afterward the watches, chosen from the boatsteerers and crew by the chief mate and second mate, were set; the chief mate had the first choice; the second mate, who heads the captain's watch, succeeded him: at the same time the boats' crews were chosen by the officers, as before, the chief mate having the first choice, and so in succession according to rank, until the fourth mate had chosen. In many ships that carry four boats the captain heads his own; but most, like us, have a fourth mate, who supplies his place. But to return to setting the watches, which took place at seven o'clock, P. M.; the starboard, or captain's watch, headed by the second, assisted by the fourth mate, comprising half the foremast hands and two boatsteerers, had the first turn in. On being ushered into the steerage or forecastle, those who had been in the habit of having soft beds and comfortable bedding provided for them by the hands of affectionate mothers, although somewhat prepared for a difference, were surprised at their sleeping accommodations—rude boxes, or rather berths, built to the sides of the ship, about five feet long, and two and a half in width, furnished with a pair of blankets, a quilt, and a bed, which, according to the amount of attention paid to the outfit of the occupant, varied from a hair mattress in one case, to the common corn husk or straw tick. However, this was no time to soliloquize over past comforts, so all bundled in without ceremony; and in a short time, from the unusual exercise of the day, to judge from the nasal organism floating through the air, profound slumber reigned throughout the between-decks of the ship. And now, that one half the ship's company are enclosed in the embraces of Morpheus, we will glance round and take a peep at our vessel and crew. The vessel, as I before mentioned, is an old fashioned barque, built to ply as a packet between New York and Liverpool, which duty she performed with faithfulness and satisfaction to her owners; and in her palmiest days bore the reputation of being the fastest ship out of New York; but the improvements in shipbuilding necessitated her owners to dispose of an old and faithful servant, and replace her with a modern modelled craft—safer could not be. She was bought by a New Bedford merchant, who, after altering her for the purpose, put her into the whaling trade, where for years she maintained her reputation as a swift sailer, until clippers were introduced to compete with her, when, of course, she was obliged to succumb. From this port she made many successful voyages, enriching her owners and increasing her good name, until 1855, at which time she was fifty-three years old, and with the exception of being new topped and coppered, the latter at the completion of each voyage, she had undergone no repairs. Her great age attests to her staunchness and seaworthiness, and by all who had sailed in her the greatest confidence was ever expressed.

On board of her was every article for the maintenance of men whose principal resources for forty months lay in her cargo. There was, in the iron implement line, everything that is used at sea, from a needle to an anchor; clothing of all kinds and sizes; provisions, muskets, ammunition; tawdry articles to trade with the semi-civilized natives of the East India and Madagascar Isles; tin ware, soap, shoes, tobacco, and saddles for the inhabitants of Australia; also sails, rigging, spare boats, and all other necessaries to equip and enable her to sustain herself for three years. Whalers, unless some serious accident befalls, do not usually enter ports where their necessities can be supplied at other than exorbitant prices, except the last one, where they always calculate to dispose of surplus provisions, boats, and rigging: being in a hurry to get home, they make some port of note so as to be detained as short a time as possible in getting rid of them. The reason for touching at obscure places, is the great danger of losing men by desertion, which always occurs in commercial ports.

Besides all these she carried outboard four boats pendant from davits, resting on cranes; one on the starboard quarter, which gives it its name; one on the port quarter, called the larboard boat, is the chief mate's; directly forward of it, on the larboard side, are the waist and bow boats — the former headed by the second, the latter by the third mate; the starboard boat is headed by the Captain or fourth mate, as the case may be. Each boat has a crew of four men, beside the boatsteerer and officer, and carries two tubs of line, harpoons, lances, boat spade, hatchet, knives, keg with water, keg containing lantern, matches, candles, tobacco, pipes, bread, and a drug. Having now pretty closely analyzed our vessel and her cargo, we will glance over the inmates. The Captain, a large, powerful man, with a face apparently expressive of frankness and good nature. The chief mate, J. B. H., a young man of twenty-six, rather below the medium height, with an eye like a hawk, quick to think and quick to act—a first-rate officer. D. E., the second mate, a corpulent man, below the average height, with an excellent mind and noble heart. The third mate, J. D., formerly boatsteerer in this ship on her preceding voyage, and the fourth mate, C. A., both powerful, hearty fellows, energetic and pushing, putting their shoulders to the wheel on all occasions where strong hands and brave hearts are wanted; these, with the steward, inhabited the cabin or after part of the between decks of the ship. All were Massachusetts men; none of them had ever learned trades, or been employed in business ashore, but had pursued their perilous profession from boyhood up, in every ocean and in every clime, from the frozen north to the frozen south, and, hitherto, had always been successful.

The boatsteerers were four in number, two of whom had before steered boats and made voyages in that position; the remaining two had each sailed one voyage before the mast — one of them in this same good old barque, to the frozen realms of the Ice king, in the Arctic Ocean, whence the vessel returned, in the course of thirty months, with four thousand five hundred barrels of oil; these four, with the cooper, occupied the steerage, an apartment directly forward of the cabin.

The foremast hands, eighteen in number, of whom but four had ever been to sea before, were a youthful, reckless, merry set, from all over the Union. We had but two foreigners, Germans, in the ship — the cook, and one of the crew. Many of the youngsters were New Bedford boys, performing this voyage as apprentices. With the exception of the Captain and old Jack Miller, as hardy an old tar as ever stepped a ratline, and who could spin a yarn to order that would put Baron Munchausen to the blush, there was not a married man, or one who was over twenty-six years of age aboard the ship. To attempt, with the exception of the Massachusetts men, to assign a reason for any of our shipmates' choosing whaling as a profession, would be mere conjecture. Any one could see at a glance they were neither poverty-stricken nor indolent; but on examining their features, a roving unsettled expression might be detected by a close observer, on the lineaments of each — a certain love of change, so all-absorbing with most young men; nor were they on the whole ignorant, as I found by conversation — all being thoroughly conversant with the leading topics of the day, and each, like every true American, had his individual opinion of the merits of newspaper notorieties, politics, and other matters that engross the American mind; but we left them fast asleep, and as I, in the interim, have spun a long yarn, it is time to conclude, as the helmsman sings out "Eight bells." A hoarse call is now heard at the forecastle of "Starbowlines, ahoy!" and as the breeze has freshened and the vessel is gently pitching, we will step into the forecastle and criticise the appearance of our green hands. Part of them are out of their bunks indulging in the most lachrymose expressions, scarce able to dress, for fear the vessel's motion will destroy their equilibrium — and "I wish I was at home," is the general cry; some cannot muster resolution enough to get out of their berths, others have thus far succeeded, but only to resume a recumbent position on their chests, whilst a few with set teeth and praiseworthy resolution, manage to get upon deck, and grasp the rigging on the fife rail enclosing the foremast; there they stand, incapable of altering their position, hanging on with a pertinacity worthy of a better cause, staring in stupid vacancy at all around them, and when receiving an officer's order, acknowledging it by a sickly, unmeaning grin, to express their willingness, but inability to perform. Officers are required to exercise the utmost patience and forbearance in the management of such a crew; instead of an active, able ship's company, such as they have been accustomed to sail with, here they have an assortment of men, ignorant of a single rope in the ship, who are just as much acquainted with the rigging as with Greek and Hebrew, knowing as much about the cook's leg as the cook's nose, and more about the boy than the buoy, and as like as not when ordered to heave the buoy overboard to heave the boy. I have seen many laughable mistakes occur amongst our boys when first out; do not think I take a sailor's privilege and draw a long bow, as I am at the same time included with these worthies—I being, at the time of leaving home, as verdant as any of the rest. I have seen them when ordered to haul down the flying jib, grasp the spanker halyards, and spend any quantity of pulling and hauling upon it, wondering at the same time why the darned thing did not come down; their only mistake in this case was hoisting the aftermost sail in the ship instead of lowering the foremost. With our officers, as a general thing, these errors passed off good humoredly; but, as I said before, they were required to use all their forbearance to repress their anger at our lubberly mistakes; nor would it have been surprising, all things taken into consideration, had they let out at us occasionally, and I doubt much if Job, who, by the Book of books, is spoken of as the most patient man of antiquity, were he afloat with a green crew, who misunderstood all he said to them, and who in the multiplicity of their ideas would attempt to haul up the mainsail with the spanker vang, or clew down a topsail with the slab line—I say, I doubt whether even he, the said Job, would not find his stock of patience, noted as he was for that virtue, oozing out at his fingers ends, and be tempted to anathematize their lubberly eyes in a heartfelt and seamanlike manner. In a short time, however, things began to wear a totally different aspect; improvement was the order of the day — each tried to excel the other. This spirit of emulation was productive of the most beneficial results to everybody, and in a short time we had an efficient crew, perfectly competent to battle with the combined forces of Boreas and Neptune.

When three days out, we spoke the ship Monmouth, of Bath; she was a fine-looking ship, running free, with the wind on her quarter, and everything alow and aloft drawing, presenting a beautiful sight.

On the fourth day out, whilst crossing the Gulf Stream, we were struck by a squall, prevalent in that latitude. All hands were called, and as this was our first trip aloft, we ascended the rigging with fear and trembling — holding on to the shrouds as if it was our intention to squeeze all the tar out of the rigging. When on the yards we were of little use, carrying out the landlubbers' motto to the letter, of both hands for yourself and the rest for the owners. We all hung on like good fellows, and if it had depended upon us to reef the sail it would not have been done till now.

The first Sunday intervening after our departure from home, proved a bright, beautiful day, the sun rising in gorgeous splendor. After breakfast the chief mate went throughout the crew, and gave to all who were not already provided, a Bible or Testament, also tracts and religious papers. These books, I believe, were supplied by a Tract Society, in New Bedford, who customarily place the word of God aboard every ship that leaves the harbor. The books were all received with thankfulness; and I will here take occasion to state that I never heard a sailor speak irreverently of the Bible. Men aboard ship I have heard do so, but only in three instances, and in those cases they were neither sailors nor landsmen—incapable of filling a respectable position on either element; therefore their opinions were of little weight.

Directly after we got outside, the peculiarity of the great Yankee nation began to manifest itself, and divers trades and speculations were set afloat; the ship's company having been transformed into an Israelite assemblage worthy of South Street, Philadelphia, or Chatham Street, New York, bartering for and exchanging old and new clothes. Money is not a medium aboard a whale-ship, and the possessor of it usually stows it away in the corner of his chest as so much dross, of no value to him. Tobacco takes its place and is the currency; an article being valued, not at so many dollars, but at so many pounds and plugs of tobacco — thus substituting a vegetable for a metallic currency; and as most men coming to sea, whether they use the weed or not, provide themselves with a considerable quantity of it, some of the old hands accumulated quite a stock; several of them numbering their acquisitions by the hundred pounds. As they did not assign a motive for hoarding it, I wondered at the propensity, but was not enlightened until we made an Australian port, where, on account of the inferior article imported, and the high duty, making the price per pound treble of the best tobacco in the States, theirs, by smuggling it ashore, was readily disposable at a good return.

Gambling, too, soon developed itself, and after a hard day's work, or when the gale was piping through the rigging, and the waves surging and hissing in ocean's cauldron, rendering the vessel's motion unsteady, so that the participators in the game could scarce retain their seats, I have seen a half-dozen seated around a chest (or, in sailor's parlance, donkey), a pile of tobacco in the centre, shuffling a pack of dirty, greasy cards, playing bluff or all-fours, and watching the game as if their very existence depended on the winning or losing a few pounds of tobacco. By this operation the green hands were the losers, of course; those who had been to sea before working together, and always making the game profitable to themselves; therefore, those who had not strength of mind to refrain, were soon stripped of all their tobacco; and I remember, one evening, seeing a man, after losing all his stock, pull his shirt off his back and sell it for tobacco to continue the game. This being speedily dissipated, his under-shirt was disposed of in the same way. We, who did not take part in the game, stood it as long as we could, as the usual attendants to a game of chance, high words and quarrelling were rife; we finally began to complain, when the captain, to avoid disturbance, offered a pound of tobacco for every pack of cards that should be brought to-him. This had the desired effect, and we had the satisfaction of seeing the cards hove overboard and lightly floating astern. We congratulated ourselves on this amelioration of discomfort; but an inventive genius from New Jersey, becoming, as he said, oppressed with ennui, manufactured a set of dominoes from a sperm whale's jaw; another contrived dice; whilst a third made a checker-board; a fourth originated a sweat-table; and thus we were attended by this evil throughout the voyage—the only intermission being Sundays and the time occupied in capturing and taking care of whales.

When a week out from home a false alarm was raised of "There she blows! There she blows!" continued for some twenty or thirty times in succession, at intervals of about thirty seconds. The boatsteerer on the maintopgallant crosstrees, on being asked "Where away," by the captain, answered, "Two points on the lee bow, about two miles off." All hands were called, the lines put into the boats; they were then hoisted, swung and lowered, the crew following the boats down the sides of the ship, and leaping in the moment they touched the water; then shoving off and pulling in the direction of the fish. Soon the boatsteerer was ordered to stand up, then to give it to him, then to give him the other iron; and then we found that there had been no whales seen, but that the whole affair was arranged to familiarize us with boat duty, so that we might be acquainted with the rigmarole when occasion required. At first but little order or regulation was observed, each one pulling on his own hook; but after some little instruction we managed to make the boat go ahead without describing half a dozen circles before starting. As we became warm with the exercise, the old hands grew excited, and gave their short, quick orders of " Give it to him! Stern, stern all—hard! Stern, men, for your lives!" with as much enthusiasm as if a sperm whale was in reality spouting under the head of the boat. The day being fine all hands were delighted with the sport, particularly so our New Bedford boys; and after coming aboard and hoisting our boats to a merry song, no doubt more than one aspirant to the heading of a boat, went to his pillow to dream of future successes, and turn up whales in imagination by scores. Their ambition is pardonable, too, as, in the section of country in which they reside, a successful whaling skipper is looked upon as a much more important personage in the community than is a member of Congress; and I do not doubt that if the choice of the appellations Honorable and Captain were tendered to the youths of New Bedford and its vicinity, nine-tenths of them would prefer the latter; nor does he, in thus devoting himself to whaling as a profession, embrace an easy mode of gaining a livelihood. He must be no mere carpet knight, but must stand prepared to give and receive hard knocks; and combat, not only with the winds and waves (the task of ordinary sailors), but with the monarch of the seas — the great sperm whale; nor must he betray, no matter how perilous his position may hap to be during an encounter with leviathan, the slightest evidence of fear, as such a symptom would make him a butt for rude personal jokes, which would drive him, by their pointedness and sarcasm, out of the service; but he must view every position into which he is thrown, and every peril to which he may be subjected, with as much indifference as if it were of no importance to him, and he will acquire a reputation for fearlessness and coolness, which invariably, no matter what his faults may be, will gain him respect both from officers and crew; sailors, as a class, admiring reckless courage, and although they will always follow where an officer in whom they have confidence leads, the slightest suspicion of their leader's capability or courage is sufficient to damp their ardor, and cause them to act with lukewarm efforts. I do not mean to cast a stigma on the well-won reputation of seamen for courage, but from the discipline of a well-regulated ship, the seaman is taught to look up to his officers, who, in his eyes, bear all the responsibility, and thus in a measure he regulates all his motions by that of his superior, and if anything goes wrong, imputes the error to its proper source. They possess an old and familiar proverb — viz., " Obey orders if you break owners," and nine-tenths of seafaring men adopt it to the letter, and thus avoid blame.

Two weeks after leaving home we were startled at about six o'clock A. M., by the look-outs at the fore and maintopgallant cross-trees singing out, " There blows! there blows! there blows!" continuously, at intervals of about thirty seconds. After about ten minutes of vocal execution, they cried out, " There goes flukes," emphasizing with great force the second word in the sentence. This was confirmatory of the presence of sperm whales, and as their yield is by far greater in value than that obtained from any other fish, we of course were anxious to capture one or more of them. After considerable manœuvring on our part, attended by excitement and bustle, three boats were lowered away. Several hours were fruitlessly spent in pulling and sailing, when the chase was given up as hopeless, the whales going faster to windward than we could pursue them. The weather was threatening, the sea boisterous, and therefore our seats in the boat were neither pleasant nor dry; consequently, at the expiration of three and a half hours, we returned to the ship. As I stepped aboard of her I felt that I had reached home, and ever after that, as long as I belonged to her, home and the old barkey were to me synonymous terms.

Whilst in the boats I saw a whale breach or leap bodily into the air, his vast bulk appearing in bas relief, suspended for a moment in mid air — the sky above, the sea beneath — and although it was not so perfect a display of the creature's immensity and power as I often afterwards witnessed, still I was struck with the greatness of the Creator's works in this, to us, almost unknown element.

Soon after our incursion on the sperm whale territory we lowered for blackfish, but were unsuccessful. This is not our legitimate pursuit, but is always done in good weather when a ship has a green crew; and in many instances the captain makes it a point to lower for and capture them whenever the opportunity presents itself. This is a beautiful fish, from twelve to twenty-five feet in length; always seen in immense numbers herding together, as if for mutual protection; they have a jet black, smooth, and shining skin, unmarred by a wrinkle, which in the sun presents a beautiful appearance, and from it they derive their name. The shape of their head reminds me of a pug-nosed dog. Unlike the sperm whale they have both jaws furnished with teeth. A full grown fish yields from two to five barrels of oil. Their meat is palatable to my taste, although I could not recommend it to an epicure ashore; nor would I, I think, partake of it anywhere but on board ship, when long deprivation from fresh food makes anything, not saturated by salt, a luxury. It is in appearance somewhat like beef, but coarser; it is minced with pork and fried in balls about the size of the sausage exposed for sale in our markets, and in this state its advent is hailed by all aboard with great gusto.

Their oil is very little inferior to that of the sperm whale; indeed, although I have never analyzed it, and speak merely from observation, I think if the same care and attention were paid to trying out the blackfish oil as is accorded to the preparation of sperm oil, it would be found that the oil of the former possesses all the good qualities of the latter. At least the experiment is worthy a trial.

On the 12th of August, 1855, we novices saw for the first time a foreign shore. Its appearance was detected by an experienced hand long before our eyes could discern it, and when, finally, they were pointed out to us, it was with no little difficulty that we could be led to believe the two islands other than clouds. They proved to be Corvo and Flores, of the Azore group, or as they are familiarly known, the Western Islands. They belong to Portugal, which rules them with an iron hand, carrying away the flower of the youth born here to support the throne in Europe. The next day we made land, and signaled the barque Henry Taber, that left New Bedford on the same day as ourselves. We passed her and stood close in to the Island of Flores. When within about ten miles of the land, a boat containing a dozen swarthy, grinning, chattering Portuguese, boarded us, who, immediately on touching deck, made for the forecastle, and dove into the bread barge, devouring all it contained and greedily inquiring for more. This modest demand not being complied with, they offered for sale fruits, comprising apples, oranges, lemons, limes, figs, melons, grapes and tomatoes; also straw hats, milk, and aguardiente. They brought us, amongst other edibles, an anomaly known to sailors as jackass cheese; it is in round cakes, about three inches in diameter, and of the color of cheese made from cow's milk, although totally dissimilar in taste to any other cheese I have eaten. As regards its origin, whether produced from John Horse, goat, or cow's milk, I cannot aver, neither do I care; but its general good taste and appetizing qualities I can vouch for from having partaken of it. After a short time another boat appeared, bringing us eggs and fowls (and knowing a sailor's preference for potables), aguardiente and sour wine. These additions to our usual sea fare, made us an excellent meal. For all these dainties these people were willing to receive tobacco, which, on account of the monopoly of the trade in that article by the government, commands a high price. They are obliged to smuggle it ashore, but from the careless manner in which they stowed it away I should think that little surveillance is exercised towards the inhabitants by the excise officers; whilst an American or European is pretty thoroughly searched on landing, to see that he does not carry the contraband article.

At about ten A. M. the captain went ashore with a boat's crew, for the purpose of purchasing stores for the ship, excellent potatoes and onions being produced in this genial climate, and from the little intercourse these people hold with the rest of mankind, can be obtained at a mere nominal price. On nearing the shore we found the coast rocky and precipitous, covered with herbage of the richest green; a heavy surf was beating on the rocks, but we landed by the assistance of the Portuguese, who fearlessly plunged into the water and hauled our boat ashore. We found on the beach a concourse of dark and light, young and old, male and female, assembled to meet us; all shoeless, and many of them hatless; all making a noise and bounding from cliff to cliff with little less agility than the goats, of which great numbers are kept for the sake of their milk and skins. On proceeding to the town, the name of which I never could discover, not having seen an American who knew, or a Portuguese who could tell me what it was, although I have asked the question frequently, always with the same result, we found that it was built without regard to order or regularity — the buildings of stone. Many plats of ground were surrounded by immense stone walls; some of these plats are not more than sixteen feet square, but are enclosed by walls two feet thick, reminding one of the masonry in the German castles of romance. At the town we saw little to attract except the merry appearance of the female, and scowling expression of the male inhabitants; the men looking upon us, it seemed, as intruders, and desiring but little intercourse with us; the women, although barefooted and with hair unkempt, their negligent dress exposing rather more of their persons than accordant with modesty, were more than affable; every article of our apparel that was exposed to their view being made by them a price for which they were willing to prostitute themselves; and so pertinacious were they, that it was with difficulty a sheath knife was wrested from one of them by a blushing boy of our party to whom their immodest offers (having but three weeks previously left the bosom of a virtuous family of mother and sisters), sounded like sacrilege, and, as he afterwards expressed himself, absolutely appalled him. We saw little evidence of cultivation in the town; but upon inquiry were informed, as well as their broken English could enlighten us, that the produce grew higher up—in the mountains. To scale these we were not adventurous enough; so we sat down, and, after some bargaining, procured boiled eggs, fruit, bread, and sour wine, on which we made a hearty repast. I observed about the town cows, pigs, and dogs, but neither jackass nor donkey; so I do not think the aforesaid long-eared gentleman possesses the right or title to claim the paternity of the world-renowned jackass cheese; although seamen, in a spirit of vagary, have given to it the appellation of that intellectual animal.

In the afternoon we went off to the ship, got our onions and potatoes aboard, and carried with us two Portuguese boys, about seventeen years of age—one of whom goes into the forecastle to do duty as a foremast hand, the other, into the steerage as steerage boy. Great numbers of young men are carried off from these islands annually, by American whale-ships, the government demanding of each young man, born in the islands, a certain amount of military duty in Europe. To emancipate themselves from this irksome service they join whalers, as after an absence on the part of one, during which he has acquired the English language, he is exempted from military duty. Whether the government does this to encourage the development of knowledge, or that, after a tarry on his part amongst the republican Americans, they think him too liberal in sentiment to mingle with other servants of their despotic rule, I cannot say. When these people first come aboard the ship they are indifferently dressed, and invariably barefooted; when those we shipped were supplied with an outfit of sea clothes, they were greatly astonished and delighted. They are a very economical people, and by dint of washing for others, patching, at which in a short time they become adepts, and other little jobs, they soon become possessed of a large amount of clothing, which they hoard up and gloat over as a miser would his gold. They are shipped for little or nothing as regards remuneration, scarcely anything being said about a lay on either side; but the captain, if generous, will always make them a liberal allowance on the ship's arriving at New Bedford. They are generally strong and able-bodied, and make good working-hands to pull and haul, but, except in rare instances, do not rise in position above steering a boat; although there are several ships at present sailing out of New Bedford whose masters are Portuguese by birth, yet in each instance, I am informed by good authority, they were taken from the islands at a very early age, and sent to school in America between voyages. When they first come aboard they look thin and cadaverous, probably from their almost entire diet being vegetable; but in a short time, from prodigious indulgence of their appetites for flesh, they become round and sleek. Their attenuated appearance has led to the standing joke amongst sailors, that if you want a Portuguese crew, all you have to do is to run close in to one of the Western Islands, heave a hook and line overboard baited with fat pork, and in a few minutes you will catch as many as you want. To tell the Portuguese this is considered by them as a bitter affront, they always magnifying their position ashore, I do not know how many times, making everything *grand*, as they express it. To illustrate their passion for meat, I shall not go into figures as regards the consumption, as few, if any, would credit my bare assertion; but I will state that one of the boys gained sixty pounds in weight during the first five months he was with us.

If there be only one or two of this race aboard, and they are separated in different parts of the ship, and not allowed too frequently to converse with each other, they soon acquire English and become useful; but if there are half a dozen together in the forecastle, they jabber and chatter their unmusical jargon from morning until night, and will go a three years' voyage, knowing at the end of it little more English than is embraced in the technical terms of the service, which, being impressed on their memory with a kick or blow by way of injunction, they are apt to retain.

These people are, or profess to be, devoted to their padres or fathers in the church, and from my light observation of them and their peculiarities, I should be inclined to give it as my opinion that they are totally under the sway of their Jesuitical advisers; but I must about ship and resume the thread of my narrative.

Whilst lying here off and on shore we gammoned the ship E. L. Jones, of New Bedford; the barque Sea Flower, of same port, and schooner Antarctic, of Provincetown. This is an excellent whaling-ground — numbers of large and small craft are continually cruising here, and in the course of a voyage generally do well. Gammoning at sea is the term for an interchange of civilities between two or more ships, and is much in vogue amongst whalemen, who have so much time that hangs heavy on their hands, and are glad to vary the monotony by the sight of a stranger, or, if a later arrival, receiving intelligence from home. When a ship wishes to gammon another, or, as it is pronounced at sea, gam', the second syllable being dispensed with, the *lee* ship hauls aback her mainyard, or sets a signal signifying her wish, the *weather* craft squares her yards, puts her helm up, runs across the other's stern and speaks her. Then the captain of one lowers away and boards the other, the mate returns in the boat with a fresh crew, the officers resort to the cabin, the boatsteerers to the steerage, and the crew to the forecastle. As soon as breathing time is allowed to the visitors they are beset by a dozen querists, who, all at once, want to know how long they are from home, what success they have had, and the birth-place, or place of residence of each. For instance, here one steps up and inquires, "Any New Yorkers here," or "Any Philadelphia, New Bedford, or Boston chaps," whichever place to him is best known; and if, perchance, he finds a townsman, in a few minutes they are as thick as lovers, and as far advanced in friendship as an acquaintance of twenty years ashore would warrant; and ere they part chests are thrown open, with the injunction to help yourself added, and do not be backward about it either. Soon after some one calls for a song, and in a short time, after some pressing and coaxing, which is as necessary here as in more select circles, the time-worn, but sweet melodies of the sea are sung, if not with artistic correctness, with spirit — all hands joining in the chorus, till the old ship rings again. Meantime, the officers in the cabin are rehearsing old memories of whaling, telling of the largest, wickedest and quietest whales which they have borne a hand at taking; dire and wonderful are the *fish* stories that in this manner receive birth. These relations, assisted by the genial influence of the bottle and the pipe, soon while away the time, and ere one would have thought it, the signal is up for returning. The boatsteerers are killing time in much the same manner, lacking only the ardent; whilst the crew, if a merry set of fellows, have, ere this, got the fiddle or accordeon player, if one is aboard, on deck (providing that it is good weather, and the ship on an even keel), and are breaking down in the waist at a rate that would set a French dancing-master crazy; but it is all the same to them — they enjoy, and are bound to make sport of it. The signal for returning being set, books are exchanged, tobacco, pipes, and in cases of need, articles of clothing are freely presented, and the visitors go over the rail into their boats, with "God bless you. *Greasy* luck to you. Take care of yourself, my hearties," or some other equally expressive and kindly wish following them; and the two ships resume their courses in different directions to different quarters of the globe.

CHAPTER II.

The next day after leaving Flores we passed within sight of Fayal. This island presented a gorgeous appearance; the many vineyards on the sloping side of the mountains, looking to us like so many squares in a quilt of the most luxurious green, forming a patchwork of Dame Nature's handiwork, in inimitable colors. An hour after, we saw the Peak of Pico, rearing its cone-shaped pinnacle high in the clouds. At its extreme summit, I noticed an appearance resembling a chimney, into which, I was informed, steps were hewn for the convenience of those whom curiosity led to ascend or descend the acclivity.

About this time, I recollect, we had our first experience of bending on to a sleeper. It is customary in good weather (particularly whilst running down the trades, when, from the regularity of the winds, there is scarce any working ship to be done) for the members of the watch, with the exception of the man at the wheel and another on the look-out, to come on deck, provided with two or three coats, for the purpose of indulging in a caulk or sleep on deck. As soon as the watch is all out, and the officer has had a look to assure himself of the fact, a soft plank in the deck is selected on which one spreads himself, covering up snug with the coats; an example religiously followed by the others. Soon they are as soundly asleep as if in a comfortable bed at home, unmindful of the noise made by the creaking of the yards and rigging, or the hissing of the sea. This practice is winked at by the officer of the deck, so long as all are at hand on a call; but on the night to which I now have reference, all the comfortable places under the lee of the weather rail being occupied, the unlucky wight whose dilatoriness in turning out when the watch was called, had excluded him from forming one of the caulkers, attracted by the inviting appearance of the forecastle, and thinking himself unnoticed, slipped down, deposited himself on the chests, and was soon fast asleep. The man on the look-out having seen him descend the ladder, waited in vain for his exit, and after allowing him sufficient time to get into a deep slumber, went down, assured himself of the fact, and then woke up two or three of the sleepers who were noted for their indulgence in practical jokes, and who at any time would forego a good nap to enjoy a hearty laugh. Having informed them of his intentions, the mischievous trio lashed a tail-block to a barricade of spars over the forecastle, rove a spare piece of rope through it, and attached one end to the sleeper's leg. When all was in readiness they awoke the remainder of the watch, and having manned the fall strong, with a long pull, a strong pull, and a pull altogether, the poor fellow was jerked half way up the companion-way before he was fully awake. Discovering his position, he grasped the ladder to retard his ascent, and, like the Knight of Snowdon, bade them —

"Come one, come all, this rock shall fly
From its firm base as soon as I."

For a minute the jokers were non-plussed; their victim having the laugh on his side; but this was soon remedied by the fastenings of the ladder giving away, and the pendant caulker was whipped up on deck amid the jeers of his companions. This remedy is generally effectual; but I have seen a case of persistency in this, to a seaman, odious habit, which after everything else had failed, was eradicated by tying the caulker's leg fast to a large pig, which, upon being roused up by the tormentors, travelled fore and aft the deck with Kedge Anchor in tow. Previous to this he had been repeatedly soused with water, bent on to, made fast to the bell, getting a reprimand for the *peal* he unwittingly rang, and lashed to the studding-sails on the forecastle, where, at times, he would remain the greater part of the night; but all to no purpose, until a humorous genius one night, when nothing else was on the carpet, proposed uniting Kedge to the porker, and, as I before stated, the remedy was effectual.

Our cook, a German, who had been to sea before, having an eye to creature comforts, purchased, whilst at Flores, a number of jackass cheeses. These he had carefully saved, intending to make them last as long as he possibly could, and for this purpose he locked them up in his chest; but, unfortunately, during the night some person or persons went clandestinely to his chest and feloniously appropriated the cheeses therein to his or their benefit. The cook, on the whole, was a good-natured fellow, but losing his cheeses soured his disposition, and he swore vengeance. His Dutch oaths soon attracted attention, and old Jack, as the oldest man in the forecastle, was appointed inquisitor, to find out the perpetrator or perpetrators of the heinous crime; sailors viewing theft from a shipmate, even of the slightest article, as an offence second in enormity only to murder; and woe betide the poor wretch who is detected in the act, as he can never recover an intimate footing with his shipmates.

I said that old Jack was appointed inquisitor. He went about his task very methodically. Taking a number of matches, he handed one to each of the denizens of the forecastle, stating that he would call on them to return them in half an hour, and that the one who should then have possession of the longest one would be considered the culprit. On calling the matches in, one was found to have been broken off by its recipient, and information was immediately given to the captain by old Jack, who had satisfied himself regarding the guilty party. The boy was questioned, but denied the point so strenuously that we did not know whether to think him guilty or not. The captain let it pass without further remark, and some twelve months afterwards we discovered the offender; then the boy who had previously been suspected, acknowledged that he had broken off his match so that there should be no question about his having the longest one; and in his endeavors to ward off suspicion, took the readiest means of arousing it — old Jack saying that his conscious guilt caused him to break his match.

When our North latitude had been almost run out we were struck by a very heavy squall. By working smart we managed to get all snug without being damaged. On the succeeding morning we saw three merchant vessels, one of whom had lost her maintopmast; a second, her foretopgallant mast; and the third a whole suite of sails. A fourth vessel, that we saw to windward in distress, with several vessels around her, appeared from her heavy rolling to be water-logged. During the night she fired rockets and blue-lights. All these vessels, as we ascertained, had met these casualties in the squall that we experienced. It is customary with merchant vessels to hang on to their canvass until the very last minute, and, as in nine cases out of ten these ships go shorthanded, the consequence is, that when a heavy squall breaks upon them, something must go before they get their sails stowed. If asked their reason for crowding sail in such a manner, they will answer you with a shrug of the shoulders, that "Time is money;" but it is not so with a whaleship, except when homeward bound—then everything that a ship will drag or carry is packed on to her to make her keep pace with the impatient spirits aboard. When on the whaling-ground, however, the ship is allowed to glide along under easy sail, royal yards, studding-sail booms, and, if in boisterous latitudes, the foretopgallant mast is sent down, and the flying jib-boom is sent in, so that if bad weather comes on suddenly, the little canvass spread makes her easy to handle. Another advantage the whaler possesses, she has thirty-four or five men to handle a vessel of three or four hundred tons, whereas a merchant ship of the same size would not have more than a dozen; hence the great proportionate disparity between the accidents to whalemen and merchantmen. The whaler is better manned, and is not drove under by a press of sail, whilst the latter is groaning under her burden from the time she leaves dock until the time she returns to it; providing there is breeze enough to keep her going.

From this time until we reached the Cape of Good Hope, little of interest transpired. Occasionally we were called to look over the rail and see the fin-back whale sending his spout in a spiral column towards the clouds; or the blackfish, grampus, or porpoise, gambolling amongst the great waves. At times the scene was diversified by the appearance of the shark, dolphin, benita, and flying-fish, each preying on the other. The last three mentioned are easily caught, and are eagerly angled for by seamen. The manner of catching the dolphin and skip-jack is to bait the hook with a piece of white rag, and allow it to sway with the vessel's motion. The fish thinks it a flying-fish taking its flight, rushes towards it and gulps it down. I had often heard stories of the dolphin's extraordinary change of color when dying, but must confess myself so unromantic as to say, I think there is so little change in his colors that none but the most acute observer could detect it. His beauty is confined to the period when sporting in his native element; then his motions are full of grace and vigor; but caught and landed on deck, he is a flat fish with a round head, and great, goggle, staring eyes. His flesh, however, is indifferent eating, as is that of the benita. The latter, when caught, goes into spasms, shaking like a man with an ague fit, sometimes disjointing the vertebra in its throes. They are at times so violent, that if the fish is large a man cannot hold one.

The flying-fish, the last that I mentioned, has been

so often described, that I shall not attempt it. It is preyed upon both by larger fish and by the birds. I have seen the tropic birds and dolphin acting so nearly in concert, as almost to convince one that they understood each other's mode of operation. The dolphin would chase the little creatures until they would take to their wings, when the tropic bird, or garnet (which is a beautiful white bird, about the size of our common pigeon, with red legs and bill, and a tail resembling a marling-spike, by which name they usually go amongst sailors), would pounce upon them; and, tired with their ærial flight, they would again resort to the water, only to become a prey to their finny enemy.

With the usual variations of weather we wended our course through the South Atlantic—at one time becalmed, at another struggling with a heavy gale, until we arrived in the vicinity of the Islands of Tristan D'Acunha, when one morning we were startled by our mastheadsman shouting, "There blows! and a forked spout, *sir.*" This informed us of the presence of right whales; their spout, unlike that of other whales, being forked. Our boats were lowered; but we had no sooner got in their neighborhood than they peaked their flukes and went to windward, eyes out—which means as fast as the wind. It was useless to follow them, and we returned aboard with fishermen's luck—a wet skin, and hungry stomach.

When down in the boats at this time I had a *near* view of a whale. We were not more than a boat's length from a large one, when he sounded, and, as he threw his tail in the air, I had an excellent sight of his small and flukes. What I felt I cannot describe; but the shining skin covering all, and the manifestation of power and bulk, in every movement, made me think of some vast piece of iron machinery; and I cannot imagine a more effective battering ram than a whale's flukes employed by himself.

In these latitudes we saw numbers of varied specimens of the ornithological family. The albatross, monimoke, old horse, noddy, cape pigeon, garnet, mutton bird, and Mother Carey's chicken or petrel, all existing here in great numbers. The albatross I have seen measure fifteen feet from the extremity of one wing to the tip of the other. It is a beautiful bird, and comes around a ship in great numbers when a whale is alongside. They are ever on the alert for something to eat, appear at all times hungry, and their voraciousness makes them an easy prey. They are often caught. Their quills are not fit for pens, but are used by sailors to splice their pipes; their feathers are used in making beds and pillows; their feet are skinned and made into tobacco-pouches; whilst the head and bill are cleaned and taken home as a curiosity. As a general thing they are not eaten; but our cook at one time agreed to cook them, if we would catch and dress them. They were soon ready for him; and after being cooked they were very palatable, although they had an oily flavor, somewhat resembling that of the canvas-back duck. The mess having succeeded so well, it became a favorite, but was indulged in so often that it soon fell into distaste, and the practice was not again revived; the more so, as the captain had a peculiar regard for the birds, and professed to place implicit confidence in the assertion, that if they were misused by a ship's crew, those who maltreated them would assuredly meet with some evil fortune.

The Cape pigeon is a beautiful bird, about the same size as our domestic bird of the same name. They are uniform in color, alternate stripes of black and white coursing their plumage.

The monimoke, and old horse, resemble in appearance the albatross, but are not more than half its size. At times, from the similarity of their appearance, I have been led to suppose them their young; and as regards the monimoke, I am still at a loss to determine as to whether the goney has a claim to its paternity or not: but the old horse or stinker, by both of which names it is indiscriminately known, is a totally distinct species; and when handled, it emits a most offensive odor, which clings with tenacity to its feathers long after being separated from the bird.

The diver is about the size of the pigeon, and is only remarkable for the great depth to which it descends in search of food. The spectator may be watching the bird gracefully sailing on the surface of the water, when suddenly it disappears from view, and if the water be clear, he may be seen, with his pinions spread, pursuing his course through it with as much facility as if he were in the air, for fathoms below the surface. After a short time he gradually ascends, until, emerging from the water, he takes wing and skims through the air, unwearied by his immersion.

The petrel, or Mother Carey's chicken, is a pretty

bird, smaller than the swallow, and quick as lightning in its movements; although so small, it is found in company with the larger birds unmolested.

At sea not only do we see marine birds, but often, when near any point or headland, we are visited by land birds, who, blown off from the land, pursue their bewildered flight until exhausted, or, meeting a vessel, they alight upon it to refresh their wearied forms. At first they fly around and around the ship, as if fearful of molestation, when, overcome by fatigue, they forget their natural dread of mankind, and alight in the boats, or on deck, unable to move farther. Their wants are supplied by the sailors, and fresh water, of which they appear most in need, given them. After a stoppage of twelve or twenty-four hours they renew their flight, always in the direction of land.

After doubling the Cape of Good Hope, which we effected without experiencing extraordinarily heavy weather, we spent several weeks in beating up towards Port Dauphin, in the Island of Madagascar, off which is a noted locality for the sperm whale fishery. Finding that we made but little headway, we kept away for the off-shore, St. Paul's ground, and after a fine run found ourselves among the right whales. Here we saw several vessels — the Pioneer and Catharine, of New Bedford, and the Monmouth, of Cold Springs. These vessels had been absent from the United States twelve months each, and had aboard from one hundred to five hundred barrels of oil. The Monmouth reported having lost a boat and a boat's crew, a few weeks previous, at the Island of St. Paul's. The boat was headed by her second mate, who had remained fast to a whale until drawn into the breakers, which left not a vestige of the boat or crew in their pitiless destruction.

On this ground, after numerous lowerings away and coming aboard — after seeing whales almost daily, although we found it impossible to get within gun-shot of them, they appearing shy and not at home — one Sunday afternoon the mate and fourth mate lowered away, the other boats being retained aboard the ship. No sooner were we down than, encouraged by the regular movements of the fish, we were convinced we should make a capture, and therefore the chase was conducted with an eagerness not displayed in our former lowerings away. No sooner had we touched the water in the larboard boat, than the mate, after glancing at the spout, gave us orders to shove the boat clear of the ship; then "Out with your oars, my hearties;" and to make us the more eager, he offered us a dollar apiece should we make a capture. As we neared the whale, sinking his voice to a whisper, he urged us to greater exertions, by continually speaking of the whale. "There she lays, my boys; an old soaker, with a back as broad as the deck of our ship. Pull, lads, pull with a will! Give way! every man, fore and aft. Do pull! The boat scarcely moves. Now one more try. She is only two seas off. What do you say now. Put the boat right on top of her. Pull hard, do pull!" Now we draw nearer and nearer, and his enthusiasm is at a boiling heat for fear that we will yet lose the whale; and determined to give vent to his excitement, he offers all his clothes, all his tobacco, and all his money, if we will only get the boat alongside the fish, which by this time is done. Just as the mate heaves his hat over in despair, the boat glides against the monster's unwieldy carcass at a portion of his body which secures us from the sweep of his immense flukes, and the boatsteerer springs to his feet, and, with nervous arm, drives his harpoon to the socket in the yielding blubber. The mate now loses his excited manner, and, throwing the boat from the whale to escape the mighty effort he makes for our destruction, again becomes the cool and steady whaleman; but our work is not yet done. No sooner is the fish struck, than off he goes, like a charger with the bit in his teeth, perfectly unmanageable, and for an hour we dash through the water at locomotive speed, until the whale exhausts himself with the violence of the effort. Now comes the order to haul line, and the boat is gradually drawn into the whale's neighborhood, when a bomb lance is discharged, and, fortunately, is lodged on the line of the vertebra, disabling his whaleship from farther flight. They were cognizant of our operations aboard the ship, where the mastheadsman sung out, "There he gives it to him," the moment we fastened; and immediately after, "The larboard boat's fast." The two boats on the cranes were lowered away, manned, and pulled for the scene of action. They arrived in about fifteen minutes after the whale was struck. The waist boat was the second fast. The fish was bleeding at every pore, handlances having been darted into him. He attempted to descend, but his debility from loss of blood prevented him going but a few feet below the surface; he lay and rolled, opening wide his huge jaws, displaying his flabby tongue, lashing the water with his gigantic flukes, and bellowing like a whole bevy of mad bulls, from the intense pain he suffered in dying. The other boats, on coming up, fastened, and soon the bloody discharge from his spout holes became thicker, until it had obtained the consistency of tar, when the suffering brute, moderating its bellowing to gasps and sobs, slowly described a circle, throwing its head toward the sun, and after a brief but terrific struggle, rolled fin out, without life or motion. We then cut a hole through the flukes and towed him in triumph to the ship.

I will now, before going farther, describe the demeanor of a boat's crew when fast to a whale. In the first place the officer goes close enough to the whale to give the boatsteerer a good opportunity to strike him. As soon as the irons leave his hand the head of the boat is thrown from the whale, to avoid the sweep of his tremendous tail, which he invariably exercises the moment he is struck. The officer and boatsteerer now exchange positions, the boatsteerer assuming the management of the boat, whilst the officer takes his position in the bows, and, by the assistance of the bow oarsman, clears away a lance, preparatory to striking the fatal blow. The whale, on being struck, either sounds, or rushes with great rapidity over the surface of the water. In either case the line runs out with marvellous rapidity, and water is continually poured upon it to prevent the wood from igniting by friction. Shortly afterwards, if the whale has moderated his speed, the line is manned by all the crew of the boat, with the exception of the boatsteerer and after-oarsman, who are busily occupied coiling it away in the stern sheets of the boat, so as to prevent its entangling, if again run out by the whale, and the boat is hauled close to him, so as to give the officer an opportunity to lance and despatch him. If he shows a good chance, this is the work of but a few minutes, and the monster is turned up with little or no trouble; but it often happens that hours intervene, before you have an opportunity to kill the whale, and oftentimes are obliged to cut, from the near approach of nightfall. But to return to our whale. We got him alongside, and made him fast by a strong chain, encircling his flukes, passed through the hawse-hole, and secured to the bitts on the forecastle; then a hole was cut close to the whale's eye, the tackles attached, the cutting fall taken to the windlass, and with a merry song we bowsed his jacket in, stripping the blubber from the carcass, and allowing the latter, with the flukes, to go adrift. Next the head was hove in and lashed on the quarter-deck, then several men with axes split the bone from the jaw, to which it was attached by an adhesive substance known as the gum; it was then scraped, in preparation for the home market, and, after scraping, stowed away in the hold, where no moisture could reach it. The appearance of this bone in the jaw, before separation, is beautiful; its regular arrangement, and long, fringe-like edging, giving it the appearance of an artificial grotto. After disposing of the head and heaving in all the blubber, this, as fast as stripped, is deposited between decks in the main hold — which apartment is designated as the "blubber-room." The try works being started, two men go into the blubber-room, and, with sharp spades and knives, cut off the lean from the blubber, and divide the fat into pieces about six inches wide by eighteen in length, suitable for the mincing-machine. They then, with pikes, pitch it into a tub placed on deck for its reception, whence it is carried to the machine, where it is minced into pieces half an inch in thickness, and consigned to the pot. After all the oil is separated from it, the scraps are taken from the pot and the oil poured into a copper cooler, whence it runs into a cool try pot, and thence is bailed into casks, which are rolled on to the quarter-deck, where it is allowed to cool preparatory to stowing below in the hold. Meantime the pots are again filled up, and the scraps from the preceding pot are used in heating the works — these scraps forming an excellent and remarkably economical fuel; for if the whale did not furnish material for rendering its own oil, the fuel which would have to be substituted would be a costly item. From the embers, united with fresh water, an excellent lye is made, which is useful in extracting grease from clothes, washing the paint work and so forth. The oil is usually allowed to stand for twenty-four hours before stowing below, and when ready a trap is removed, which is cut through the deck, a tub lashed under it between decks, and a hose with a cock attached; a cask is now rolled on to this trap, the bung extracted, a vent pipe introduced, and soon the whole produce of the fish is in the hold, never to be removed, except in case of leakage, during the remainder of the voyage. This whale made us ninety barrels of oil. After capturing him, we remained on this ground for several weeks, without farther success in increasing our cargo; in two instances the boatsteerer missing whales, and in a third striking one with the irons, causing him to spout blood; but most of the chief mate's line being run out, he bent to his that belonging to the bow boat. On its passage from the tub, it brought with it a formidable array of harpoons and lances, with which it had become entangled. "Foul line," was sung out, the line severed, and the whale allowed to go adrift. We saw him for some time afterward, and bending to our oars, we pulled to windward with a will, in pursuit of him, but to no purpose. Whilst chasing him to windward, the bomb-lance gun, in the mate's boat, went off without leave, and pierced a hole through the head of the boat, so disabling her, that she had to return aboard; as we all did at noon. Afterward the whale came close to the ship, and, peaking his flukes, gave us a view of our line, wound in a thousand contortions around his small and tail. We again lowered for him, but without success.

On the 12th of November, a merchant barque ran across our stern, which, on speaking, we discovered to be the Eliza Carrew, of Boston. So far, all was very well; but on crossing our stern, she luffed up under our lee, and, our sails taking the wind from hers, she became unmanageable. The next moment she was aboard of us, crushing the lee boats to pieces, carrying away cranes and davits, snapping off the spanker-boom, and carrying away the entire larboard mizzen rigging. After a short interval she got clear from us, when we found that she had not escaped scot free. We saw that her maintopsail yard was snapped off outside the head ear-ring, her foreyard carried away in the slings, and about twenty feet of her bow rail, on the starboard side, stoven to atoms. After the two vessels had swung clear from each other, the third mate and his boatsteerer jumped into the bow boat, which had broken down and lay floating alongside, for the purpose of saving the craft. Almost as soon as they got into her, she became detached from the ship, drifted astern, and capsized; so that we were obliged to lower away our only whole boat, that on the starboard quarter, to rescue the two adventurers, who were taking it very coolly, seated on the bottom of the wreck. In a short time we had them aboard the ship; but in the operation, the bow of the starboard boat came in contact with the stoven one, and had a hole knocked into it. So here we were on a whaling-ground, in the height of the season, with plenty of whales around us, without a single whole boat on the cranes; and were it not that we had spare boats, the damage would have been irreparable; as on this side the Good Hope, whale-boats cannot be procured at any port nearer than Hobartown, and this, involving a long run, loss of time, and port expenses, to compass it, would have caused a total forfeiture of the whole season's work. The broken boat was hoisted aboard, and then the Carrew ran close to and spoke us, asking if all was right with our vessel and men. Our captain answered quickly and curtly, and in an undertone desired him to take his departure, for, should he repeat his manœuver, he would give him occasion to regret it. During the whole of this time, and for weeks subsequent to the accident, we were under the impression, as she had shown no colors, that she was a Johnny Crapeau, and sailed under the tri-color; but we learned afterward that she was a Boston ship. Different reasons were assigned by different individuals as to the cause of the unseamanlike conduct in managing the Carrew; some stating that they distinctly heard her captain ask ours for a porpoise iron, and supposed that he came close to us in order to have it handed aboard without the bother of lowering a boat; whilst others, less charitable, stated that she was loaded with liquor from the Mauritius: that the captain had broken bulk, and imbibed so much that it had set his wits wool-gathering. As to the first reason assigned, having heard nothing regarding the iron, I can give no opinion; as to the second, not having data sufficient to draw so sweeping a charge from, I will not advance so gross an accusation, but allow the matter to rest: the public, of course, having heard from the master of the Carrew his version of the matter, as we saw by the papers that he had reported the collision on his arriving at port. On the whole, both vessels were extremely fortunate in escaping with so little injury; as two vessels seldom come into contact, even in port, where they are in smooth water, without the result being much more disastrous than in our case.

It is said that misfortunes seldom come singly; and, indeed, in the experience of a lifetime, circumstances seem to justify the correctness of the adage. So it was in our case. A short time previous to our last misfortune, the larboard watch was sent aloft to double reef the foretopsail. It was about half an hour after eight bells, in the first watch at night—the watch below had turned in, but were not as yet sleeping— when, directly after the watch had manned the foretopsail yard, the men in the forecastle were startled by the fall of a heavy body on deck, directly over their heads. A rush was made for the ladder, and on getting on deck, a youngster, who belonged to New Bedford, was found prostrate, without sense or motion. By the orders of the first officer, who thought him dead, he was immediately carried into the cabin. The watch on the yard were instructed to lay down from aloft. On carrying the sufferer into the cabin, it was found that his heart beat; he was bled, and in the course of a few hours he regained consciousness, and continued gradually to mend, until, after the lapse of a few weeks, he was perfectly recovered, without, apparently, any serious effect from his fall, except the increase of an already craving appetite, and corresponding augmentation in length and breadth of person. His fall may be attributed to a superabundance of heavy clothing, beside a coarse, heavy pair of boots, united making him clumsy and unwieldy aloft. Although, from his account, it would appear that, at the time of the accident, he was very nearly, or quite, asleep, as he retained no remembrance of their having occasion to reef the topsail, and no recollection of having been on the yard, or any other circumstance connected with his fall, the only reason that we can assign for the slight injuries he sustained, is the supposition that in his descent his fall was broken by his striking against the foretop, the mainstay, and a barricade of spars that were lashed forward. I think you will agree with me that he required some easing down, when I state that he fell from the weather yard-arm, close by the bunt, at least forty-five feet from deck. A few weeks after this we had another specimen of lofty tumbling whilst we were gammoning with the barque Pioneer, of New Bedford. The watch had gone aloft to furl the foretopsail, and had so far progressed as to be ready to pass the yard-arm gaskets. Jose, a Portuguese, was at the end of the starboard yard-arm coiling the outside gasket, preparatory to encircling the sail with it, when his feet slipped from the horse; keeping firm hold of the gasket, which reached about half way to the water, he slid to its extreme end. The weather was light, and the ship pretty steady. He remained suspended for a moment, when, watching for the weather roll, he let go, descended into the water, rose, and struck out like a good fellow. The second mate ran on to the house, caught up a boat's fall, made a bowling in the end of it, and hove it to him; he slipped it over his head and under his arms, and was soon hauled aboard, without other damage than a good wetting, of which he made very little account.

Having recorded several instances of a serious character, I shall take occasion to speak of the numerous practical jokes that are enacted aboard ship. The monotony of the life at sea renders a hearty laugh somewhat of a relief, and assists in passing away the time; and this end is desirable on the whaling-ground on account of the many hours of inactivity. At night, in the vicinity of a place of known resort for the fish, sail is shortened, and all hands, except one boat's crew and its boatsteerer, go below; the officers remaining all day on deck, and standing no watch at night. In a four-boat ship, the night is divided into four watches. The night watch, therefore, is so short as to be anything but onerous; hence the early part of the night is devoted to singing, yarning, &c. But I set out with the intention of telling a joke, and as I have digressed a little I hope the reader will pardon me. One fine Sunday morning Kedge Anchor expressed a desire to have his hair cut. Here was an opening—and a conspiracy was immediately formed against his cranial adornment. One went to work and cut his hair. When finished, a dozen voices exclaimed against the barbarian who had put so *outre* a cut on his poor head; others recommended a little more off behind. The victim acquiesced, and submitted to the operation. A second, third, fourth, and fifth, lent their aid in denuding his skull, and by the time the last had finished he was a picture for a painter. The poor fellow had not a hair on his head more than a quarter of an inch in length, and, as his forehead was receding, his appearance can be better imagined than described. Suffice it to say, that for weeks after the shearing his appearance was greeted with hearty laughter; and, as with him laughter was contagious, he always joined in the shout. For a long time he did not discover that he was the butt, but when he did discover his loss he was rather pleased than otherwise at the singularity of his appearance. This is but one of the many tricks of this kind that I have witnessed. I remember seeing a green hand sent to tell the steward to overhaul the captain's chronometer box for a swab to clean up the forecastle. Another sent to the masthead to ask the man stationed there the time of day, or to see if the sun had risen. Another to the officer of the deck to advise him to secure the barometer, or to tell him that the masts were working. And I remember one poor fellow, who prided himself much on his agility, giving us a specimen of the movements of the kangaroo, sweating and exerting himself for a whole afternoon, delighting us, as he supposed, with his farcical antics, until he discovered on his back a large paper figure in imitation of himself. He said not a word at the time, and sat down totally abashed; but ere long a paper Punch figured on the back of the supposed instigator.

CHAPTER III.

FINDING but little could be done amongst the whales on this ground, early in December we resumed sea watches, and steered a course for the coast of New Holland, intending to cruise off its south-westernmost point for sperm whales. On the fifth of the same month, whilst pursuing our course to the eastward, we sighted the Island of Amsterdam, in 40° South latitude, 77° East longitude. At daylight the ensuing morning, we lowered away three boats, each member of their respective crews provided with fishing-tackle, for the capture of much smaller members of the finny tribe than our usual game. Before arriving at the island, we saw, and gave chase to an otter, but he eluded our pursuit. This was the first animal of the kind I had ever seen; it absorbed my attention, whilst in sight, to the exclusion of all other novelties. His face, in expression, reminded me of that of a pug dog, in which opinion all my companions united. I also saw here the first of those peculiarities, viz. penguins, or waugans, as they are called by seamen — their hoarse cry and long immersion in water excited my wonder and attention. Here also were the osprey, sea hen, albatross, monimoke, right and sperm whale birds, and numerous minor specimens of the family, flying in and out of their eyries in the cliff, carrying food to their young, and occasionally disputing for the possession of the finny prey, which they capture with much dexterity. Sometimes they wheeled in circles around our boat, apparently viewing us as intruders on their domain.

On approaching the island, we found it a rock-bound precipice, almost inaccessible, with a scanty vegetation dispersed over its summit. It has a desolate appearance, is uninhabited, and only visited by whalemen and those unfortunates whom Neptune, in his furious mood, casts upon its desolate shore. On the cliffs a few goats were to be seen, set ashore some time since by the humane captain of a whaler, who opined that they would increase, and afford sustenance to any shipwrecked mariners who might be cast away here.

We went close to the rocks, over which huge breakers gambolled, and made our boats fast to the kelp. Then out lines, and on the instant were busily engaged in hauling in noble fish, varying in weight from five to twenty pounds, of all varieties and colors: cod, trumpeter, and many species unknown to us, white, black, blue, yellow, and red. In the course of a few hours we had secured as many as we wanted; the other boats experiencing like success, the fish biting with the greatest avidity; it only being necessary to bait, heave the line overboard, and haul up, and, ten chances to one, before it reached the surface, a fish was attached to it. On an eminence on the island, a royal mast is erected, it having been the signal pole of the crew of the whale-ship Tuscany, of Sag Harbor, which went ashore on this island.

It appears that the English ship Meridian, returning from Australia, was cast away here. The principal part of the passengers and crew reached the island, and scaled the cliff; here they remained for several days, existing on a wild cabbage that is indigenous to the island. They were much depressed, until one morning they descried a ship beating up for the island. She proved to be the whaling barque Monmouth, of Cold Springs; her captain, all honor to him, and no less to his faithful messenger, sent one of his crew across the island to communicate with the distressed ones. He directed them to cross the island, as at the side they then were it would be impossible to land a boat. This, although comparatively a short distance, they were all one day and part of the next accomplishing — the rugged, steep way, their enfeebled condition, and the presence of ladies and children, delaying them. The Monmouth's boats, as soon as possible, conveyed them aboard their vessel, where they received every attention their condition required, and were conveyed to the Mauritius, where they were disembarked. Now for the romantic part of the story. It appears that in the general confusion, several bags of English sovereigns, that were carried from the wrecked ship ashore, were deposited, as it was supposed, in a secure place, and left on the island. This was communicated to the captain of the Tuscany, and, as the report goes, he had run close in with his ship, landed, and found the money; but at the moment of his grasping it, he discovered his ship in a perilous position. The second officer, who was left in charge, from incapacity or ignorance, had run her ashore. Circumstances occurred, during his stay on the island, that rendered it impossible to bring away the gold, the existence of which, whether chimerical or otherwise, is still a favorite theme amongst the whalemen who frequent this latitude; and in January, 1856, a whale-ship that then lay at the Vasse, had engaged one of the Tuscany's former crew, and anticipated having a search for it.

Our second mate went ashore, near the spot where the Tuscany was stranded, captured a right whale bird, and procured a number of eggs. On examining the bird, we found that the substance composing its jaws exactly resembled right whalebone, and its tongue was precisely similar in shape to that of the right whale. These peculiarities I had often heard attributed to the bird, but considered them fabulous, as did most of our ship's company; although many of them had been engaged in whaling for years, but never previously had an opportunity of making an examination. Having procured as many fish as we could take care of for the nonce, at eleven o'clock we returned to the barque and commenced cleaning and salting them. In the afternoon we sent another boat in, and when all were taken care of we found that we had seven barrels, and visions of good fare rose before us; but alas, for the uncertainty of human expectations — three months afterward the whole of them spoiled, and we were forced to consign them to Davy Jones' locker.

The next morning after our fishing excursion we saw right whales and the Island of St. Paul's. The whales we lowered away for and chased, without success. The Island of St. Paul's lies in the same longitude as Amsterdam, but is a degree farther north. Like Amsterdam, it is barren, but is occupied by a French company, whose agents reside here for the purpose of fishing. They cure their catchings, and at periodical seasons a vessel visits them, bringing them supplies and carrying away their accumulations of fish. From the quantity and quality of their prey in the vicinity, I should think the business must be lucrative, and, indeed, it ought to be, to compensate for the isolation men must feel in this out of the way spot. This island being only sixty miles distant from Amsterdam, is easily distinguished on a clear day.

Nothing occurred from this time until Christmas day, when, of course, we who were brought up to the southward of the New England States, expected some observance of the time-honored customs of the day; but what was our surprise to see the work going on as usual; no difference being made, except breaking out a cheese, and distributing it amongst the crew, fore and aft. This humble fare, being so long deprived of, we hailed with acclamation, and partook of with avidity. This method of observing Christmas was persisted in during the voyage; on one, however, nothing either in the fare, or relaxation of discipline, served to mark the anniversary; on another we were agreeably surprised by the steward's making mince pies for the whole ship's company. New England men pay very little heed to the coming of Christmas day, they having been accustomed from childhood to regard Thanksgiving as a much more important holiday; and as they cannot tell at sea when Thanksgiving day comes, the only holiday left is the Fourth of July; and two out of the three recurrences of this glorious day, whilst I was aboard the ship, were unmarked by a single circumstance to note it; I well remember the mate's answer to one of the crew, who in reply to his order to get up the spun yarn machine, laughingly said that it was Fourth of July. The curt answer was, "Yes! it is Fourth of July at home, but not here." In the evening, after the quarter watch was set, the accordeon, drum, fife, tamborine, fiddle, and triangle, were pressed into service, and all the national airs performed thereon with great glee.

The New Year found us on the coast of New Holland in sight of Cape Leuwin. This portion of Australia presents rather an indifferent appearance, viewed from the ocean; it being barren, apparently, over a great part of its extent, and where vegetation does appear, it is low and scanty. Off this cape is a great resort for sperm whales, and at almost all seasons of the year American whalers are to be seen, standing off and on, patiently awaiting the appearance of the cachalot. At the time that we reached this ground, the ships were just resorting here from the coast of Africa and Island of Madagascar, we spoke and gammoned a number, varying from eight to thirty months from home, and having from one hundred to two thousand barrels of oil aboard. On the fifth, a gale of wind having but just abated, leaving a heavy swell on the surface of the ocean, we saw sperm whales. We lowered for them at $7\frac{1}{2}$ o'clock A. M.; at 8 the starboard boat fastened to a large one, and a moment afterward we followed with the waist boat. The larboard boat, in trying to imitate us, was struck by the whale's flukes and stove. She filled, and her crew were obliged to swim for their lives to the bow boat, in which they were conveyed to the ship. They had managed to get one iron into the whale before being stoven; but the boatsteerer, undaunted, when up to his waist in water, darted his second iron at the animated target, striking his mark, but not with sufficient force to fasten solid. Their line entwining around ours, prevented us hauling on to and despatching him; and whilst we were dallying, away he went to windward, towing us faster than a steamboat, the water breaking completely over us. Our boat was one-third full all the time, and it was only by unremitting bailing, by two of our number, that we kept her afloat. This continued for hours, until the ship was only seen as a speck in the horizon. The whales were darting here, there, and everywhere —ahead, astern, and under us—and the officer only prevented their getting afoul of us by repeated lancings; whilst our boats were tossed to and fro. The boatsteerer of the starboard boat was pitched out, but he caught the gunwale and soon recovered his position. Immediately after the line ran foul, our boat capsized and was taken down. I jumped, as soon as I found that she was going over, kicked off my shoes, and swam for the other boat, the line of which had been cut as soon as they discovered our mishap. On getting into the boat, I found that three others were all right, and directly our second mate made his appearance and was assisted in. He stated that the line had become twisted around his ankle, but, fortunately, he had the sheath-knife in his hand when he went down, and cut himself loose. The tub oarsman got in with his hand seriously cut, evidently by a lance which he must have come in contact with under water. As soon as we counted those in the boat, the amidship oarsman was found to be missing, and as we knew that he could not swim, we were apprehensive that he was drowned; but on the instant his head made its appearance, and I shoved him an oar, with which he supported himself until picked up. After finding all safe, we laughed at the accident, and looking around for the whale, discovered him apparently taking a view of us—his profuse bleeding rendering it impossible for him to sound. On our approach he gradually receded from us stern foremost. We were twelve in a boat, almost out of sight of the ship, and had anything happened to our boat at this stage of the operation, some, if not all of us, would have lost the numbers of our mess; but Providence protected us, and we came off harmless. On going on to the whale to lance him, the monster would roll on his side, display his enormous jaw, and attempt to seize the boat with it. This was repeated a number of times, when those in the ship, which had been gradually nearing us, discovering only one boat, and that full of men, they lowered away two boats. One went in pursuit of the capsized boat, while the other came to our assistance, and fastened to the whale, discharging three-bomb lances into him. These caused him to roll and groan, but not producing a fatal effect, our boat returned to the ship for more, which were likewise deposited in his carcass; but it was not until sundown that he rolled fin out, and was brought alongside. We secured him for the night, and the next morning proceeded to cut him in. This is a very different operation from cutting-in a right whale; the two species being totally dissimilar. The first move with the sperm whale is

CUTTING IN A SPERM WHALE.

to separate the head from the body, and when the jaw is loose, heave it in. Cutting off the head consumes, if a large whale is the subject, from two to four hours, according to the dexterity of the manipulator; if a proficient handles the spade, it is a work of but little trouble, but if a bungler, he wearies everybody's patience out beside his own. The head, when completely clear, is made fast to the ship's quarter by a strong chain, and the body then hove in. When the small is cleared away, the head is hooked on to and hove out of the water, then separated into two portions, known as the case and junk, and separately hove in. If the whale is very large the case is bailed overboard, so as not to endanger the ship's spars by so heavy a heave — in this case we hove it in. Whilst heaving in our last body piece, to which the flukes were attached, they swung around and knocked the second mate and a boatsteerer overboard, with spades in their hands. They soon were recovered and on deck safe again.

We now had him all aboard. The jaw was dragged forward and secured, and several employed in cutting the blubber from the pans; it measured twenty feet in length and had in it forty-eight ivory teeth, many of them weighing a pound or more. The case was then opened, and a boatsteerer jumped into and prepared to dip out the unctuous matter, which in this part of the head is fluid; for what purpose designed I know not, but no doubt it is a provision of Providence that has its uses, although we cannot discern them. From this vast receptacle for oil we bailed some twelve barrels of the pure spermaceti. The junk was then cut into horse pieces, and these, with the other blubber from around the head and jaw, were rendered out and stowed in casks marked "head;" it being by far the most valuable portion of the whale, and commanding a better price. The head of the sperm whale generally yields about two-fifths of the oil procured from the entire fish. After finishing with the head matter, we proceeded with the residue the same as with the right whale formerly mentioned. On boiling the body blubber, we found it exceedingly poor, and were not at all surprised at the whole yield being only seventy-two barrels—his size auguring at least a hundred. He was seventy-five feet long.

In appearance, this whale does not bear the slightest resemblance to the right whale—its massive head differing from the latter; neither has it the bonnet, as the right whale, infested by barnacles and vermin; its body is not so thick; it is longer, and on the back, near the small, a ridge rises which is known as the hump; the flukes, too, are smaller; and the skin, instead of being black as ebony, is of a slate color, frequently mottled with white—around the head presenting an appearance like marbling; beneath the skin, on the head, is found short, stiff, hair, and between the hair and skin an alkaline substance which is a solvent for oil—it is used for washing clothing and the paint work.

After our whale was stowed below and finished with, we remained off the Leuwin for a few weeks, seeing whales but once, and then just at nightfall. So the captain said, one fine morning, that he thought he had waited long enough for the whales, and that now they might wait for him. He ordered the helm hard up, and we went bowling away before a ten knot breeze toward Vasse — a settlement situated in Geographe Bay, a short distance to the northward of Cape Leuwin. Soon we could see the breakers dashing and surging over the inhospitable coast, and at 7 o'clock P. M. let go our port anchor in three and a half fathoms of water, about three miles distant from the shore. We found several other whalers at anchor, and two more came in the same evening. From the ship the country looked low, sandy, and bushy. The next day we went ashore for the purpose of procuring fresh water, and found that we had an onerous task; as the casks were towed ashore and rolled about a quarter of a mile to the wells, over a sandy, uneven road, into which the pedestrian sank knee deep at every step. On arriving at the wells, the water had to be dipped up by bucketsful from a depth of twelve feet; nor was the water very good, it being produced from the sea by filtration through the sand, which deprived it of its saline matter. On filling our casks, finding it impossible to roll them through the sand, we took our raft rope and laid it in a continuous line, rolled a cask upon it, brought the end of the rope over it, and thus, all hands taking hold, we succeeded in parbuckling them, one by one, to the beach. I had often heard it sung that Jordan was a hard road to travel, and whilst engaged in this occupation, beneath a burning sun and over the scorching sand, I thought that it would not have been inappropriate to substitute Geographe for Jordan; as a harder road to travel I defy any one to point out. Thus we toiled, day after day, until we had four hundred barrels of water

7 *

in our ship's hold, when liberty commenced. This is always a season of rejoicing amongst sailors, but it would be impossible to give a perfect description of the manner in which they enjoy themselves, and the mad pranks they cut whilst their liberty lasts. Imagine, if you can, a school of the most mischievous urchins let loose, with perfect freedom to enact all the mischief they are capable of, and you can form a faint idea of Jack ashore in a foreign port. Some have hired horses and are riding double, one facing forward, the other in the opposite direction, kicking, spurring, and urging the nag onward, occasionally getting a fall which is productive of nothing but a hearty laugh, the loose sand protecting the dismounted cavalier from injury; and ten chances to one, after recovering his feet, the unseated one would grasp the animal's tail to mount again. I remember a case of one of our crew, who, burning to distinguish himself, went ashore, hired a horse, and rode off into the bush at full speed. The beast, being better accustomed to bush ranging than his rider, in the course of an hour made his appearance alone; and, on search being instituted, the gay horseman was discovered hanging in the forked branch of a tree, in such a position that he could not extricate himself without assistance, and even then his garments were rather the worse for wear.

The oldsters, when ashore, of course, resorted to the grog shop and got merry; the younger ones, burning to emulate them, were soon half seas over, and rolling around in too heavy a style even for a sailor. The first day, however, settled the affair, as on the following one the youngsters discovered that the way of the transgressor is hard; for they had to pay the penalty of a disordered stomach and severe headache. On the next liberty-day Bacchus had but few votaries.

I will now endeavor to give a slight description of the town of Vasse. The town and bay take their name from a French vessel and her master—the town from the captain, and the bay from the vessel. She was cast away here years ago, and remnants of her timbers are still to be seen. After half a mile's wading through the sand, we came to the outskirts of the town; the first house was a grog-shop, the second a smithery, the third a grog-shop, and, half a mile farther on, another groggery; so that it was easily to be seen that the Maine Law had not yet gone into operation in this vicinity. Three grog-shops, in a village of about one hundred inhabitants, are rather more than one would suppose were needed; but all seemed to be doing a thriving business, everybody, men, women, and children, indiscriminately going to the bars and drinking miserable spirits, for which they pay six-pence sterling, equivalent to twelve cents of our money, per glass. Then again, within a compass of a few miles, numerous sawyers are employed, who, after laboring hard for two, three, or six months, and accumulating a sum of money, resort to the village, and, to use their own expression, proceed to knock their earnings down. This they soon effect, and return to their old employment, when forced to, for want of funds to continue their carousal. The ticket of leave men, too, who are mostly employed in this section by the government, in repairing roads and public works at certain seasons of the year, are allowed a short time for recreation; and recreation to this people is only known in intoxication, and hence they too are amongst the publican's best customers.

The aborigines are a slender made people, with faces and bodies as dark as a negro's, but with straight hair. Their features, to me, are unpleasing, and they heighten the disgusting expression by besmearing the cheeks, forehead, and the fore part of the hair with a reddish clay, resembling Spanish brown, mixed with oil. They are very filthy, being alive with vermin. Their only clothing consists of a kangaroo skin, with the hairy side turned in, thrown over the shoulder; this they call a bouka. The paint they put on their faces they call willagee. Their weapons consist of a hard piece of wood, shaped like a half moon, called a boomerang, which they send whizzing through the air, striking any object they aim at with the most unerring precision. The spear, too, they dart with exceeding accuracy from a diamond-shaped piece of wood which they call a womara; they also dart it from the hand. One morning I had half a dozen children darting for small pieces of tobacco, which they invariably struck. They have a passion, like all uncivilized nations, for rum and tobacco. The former they are debarred from using, from the fact that the government inflicts heavy penalties on any person who supplies them with the smallest quantity of alcoholic stimulant. Our fellows, in several cases, got a bottle and carried it into the bush, and gave them small quantities for the fun of seeing and hearing them dance and sing; and, indeed, a very small portion of spirits causes them to act more like demons than members of the human family.

One afternoon I witnessed a sham battle between about a score of them, equally divided. Twigs were substituted for their spears; the latter being pointed, and armed with glass attached by means of a red gum, are rather dangerous weapons to play with. They charged each other, rallying and retreating, and, when opportunities presented, darting their weapons, all the time making a hoarse guttural sound, and becoming much excited. The sport continued for some time, and, after they had finished, tobacco was given to them. One of them demurring at the quantity in rather an outrageous style, was cooly knocked head over heels, and this arousing a combatant spirit amongst our crew, the whole of the natives, in a few moments, were flying as if for dear life from the vicinity. From observation on different occasions, I should say that the men are possessed of no courage; the women fight brutal battles with each other, armed with sticks, and never succumb until powerless from exertion or injury. But few, if any, of the females whom I have seen, were not covered with welts, thicker than one's finger, on the back and breast, the result, no doubt, in many instances, of these encounters: but they have a custom, I am told, of abrading their flesh on the death of a relative, and to this cause is assigned most of the scars they are covered with. They, like the men, are dressed with the bouka or kangaroo skin, and are squalid, dirty, lewd, and ignorant. Anything, a chew of tobacco, or a mouthful of biscuit, will cause these libels on the name of women to forget the allegiance due to their lords.

In the summer these people sleep in the open air, making, towards sundown, a fire in the bush, and sleeping with their feet to the fire. In winter they build rude huts of twigs and reeds, about four feet high, and large enough for two or three individuals, and here they, having in their hunting season collected provisions enough to subsist on, huddle together and sleep away the rainy season, which usually lasts about five months. Their food comprises almost everything that is endowed with life — kangaroos, snakes, iguanas, and grubs being their dainties; and if in the neighborhood where a bullock is killed, they greedily flock to the spot, secure the entrails, and devour them without cleansing. They are also very fond of the flesh of the whale; and if by accident one comes ashore on the coast, or they take one at either of the fisheries in the bay, they resort to the spot in great numbers and devour the meat, fresh or putrid, without cooking. The women back all the burdens, beside carrying the children; the child, perfectly naked, sits astride on the mother's shoulder, with the hands firmly clasped in her hair, and in this manner they travel miles with them. Some of the children carried in this way are of so light a complexion, as to excite strong suspicion of amalgamation with some of the whites in the neighborhood. The women, beside the child, carry a bag, into which all the surplus provision is stored. Impelled by curiosity, I one day bargained for a sight into one of these mysterious receptacles, and for a plug of tobacco had revealed to my sight half a dozen grubs, several snails, part of a toad, a snake, roots and herbs. The snakes they will not eat without they have been present at the time they were killed, being fearful that the snake, on being wounded, should have bitten himself. These people are remarkable for accuracy of vision and keen scent. For the former quality they are occasionally carried out by whaleships, for the purpose of looking out from the masthead; and I have been told by those who were shipmates with them, that they could discern a spout or sail at as great a distance with the naked eye, as a practised hand could with the glass. The last mentioned quality causes them to be employed by the government in tracking convicts who have taken to the bush, by captains of whaleships to recover deserters, and by the settlers to track up their stray cattle. In all these pursuits they are said to be infallible; although when they arrive at the runaway, if he present a bold face to them, they will not molest him; and unless they have a white man with them to urge them on, they will retreat empty-handed. They have a wholesome dread of fire-arms, and some of their race having seen a revolving pistol, has impressed on most of them the supernatural character of the weapon; and the "little fellow," as they call it, is to them a great bug-a-boo.

On the strictest inquiry I could not discover that they had any religion. The only inkling that I received of their ideas of hereafter, was the fear they expressed of jing-ge, a word synonymous to the English word devil; whether they have gleaned this idea from their intercourse with the whites, or that it is traditionary with them, I have no means of ascertaining.

These people are in the extremest degree indolent, and are only induced to do even the slightest job or errand, by promising them a meal upon its performance. If the employer good naturedly bestows the recompense when they are partly through, or the black fellow has had anything to eat previously, all efforts to induce him to return to the work are futile — words and blows being equally useless. On the appearance of whaleships in the bay, they resort to the town, and every member of said ships on going ashore is importuned for hard bread and tobacco, or an old jack-knife; and if the donor gives to all who ask him, he soon finds his stock of edibles and patience entirely exhausted.

There are no musical instruments among them; their vocal music is monotonous, and sounds harshly to the ear. At certain seasons of the year they meet for the purpose of having a "corroborie" as they call it, to which every member wears his best bouka; and when assembled they vie with each other in grotesque grimaces and contortions, both of form and feature.

These people are protected by the laws equally with the whites in this section. Some few hundred miles to the northward, at a locality known as Port Gregory, it is but a word and a blow; the blow, which is generally fatal, coming first. In the latter neighborhood, depredations committed on the settlers are the causes of their harsh treatment. Some few of them, when young, have been taken, educated and clothed in the European fashion, but in vain; they always prefer life in the bush, with their own people, to all the advantages of civilization, and only return to their benefactors when forced by hunger to do so. This often happens, as they are exceedingly improvident. Their mode is, on obtaining food, to gorge themselves to repletion, and then to sleep or hulk about until Providence sends them another supply, or hunger compels them to seek it.

These Australians contrast very unfavorably with our aborigines (the North American Indians), being possessed of all their bad qualities, without a single one of their redeeming traits; the same love of rum and tobacco, and a mean habit of pilfering, without their perseverance in the chase and bravery in conflict. I shall now, for the present, bid them farewell, though, as my narrative proceeds, I will again have occasion to revert to them.

As this settlement is part of a penal colony to which Great Britain consigns her malefactors, for from five years to the duration of their lives, to atone for offences against the laws of their country, the society is not, consequently, what we at home would call select; but, such as it is, it has its aristocracy. Although the majority of the inhabitants are convicts, some of whom have served out their term of punishment, the word convict amongst themselves is never used—it being apparently banished, by common consent, from their conversation. The convicts here form three grades — the members of the first, comprising those whose sentences have not been ameliorated, are under the strict surveillance of the government, and employed on government work. The second class are known as "ticket of relief holders;" these, for uniform good conduct, receive this ticket, which entitles them to choose their own employers and place of residence; but at the same time they are expected to give information as to where they reside to the police, and to be within doors at 8 o'clock in the evening. If these ticket holders continue to conduct themselves in a praiseworthy manner, they then receive a conditional pardon, which entitles them to leave the country, but at the same time debars them from returning to Great Britain or Ireland; or, if condemned in the colonies, from returning to the place of conviction; permission is, however, accorded to them to take up their residence in any other part of this colony, or in any colony under the control of the English government — England, by this precaution, guarding against the return of her prison population to her own shore. Hence these men, knowing that the stigma of conviction will cling to their skirts as long as they remain in this country, anxiously desire to embark in whalers — the United States being, in their eyes, the land of promise — and in this way numbers of emigrants of very doubtful character land on our shores. It is customary for whale-ships to engage some of these men; occasionally discharging their entire original crew, and shipping these in their places. We had a number of them during the voyage, and in this port we shipped two. I cannot but deprecate the practice of introducing men of such vicious antecedents, into a forecastle in which are American youths, who, by intercourse with such people, begin quickly to have very crude ideas of morality; and, unless there is some strong-minded person, with a clear, cool head, to rebut their specious arguments, they exercise an injurious influence on the minds of the young.

During the remainder of our stay in this port, we were engaged in giving liberty, boating ashore goods that had been sold or exchanged for potatoes—other vegetables not being procurable. Beef was furnished sparingly, it being alleged that a sufficient supply of it could not be procured; but as I then was, and since have been informed, that thousands of cattle were within a short distance of the town, the story requires confirmation to make it credible.

The articles chiefly disposed of here were Yankee notions—fancy shoes, soap, calicos, saddles, and other such stores. Formerly the whalers that resorted to these ports for provisions found a market for all their surplus articles; but, at the present time, over-importation has caused a total stoppage of their trade, except at ruinous prices. Every whale-ship that comes into this vicinity brings tons of tobacco in her outfit, and very little, if any, duty is paid upon it—it being mostly smuggled ashore. On the starting of a ship for port, the foremast hands always resort to the slop-chest for tobacco, which they carry ashore and dispose of at three times its original price; thus eking out their liberty-money to a respectable sum, and, much or little, expending it quickly.

The excise is guarded by the police, who, as a matter of form, look into every boat that comes in; but I have never seen any difficulty in carrying ashore, anywhere in the colony, twenty or thirty pounds of the weed about the person; and, once ashore, purchasers are readily found.

A few Americans are to be found here, in every case deserters from whaleships; who invariably, if at all attentive to business, in the course of a few years, accumulate an independence; but, unfortunately, they are too apt to imbibe a taste for that curse of this country, rum, and live from hand to mouth, until, becoming unsettled and weary, they embark aboard another whaler, and in time get home, having little or nothing due them, after a voluntary exile of eight or ten years from home and friends.

On the second liberty-day, given to the larboard watch, Kedge Anchor took French leave and fled to the bush for concealment. For some days we saw nothing of him; but, after a week's absence, he was at the beach, very anxious to get aboard on any conditions. He returned miserably filthy and covered with vermin; his clothing almost gone, and what he had left was all of one color, from wallowing in his various sleeping places. Whilst ashore, he was under the guidance of a fellow, who, by flaming accounts of the condition of the country, induced him to desert, intending to apply to our captain for his berth. On Kedge's return, he was greeted with laughter, in which he heartily joined; and, as it was impossible to get angry at him, he escaped with a reprimand; the captain at the same time assuring him, that if, at any future time, he repeated the attempt, he would not allow him to return aboard. What effect this had we shall discover as we proceed.

At 10½ A. M. on the morning of February 12th, the ship James Allen, and barque Henry M. Crapo, hove up their ground tackle and stood out to sea. The captain of the James Allen had been vaunting of the speed of his ship, and confidently asserting that she would outsail any ship or barque in the harbor, he issued a challenge. We hove up at 11 o'clock,

half an hour later than he, and in the course of two
hours had both the Crapo and James Allen on our
lee quarter. As we passed the latter, our captain
facetiously desired them to let go that *hawser*. They
were too badly beaten to answer without displaying
their chagrin; they therefore were discreet, and said
not a word. As this ship was our consort from this
time until July, 1857, I shall describe her and her
appointments. Like us, she was built from an old
fashioned model, but was a much younger ship. Her
captain was of a diminutive person, and strove to
atone for his small size by blustering; his first officer,
who, from all accounts, governed the ship, delighted
in a display of pugilistic powers, and kicked, cuffed,
and boxed the men on the slightest provocation.
She was two months longer from home than we, and
up to this time had taken no oil. One circumstance
that I omitted, in my remarks on Vasse, was the fact
of a collation and a ball, held on board this ship
whilst we lay there. Invitations were issued, and the
elite of the vicinity, for miles around, accepted them,
and at about 3 o'clock P. M. were conveyed aboard the
Allen by the boats of the vessels in the harbor. All
the vessels had their colors hoisted; the captains and
chief mates were the only guests from the vessels.
When the boats with their freight arrived alongside,
a chair that had a whip attached to it was lowered,
the ladies, singly, placed in it, and, reposing on
the American flag, hoisted aboard. Here a canvass screen was extended across the quarter-deck, just
abaft the mainmast, and, after a hearty repast, a
negro fiddler, who is an American by birth, and
the principal headsman at the bay whale-fishery, was

8 *

called into requisition, and, with the assistance of a triangle player, discoursed music for the dancers. Soon the whole assembly were tripping the light fantastic toe, on the well-worn decks that had faced many a gale. The scene was pleasing. The coils of rigging, the shrouds, and lower masts dimly lit up by the globe lanterns, reflecting a striking picture, and reminding one of the smugglers' jubilees, after a successful run; hardy, weather-beaten men, leading in the dance; fair maidens, I was about to say— but the scathing sun of Australia allows very few females to boast a fair complexion, although their nut-brown cheeks glow with health. The respectability of these people I know nothing about, except from hearsay; but that they were a motley collection I was assured of the following day, by hearing an old resident, a female, describe their efforts, or rather the efforts of some of the party, to appear covered with finery — devoting days to scouring the country and collecting it. My fair countrywomen must not think me embittered against their sex, or that I am anxious to do them injustice—God forbid; as a man and a sailor, I would scorn to do so; but as an American, I feel the superiority of my countrywomen over all of the sex in other countries that it has been my privilege to see; and to favorably compare these females with those of my native country, would, in my eyes, be an insult to the latter.

I must advert to another circumstance before taking final leave of the Vasse for "fifty-six"—that is the existence of the whale-fisheries in this bay; there being one here, and one thirty miles to the northeast, at a town known as Bunbry. At certain seasons the right and humpback whales resort to the various bays on this coast for the purpose of producing their young. A look-out is stationed on an eminence ashore, and several boat's crews being near at hand, at the appearance of a whale the alarm is given, and they start in pursuit. At times their work is very easy, but if the whale should run out to sea, after being struck, they are obliged to tow him to the shears, and frequently a day and night are consumed in this arduous employment. If the whale is attended by a calf, they always fasten to the latter first, knowing that the mother, in her solicitude for her offspring, is very careful not to use her tremendous flukes; or if a humpback, her sweeping fins: but woe betide the boat, unless an experienced boat-header directs it, that is in the vicinity when she discovers that her calf is dead. She then remains close to the lifeless body, striking right and left with flukes and fins, to avenge her loss; and as the slightest tap from these formidable weapons would cause destruction, it requires all the boat-header's adroitness to avoid them. The officers, boatsteerers, and, if they can by any means be procured, two-thirds of the crews are Americans: we having a world-wide reputation for skill in this pursuit.

CHAPTER IV.

AND now we will return to our old barque, that we left beating out of Geographe bay, having distanced both her competitors, and established her reputation as a fast ship. At night we shortened sail and stood quarter watches, and from this time until the middle of the succeeding month, little occurred to vary the sameness of our life. We were aroused from inaction by the appearance of sperm whales. The boats were lowered, and the waist boat fastening, both irons drew. A few minutes after, the starboard boat fastened to another. These irons holding, after a two hours' conflict we had a fine sperm whale alongside the ship without accident, except the voluntary discharge of the bomb-lance gun, which, fortunately, was productive of no injury. We had good weather, and soon he was disposed of in our lower hold. The following morning after his capture, we saw three other New Bedford ships employed in cutting in whales, making four of us successful in the war of extermination against the old squareheaders. The sperm whale, swimming in immense schools, and always pursuing a direct route, all ships that lay in their course have a chance at them. I have heard it asserted that at night these whales heave to, resuming their course at daybreak; but, although my informants were men who had been in the service for years,

I consider this a mistaken opinion, as during the whole of our voyage I saw nothing to corroborate it. I have seen sperm whales at dusk, and in the night, and they were always on the move, and could not be discerned the following morning from the masthead.

During this month we gammoned the barque Lexington, of New Bedford. This vessel was in a wretched state, and apprehensions were expressed by her crew that some misfortune would befall her: she leaked immoderately, was strained and very weak, and her rigging was so shattered that they were unable to carry sail, except in moderate weather. Whilst in company with us she could not hold her position, and drifted broadside off to leeward. Subsequently her captain carried her into Mauritius, where she was condemned, and sold, only to be refitted as a colonial whaler.

One day, while most of the crew were listlessly reclining on the decks, the extreme heat rendering exertion fatiguing, we were startled by old Jack singing out from aloft, "The sea-serpent, the sea-serpent!" On leaping into the rigging, we saw close to us a long, slender object, in form resembling a snake. It was of a bright scarlet color, and, although it moved, I think its motion was produced by the undulation of the waves, and although Jack assured us that he had often seen them much larger, and was willing to take his Bible oath that this was the identical sea-serpent about which so many newspaper articles are written, I am still inclined to think that it was some marine vegetable production. It was about twenty feet long, and as thick as a man's arm; and as the season advanced we saw many of them.

At another time we were startled from inactivity to see a strange monster, which the boatsteerer on the maintopgallant cross-trees, on being questioned, could give no explanation of; and it certainly did present an appearance different from anything I had previously seen. I was prepared to log the advent of a hitherto undescribed, and, at present, indescribable inhabitant of the deep, when my romance was knocked in the head by the captain, who, at the height of the excitement, stepped to the rail, saw it, and immediately decided that it was a young finback whale scooping up its food, which it did by swimming along with extended jaws.

We had now gradually worked up to the northward, until we had arrived on our cruising ground for the season. This ground is off Shark's bay, and extends between twenty and twenty-three degrees of South latitude, and from one hundred and seven to one hundred and ten degrees of East longitude. It bears the reputation of a profitable locality for whalers to cruise in. The bay derives its name from the presence of myriads of enormous sharks, and all over the ground, when a whale is alongside, thousands may be seen surrounding the ship, tearing off pieces of blubber from the whale, and revelling in his blood. They will bite at anything. I have seen them pursue our wooden buoy, which is used for attaching the hawser to the whale's flukes, as it gradually arose to the surface of the water, and attempt to crush it between their hideous jaws; and after finding they could make no impression upon it, following it up, occasionally nipping at it as if they did not understand the consistency of an object that resisted their incisors.

On Sunday, April 27th, we lowered away for, and captured a fine sperm whale. The James Allen's boats lowered at the same time with ours; they arrived first to the whale, ran on, and darted; but their boatsteerer missed, and our waist boat, seizing the opportunity, ran on and fastened. On the following Sunday we again saw sperm whales, and captured another; on the succeeding day the weather was boisterous, but we proceeded, in the face of numerous difficulties, to cut him in: just as we had got him in a good position for hooking on, the fluke chain parted, and away he went. We lowered away, and a second time secured him. In attempting to veer, the whale got under the ship, and it was only by strenuous tugging and hauling that we raised him. At length we began to cut, and towards noon had the head severed from the body; but, after various attempts, we gave up all hopes of saving it; it was then allowed to tow from the quarter; we then went to work at the body, and at 5 o'clock in the afternoon had it all aboard. The weather having moderated, we renewed our efforts to save the head, and succeeded so far as to get it in tow forward, when the hawser parted; we next attached a studdingsail tack to it; but, although the rope was large and new, it parted like packthread. A tub of line was then bent on, and the head allowed to float astern; but in a short time the strap attached to the head chain parted, and away it went, a total loss, leaving us with nothing to console us, except the reflection that we had done all that men could do, to save it. I noticed throughout this arduous day's work, the general alacrity of the crew in striving to do their utmost, and could not but comment on the advantages of giving each man a proportion of the vessel's earnings, instead of monthly wages; in our case all felt themselves personally interested, and conducted themselves accordingly.

It will be noticed that three-fifths of our whaling up to this time, has been on Sunday, and, subsequently, this day of days proved equally fortunate for us. I do not wish to defend the practice of Sunday whaling, and think that if a man makes it an invariable rule to whale only on week days, that Providence would so dispose it that he should not be a loser. We saw several of these Sunday ships, as they are called, and in each instance they had quite as much oil as their neighbors; at the same time, it takes a strong religious bias to induce a man who depends upon the capture of whales for an early return to home and friends, after being separated from all that he holds dear, perhaps for years, to forego attempting their capture on a Sunday. In fact, the temptation is strong; and, strange to say, most whalers see greater numbers of whales on the Sabbath than on any other day.

Soon afterwards we met the James Allen. Since we last saw her she had captured a whale, her first — whose lower jaw was snapped short off — probably in conflict with another of his species. These creatures are often terribly scarred, and their teeth indented and broken, as if another whale had locked jaws with them; in which case something must start.

In the month of May we gammoned the barque

Massasoit, of Mattapoisett, and from her got several terrapins which she procured in Madagascar. These creatures had lived in her lower hold for twelve months, we kept them three more; still, when we killed them we found them quite fat, and had a delicious meal off them. From this ship we also received a quantity of Madagascar beans, which were most excellent — surpassing, in richness and· flavor, the best of our beans at home. They are about the size of the Lima bean, the skin being covered with black spots.

On the 23d of May we spoke the barque Ann, of Sag Harbor, and from her received papers five and a half months old; they were treasures to us, and were read with intense interest, advertisements and all coming in for a share of attention; these papers were full of anticipated troubles with England, and, of course, this prospect of a war was the favorite topic. Like all Americans, we felt the superiority of the universal Yankee nation, and had no fears as to the result in case of a war with John Bull; and, from the general tenor of the conversation, I should infer that, in case of emergency, the whalemen would be found amongst the most strenuous supporters of both army and navy. Another light also was cast on the subject by some one hoping that we should be ordered home; and as a war would raise the price of oil, and induce an earlier return home, both topics of intense interest to us, it cannot be wondered that we were so much engrossed by them.

As I before said, we shipped two new men in the Vasse; one of these was, according to his own account, a renowned pugilist, and had fought and conquered in a dozen fights in the English ring. He was allowed to vapor for a long time, but one pleasant evening, he went so far as to offer to fight any man in the forecastle for an English sovereign. His offer was instantly accepted, and a mere boy was chosen as his antagonist. In less time than is occupied in the narration, the bully was describing some queer figures on the forecastle deck—tumbling in and out of bunks, over chests and kegs, all the time begging piteously to be let go. After a few minutes of this violent exercise, he was allowed to get up, thoroughly convinced that a Yankee hug was at any time a puzzle for an English pugilist. The following morning he went to the captain to complain of his ill usage, but the "old skipper" had already been informed of the merits and demerits of the case, and received the complainant with an order to clear out and not bother him; but he was too anxious to make himself heard, and, persisting in his cock and bull story until the captain was out of patience, he was rewarded for his pains by an application of the old man's heavy boot to his posterior, and a box alongside the ear from his powerful hand, that sent him forward lamenting, with more alacrity than he had before displayed aboard the ship. Previous to this occurrence he had quarrelled with almost every man in the ship, had refused to obey the mate and was mastheaded for it, and evidently appeared to think that, because he was an English subject, he was not bound to conform to the rules of our vessel.

On the 8th of June, we took our departure from this ground, intending to touch at the town of Balli, on the island of Lombock, an island a few degrees to the eastward from Java, about a thousand miles from our present locality—a long journey in the eyes of a landsman, but to us, who for months had been tossed and banged about at the caprice of the wind and wave, it was but a part of our customary life; the trip presenting no more perils than our ordinary daily occupation. And then again, the sea watches, which are always stood when sail is carried, afford a pleasant variation, the long-continued quarter watches having become extremely tiresome. Many slung their hammocks on deck, the excessive heat of the weather and the bed-bugs combined—the latter being always in great numbers in old ships—driving them from their usual sleeping apartments. I remember seeing our Portuguese appear on deck one night nearly nude, rubbing himself most vigorously, and swearing volubly in his own language. On my inquiring of him as to what was the matter, he answered, that "The darned bread boxes would not let him sleep." A dozen remedies were proposed with the utmost apparent seriousness. One advising him to catch them and drown them; another to pull their teeth out; whilst a third advised him to smear his bed and bed-clothes with tar, for then they would stick fast and be unable to get at him. Jeering and pestering the poor fellow until glad to be rid of his tormentors on deck, he returned to his uncomfortable couch, and resigned himself to the tender mercies of his tormentors below.

On our passage up to Balli, which climate has the reputation of being very unhealthy, the captain advised a thorough cleansing and whitewashing of the forecastle. No sooner said than done. The try works were pressed into the service, a fire made, the pots filled with salt water, and, whilst it was heating, the chests, berth furniture, bed-clothes, and every other movable article, were removed on deck, and buckets of boiling hot water dashed all over it. Then the whitewash was mixed, and with a piece of canvass, the ship not being able to boast the possession of a whitewash brush, a thorough coat was daubed over everything, and things made to wear a clean and cheerful appearance.

The old duds assembled on deck formed a curious collection, and as I noticed them I fancied that I could read the character of the owner by the appearance of each, and the circumstances under which he left home. The neatly painted chest, comfortable mattrass and quilt, prepared by the careful hands of some fond mother or sister, fully proved that their owner was a New Bedford boy, whose friends knew precisely what would conduce to his comfort when separated from them by thousands of miles of ocean waste; whilst the common straw bed, rude pine box, outfit quilt, with the padding run into one corner, and coarse blankets, testified that their owner was a reckless, careless fellow, who, at the time he shipped, cared little for outfit or anything else, except getting to sea, and, having fallen into the hands of the sharks, had been shoved aboard and sent afloat with the merest necessaries.

In the pile, too, may be noticed an assemblage of hats and caps that would make a hatter stare. During the first six months, all the hats and caps brought from home, without, perhaps one may have been saved to wear ashore, were blown overboard, for when a man goes up to reef topsails in a gale, he has as much as he can do to attend to himself without taking notice of his hat, and, unless it fit him perfectly tight, he is sure to lose it. Hence, in this collection may be seen head coverings of kangaroo skin, canvass, dungaree, cloth, and other materials, in every conceivable shape and make; also straw hats, made by the native of the Spice Islands, the Arab of the coast of Africa, the Madagascar negro, the swarthy Portuguese, and the Malay; all fabricated of different materials, and in different styles; all answering, equally well, the purpose for which they are designed — that of protecting the wearer from the seething sun, which has such power in the native countries of their fabricators.

After beating about two weeks—the variability of the winds delaying our passage thus long, while, with a favorable wind and plenty of it, we would have accomplished it in ninety-six hours — we hove in sight of the island of Sumbawa — the James Allen accompanying us. After running for some distance along its coast, delighted with the scenery —every rock and crevice being covered with vegetation of the richest green, clusters of cocoa-nut trees rising in every direction, and all the beauties of tropical verdure opening to our delighted visions—a mountain, said to be volcanic, came in for a due share of our attention. Soon we entered the Straits of Allas, and saw Balli Peak, a mountain of considerable altitude, covered with vegetation. Whilst at the mouth of the straits, we were greeted with a sight of a water-spout — a phenomena so often described that for me to attempt it would be superfluous. I will only state that sailors have a belief that the water of which they are composed, although coming from the ocean, undergoes, through the sun's rays, a distillation that deprives it of its salt. After we entered the straits, we alternately had a succession of calms and light breezes which detained us for some time; but, finally, we came to anchor about a mile from the town, in ten fathoms of water—the James Allen being within a stone's throw of us. Near us was a coral reef, which prevents craft, except of light draught of water, from approaching closer to the town. A number of the native vessels lay inside of us loading with rice. These vessels are known as proas —some of them are good sized; they are flat-bottomed, draw but very little water, and are painted in rude, barbaric style. All that I saw of any size were rigged as barques, their sails being mats, manufactured from leaves neatly connected so as to present the surface to the wind.

CHAPTER V.

Soon after our sails were stowed, a canoe from the town came alongside. In it were two Malays, who had a cargo of green and ripe cocoa-nuts, bananas, sugar-cane, tamarinds, pine apples, chickens, and cockatoos. They were desirous of bartering these articles, not for money, but sperm whale's teeth, which they term "gee gees," and use for handles to their creeses, after having neatly carved and ornamented them. They have a perfect passion for these teeth, and having at one time exposed to their view a very handsome one, I was beset and pestered by these people, ashore and aboard, to sell it. Having no desire to dispose of it, I at first only laughed at their offers, but when one plucked me by the sleeve and offered me a dozen chickens for it, and another his whole stock in trade to become its possessor, I wavered and let it go.

The cocks, of which half a dozen were purchased, displaying considerable game, two were pitted against each other, and, as quickly as one was beaten, another was backed against the victor, until they were tired of fighting, when their heads were cut off, and we supped upon the belligerents.

The captain went ashore and found that no American or European ship had been here for several years.

In the evening great numbers of the natives came down and waded into the water; at first I thought they were bathing, but afterward discovered that they were engaged in fishing for a diminutive fish, which I think, from their appearance, must have been sardines. On the ensuing morning, the captain having learned that we lay in a bad position, we hove up our anchor and ran a short distance to the northward, and again came to in the same depth of water. During this day we were occupied in getting off water, and reeving new lanyards to our lower rigging; and this laborious work in latitude 8°, was rather warm. We were visited by many boats from the shore, and at noon had a comfortable dinner of sweet potatoes, rice, chickens, &c. On the succeeding day the starboard watch went ashore on liberty, each member of it provided with half a dozen yards of gaudy-colored, large-figured calico. We walked about half a mile from the landing, and came to anchor at the market, where we found a concourse of men, women, and children, with their wares exposed to view, busily soliciting purchasers. This market was situated in the open air, near by a cocoa-nut grove. They had for sale monkeys, parrots, cockatoos, cooked and uncooked rice, poultry, limes, lemons, oranges, and figs, besides the fruits before mentioned. These last were to be bought for a song, and as we had been so long without these luxuries, they were freely indulged in; but what suited my palate best was the banana fried in cocoa-nut oil, which an old woman was busily engaged preparing— plucking the fruit from the tree and cooking it. Our appearance set these merchants agog, but they were not at all obtrusive, and waited until we directed our attention to them before they approached us; then they surrounded us, a dozen at a time asking, how much this was, all their English; but we were not anxious to part with our goods before discovering the state of the market. Soon a man joined us whose complexion presented a queer appearance, being formed of half a dozen different shades, arranged in spots, differing in size as in color, from the size of a five cent piece to that of a silver dollar, and in shade from a light yellow to a deep copper tint; he was well made, and had the appearance and manners of one of the better class; he conversed in intelligible sailor English, mixed with French and Spanish, and evidently considered himself a great linguist. From his account of himself I suppose that he was the rajah's clerk. He seemed anxious for me to describe, on the sand, some English speaking, as he termed it; and after I had complied with his request, he, in return, took the stick and drew several characters to me unintelligible. He stated that his name was Woreka, and, as this was difficult of remembrance, he was, by common consent, christened John, and seemed quite proud of his title. He assumed the office of chaperone to us, and through his instrumentality quite a number disposed of their calico. I was importuned for some time, by a native, for mine, and finally agreed to let him have it for four hundred pice. After some demurrage, he agreed to purchase it, but did not possess sufficient current funds about him. He desired me, by signs, to accompany him to his house, where, he said, he had plenty; and on my reiterating the price, he repeated, "I sabe,

I sabe," with much emphasis. On arriving at his house he handed the calico to his wife, who was as much pleased with it as an American child would be with a toy. Her spouse proceeded up stairs to procure the money, and whilst he was gone I had leisure to observe the inmates of the room. The wife, a young woman, apparently about twenty years of age, had the most perfect set of features I ever beheld, and hair, which, if loosed, would flow almost to the ground, of the glossiest black; her complexion was about as dark as that of our Indian squaws; her eyes, black and piercing — lips red as a cherry; her form full of grace, and straight as an arrow. She reminded me of the pictures I had seen of oriental princesses; and, certainly, a more graceful or prettier queen never wielded sceptre. The other occupants were an old woman and several children. By the time I had finished my scrutiny mine host returned, and presented me with a quantity of Chinese coin, which I found fell one hundred pice short of the price agreed upon. I informed him of his mistake, but as all I received for answer was "I sabe," I demanded the restitution of the calico. For this purpose he advanced to his wife to obtain it, and when she, who had been watching us closely, discovered my intention of depriving her of her prize, her pretty features contracted into a malignant frown, her eyes shone like diamonds, so fierce were their expression, whilst she stamped her little bare foot indignantly at the affront she deemed imposed upon her. In consideration of the lady's disappointment, and from the fact of my being separated some half a mile from my comrades, in the midst of a village containing hundreds of Malays, I was on the point of yielding; but the lady's rage found vent in words, which, although I did not understand, from her glances and gestures I knew were directed at me; and I have no doubt that, if I were able to translate it, it would rival the Billingsgate vocabulary. I in turn became warm at finding myself the object of vituperation, even from such rosy lips; and then reflecting how my story would sound when told to my shipmates—betraying how I, one of the oldest amongst them, was overreached by a Malay, I remained firm; and getting possession of my calico, left the house and the dusky lady—the latter to continue her vituperations to her heart's content, now that I was out of ear-shot. Some who read this may think me foolish in allowing it to nettle me; but I know of nothing more vexing, even to a patient man, than to be made the subject of abuse, when he cannot understand his villifier's language, and is compelled to submit without being able to say a word in justification of himself. I walked off with my goods, and, to avoid a recurrence of such a scene disposed of it to the first who offered, receiving in exchange four strings of pice, small Chinese coin, composed of a mixture of brass and copper, impressed with Chinese characters, each having a square hole in the centre. I met several others of my shipmates furnished in the same way. They being too bulky to carry in our pockets we were forced to carry them in our hands; one of our number had his strung on a stick and slung over his shoulder; the Malays carry them at their girdles. After having expended a few of them for fruit, and one hundred and fifty each for our dinners, the balance were thrown by handsful amongst the children, for the fun of seeing the naked little urchins scrambling for them. Our dinner we procured from our friend John, who furnished us with a very palatable repast of bread fruit, cocoa-nuts, yams, sweet potatoes, pumpkins, chickens, eggs, and rice. The chickens were stewed and seasoned to a high degree with Cayenne pepper, of which condiment these people are excessively fond, and, of course, think strangers are, or should be. After dinner a drum and a couple of gongs were produced, and several natives beat them for some time, making nothing like music to my ears. When their performance had ceased, one of our fellows seized the drum, and another, having his accordeon ashore, they began to play Yankee Doodle; this was home music to us, and was received with a burst of enthusiasm. One of our number, who had served in the Mexican war, formed the men in line, with bamboo poles in the stead of muskets, with which as many manœuvres were performed as would have excited the awkward squad to emulation. The natives looked on with great glee. Our friend John had purchased, from one of the party, a blue coat with brass buttons, and a double-barreled pistol without a lock; the coat he wore, whilst the pistol was displayed in a prominent position; and with these additions to his usual accoutrements he strutted around, the beheld of all beholders. Feeling his dignity much increased by them, a razor was shown him, to which he took a great fancy, and insisted on being shaved with it, after which he purchased it. Edge tools, such as sheath and jack knives, scissors, &c., are eagerly sought for by these people; even a

HOW THE NATIVES KILL TIGERS.

piece of iron hoop is of value, and a foot of it will procure for the possessor a day's regalement. Their creeses, one of which each male carries, are short swords, from eighteen inches to two feet in length, irregularly shaped, and made of an unpolished soft metal; they are carried in neat wooden sheaths; the handles are of ivory, beautifully carved and ornamented. This is not the work of the Malay, but of the Chinese; and the fact explains the eagerness with which they purchase whale's teeth — their hardness, and the superior whiteness of the ivory, rendering them peculiarly applicable for this purpose. These weapons are used by them in their encounters with wild beasts, more particularly the tiger, which infests these islands. Usually, when the tiger seizes his prey, they told us, he catches his victim by the calico which encircles the waist, thus leaving his arms free; then the Malay, feeling for the shoulder-blade, inserts his creese, and, piercing the beast's heart, relieves himself from his cruel enemy. Their descriptions of their encounters with the tiger I am inclined to think are, to a great extent, bombast; as from observation, I have little faith in their confidence in themselves or weapons — one of the boatsteerers belonging to the James Allen, when under the influence of their abominable toddy, driving a score of them before him with a good sized cudgel. Beside their creeses, each carries in his girdle a box containing the beetle-nut, of which he takes a large piece enveloped in a green leaf, belonging to I know not what plant, and swallows it with great gusto. This practice, which is to them as much of a necessity as tobacco is to a sailor, blackens their teeth to an ebon tinge, and, I should judge, ruined them; as few, even of the youngest of those who have arrived at maturity, have anything but stumps of teeth. They also use the tobacco which grows on the island, known to seamen as "shag tobacco." It has little taste, and when smoked, exhales an unpleasant odor; grows in threads and looks like saffron.

Here, as in all barbaric countries, the women are obliged to do the principal part of the work, and they may be seen walking in Indian file from the rice fields to the granary, each carrying on her head a large basket; the whole being under the guidance of a strapping Malay, who, from appearance, is anything but an easy taskmaster. We saw but very little of the unmarried females, except at a distance; they were, for the most part, engaged in weaving a cloth of alternate gaudy colors. On our approach the weavers would drop their work and run like deer. We examined their looms, and one who, at home, had been a weaver, said that they were on the same principle as our hand-looms. The reason ascribed for the timidity of the females was, that some years ago a Spanish vessel of war visited the town, and the crew, on getting ashore, indulging in anise until drunk, indiscriminately violated and otherwise maltreated the women. We could occasionally detect them peeping out, to have a look at us, from some secure retreat. No liberties could be taken, for the first two days, with any of them, when an acute fellow, moved by a spirit, not unlike Yankee speculation, procured prostitutes from an adjacent town; but he overshot his mark, as the liberty was then stopped, and those ashore on duty were not provided with available funds. There is a system of slavery here; and John showed me a woman, whom he said would die—indeed, she appeared in the last stages of disease—informing me at the same time that she had cost him eight dollars, but that he would sell her to me for three. Having no desire to be possessed of a human chattel in this part of the world, I declined his accommodating offer. I could not detect any difference in the races; both master and slave were, apparently, of one family.

There are two Chinese merchants located here, who appear to monopolize the whole trade of the town; they had a mart filled with china ware, vermilion, cards, and various articles of Chinese manufacture; amongst which they displayed, as very desirable articles, some disgusting licentious paintings on glass—the workmanship and coloring displaying no mean artistic skill. They were eager to display their possessions, and showed us a large camphor-wood chest, filled with pice; but, although the natives were continually passing in and out, the merchants manifested no apprehension of theft; they seemed systematic in their business, and, like all Celestials, considered themselves the only civilized nation on the face of the globe.

The houses the Malays inhabit are built of bamboo; the first floor is raised some six or eight feet from the ground, and the second about ten feet above the first; the floors are of split bamboo. These houses are airy and commodious; in the rainy season the inmates thatch the roof and cover the sides with mats, to protect themselves from the weather.

The canoes, generally, are built of tamarind-wood, having outriggers on each side to prevent capsizing; they are propelled by a paddle in the bow, and one on the quarter, and when the occupants are hurried they skim along with great velocity. One man will go out in his canoe, drop anchor, and smoke and fish all day long. Seeming to think the straits belong to them, they will neither move nor turn out for anybody. One day when we were towing a raft of water aboard, one of these canoes lay directly in our course. Finding gestures and the king's English ineffectual in clearing the way, we merely sheered our boats so as to pass; but the raft continuing its course, caught in the outrigger of the canoe, and, despite the exertions of its owner, it was dragged for some distance before he was able to extricate it. All the time he was spluttering away in Malay, until, finally, he mustered enough English to sing out, "Let go;" but, as the current was strong, we had as much as we could do to hold our own, without helping him.

Their cattle, which they call buffalo, do not, either in size, shape, or appearance, resemble the rovers on our Western prairies; they are small, formed like our ox, with slender legs, and hair the color of that of the deer. I at once pronounced them a variety of the musk ox, and when, a few days after, I partook of the flesh, my opinion was strengthened. The flesh was white and tender, but had so strong an odor and taste as to be unpalatable to us. I do not know whether the Malays eat them or not. The cows give a rich milk, which, like the flesh, tastes strong.

Their horses are undersized, but appear active, hardy, and intelligent.

Every family has numbers of poultry, and it is a favorite amusement to pit them against each other— houses for the purpose existing in several parts of the town.

The ducks are the most peculiar that I ever saw; they stand erect, with their heads high in air, and are facetiously nicknamed "Balli soldiers:" they are excellent eating.

The principal provisions we obtained here were sweet potatoes and pumpkins; the former were smaller and not near so good as ours at home, but formed a pleasant variety. We soon disposed of them; sixty bushels lasting only six weeks. The pumpkins, in shape and taste, resemble our squashes. We also managed to get a few yucas, which is an esculent resembling the potato, and, I think, a small variety of the yam.

Beside these, we carried out large quantities of cocoa-nuts, bananas, and tamarinds—the bananas, being brought aboard in an unripe state, after a few days were fit to eat; our cook attempted to boil some, but the attempt proved a failure—we preferring them raw. The tamarinds were preserved in molasses and stowed away; they are valuable for their anti-scorbutic properties, and were kept aboard for years after leaving Balli.

One day, whilst lying here, after I had pretty well satiated my curiosity in the town, I strolled into the country, and came across a cemetery filled with hecatombs — a slab being placed at the head, another at the foot of the grave, and the space between filled with stones. Near this cemetery was a spot enclosed by a high, solid, stone wall, but I could not ascertain for what purpose it was designed. Pursuing my way, I found a number of trees covered with the names of ships that had visited Balli, with date and country attached: amongst them I noticed that of the Spanish ship before mentioned, and those of several whalers, with the quantity of oil they had aboard specified. I found some one had been here before me and carved our old barque's name in large characters. Beyond this spot I discovered that a very populous country existed; but why we had not been told of it at the lower town, I cannot divine. The natives clustered around us in great numbers, and the women, after the first sight, were not afraid to approach us. In the centre of the town was a cockpit, where fowls, with steel gaffs, were plunging at each other, whilst their owners and backers were freely betting as to the result, so intensely bent on the contest, that they had neither eyes nor ears for us. Some of the men here were rather officious, and we scarcely knew what their intentions might be; probably it was only curiosity; but it induced us to beat as speedy a retreat as we could, without exciting notice.

These people are very temperate, and I did not see them indulge in any of their intoxicating liquors, which consist of two varieties; one, a scarlet-colored spirit, which they call "toddie," is made from the fermented juice of the unripe cocoa-nut. At first taste it does not appear strong, but over-indulgence in it produces either stupefaction or a species of insanity, resembling no effect I have ever seen from any other spirit. In the first case the subject is reduced to perfect helplessness and insensibility;

which does not leave him altogether for several days; if the latter effect is produced, all the symptoms of violent insanity appear, and the madman does not rest until he has had a quarrel. Hence it was called "fighting toddie;" and one who has once indulged in it shuns it afterwards, on the principle that a burned child dreads the fire.

The Anise is a colorless liquid, with a smoky, fiery taste, and has the same effect as other spirituous drinks. Neither of these liquors could be procured in the town when we first came ashore, whereupon some of us congratulated ourselves on the prospect of a temperate and sociable day; but part of our crew, determined to have a spree, by the offer of half a dozen whale's teeth, induced a native to cross the country in quest of it. The hesitation of the people in furnishing it, evidently proceeded from a perfect knowledge of its effect upon seamen when ashore, and indulging in it *ad libitum.*

The rajah of the town and his clerk visited the ship one morning. The rajah's dress and air were anything but kingly. He was a man of advanced age, and at home would have passed muster as a respectable looking mulatto; but he had little to say, not understanding our language—his clerk, Tonga, interpreting for our captain and he. The harbor duties were paid in powder, with the addition of an old musket, and the provisions in whale's teeth.

The coast is considered unhealthy by the natives themselves; the rajah's clerk expressing himself anxious to get away into the interior, saying that he was fearful of being sick. The utmost care was taken by us to prevent sickness. None of our crew were necessitated to drink the water — a cask of beer being continually on draught on the quarter-deck. No sleeping on deck was allowed, and no staying ashore at night. Even with all these precautions, our second and third mates were very ill—the latter severely so—and also one of the crew, with a debilitating fever peculiar to the climate. Several belonging to the James Allen also had reason to remember Balli for a long time after they left it — a distressing dysentery continuing to affect them for months. At Angiers, in Java, in nearly the same latitude as Balli, scarce an American whaler goes out, after a short stay, without leaving one or more of her crew to repose in death on its lovely shores: and we cannot but feel thankful for the protecting care of Providence, in guarding us from such a misfortune. This is the only objection to these East Indian ports, as I know of none where a crew of young men, if so disposed, can pass a few days more rationally and pleasantly, gleaning at the same time useful information. The climate appears to agree with the natives, as I saw numbers of the most attenuated human beings, who had attained a great age, so reduced that the student might, by procuring one of them, readily study anatomy from a living subject. I was at a loss for a long time to divine the occupation of these emaciated creatures, but soon found that they were mendicants. They never solicited alms, but seemed to make a good thing of it — the countrymen and women bestowing pice freely amongst them. Although so old and reduced, their vanity still remained, as was shown by their eagerness to purchase our gaudy calico.

These people profess the religion of Mahomet, and

their creed seems to enjoin cleanliness upon them, as they are neat and cleanly to an almost painful degree — performing their ablutions frequently and thoroughly, like all others of the same faith. Pork is their abomination, as much as it is to the children of Judea.

Parrots and cockatoos exist here in great numbers, and may be seen in the lofty cocoa-nut trees. The cockatoo is a beautiful bird, about the size of our pigeon; it is perfectly white in its body plumage; on the head is a crest consisting of three or four feathers of a beautiful yellow, which it elevates at pleasure; it has a formidable beak, is easily tamed, and can be taught to articulate. Ashore I saw several domesticated, that jabbered Malay with great fluency, and traversed the house on a perfect equality with the cats and children. Monkeys also, may be seen in these groves; they are small, but active, mischievous, and intelligent. Cockatoos and monkeys had attracted the attention of more than one of us; and half a dozen of the former, and two of the latter, were transferred to our ship, where they soon made themselves at home. The birds lived for some time, but were finally lost overboard. The monkeys not agreeing well together, one was given away, and the other committed suicide by eating putty.

On the last liberty day Kedge Anchor, from our vessel, and no less than seven from the James Allen, deserted; but their departure was soon reported, and natives despatched in search of them on the same day. After a tiresome walk of ten miles, during which they represented themselves as having been treated by the natives with the utmost hospitality, they found themselves surrounded by a score of the rajah's body guard, armed with drawn creeses; and, with some demurrage, the deserters, having no arms, were compelled to submit. No indignities were offered to them. Horses were provided for each, and thus mounted they were conducted back to the coast — their attendants easily keeping pace with them on foot. They arrived at night, and were comfortably provided with lodgings and an excellent supper, and next morning were delivered over to their respective captains, on the payment of a piece of blue cotton cloth, as a ransom for each. There was very little said to our shipmate, but aboard the Allen her deserters were handcuffed and put between decks; though after a short time they were liberated. This freak hastened our departure from the port, and on Sunday morning, at 3 o'clock, all hands were called to "Up anchor, ahoy!" With a merry song the windlass was manned, and soon the old barque was on her way out. We had several hundred chickens aboard, one hundred ducks, six cockatoos, two monkeys, and a Malay puppy. These creatures, all excited by the unusual position they found themselves in, were respectively venting their dissatisfaction in the most vociferous manner. The cackling of the chickens, quacking of the ducks, chattering of cockatoos and monkeys, the yelping of the puppy, and the merry "Yeo, heave, ho!" of the sailors, blended, formed a chaos of noises, indescribable and deafening. Our bananas were hung under the tops, over the stern, and on the stays and rigging — giving our floating home a lively appearance.

On the last day of our stay in port, the Englishman who had made himself so disagreeable to all hands, on expressing a wish to be left ashore, was discharged by our captain. He had seven or eight pounds sterling; the captain gave him several more, as also a piece of cotton stuff for which he could readily procure sale, and then provided him a guide across the country. A large, powerful man, belonging to Troy, New York, having effected his escape from the Allen, on the last day, eluding the natives sent in pursuit of him, was supposed to have accompanied him, and both took their way to Anfernande, a seaport some thirty miles distant.

In the evening of the day that we took our departure from this pleasant spot, we were favored with a strong breeze, and the crew became themselves again in the execution of their multifarious duties about the ship; lying in port always giving to Jack Tar a sluggish carriage; but the moment the sea breeze strikes the vessel, he livens up and feels himself called upon for exertion.

In the course of the ensuing week, the cocoa-nuts, tamarinds, and bananas were proportionately distributed amongst the crew, fore and aft, and these, with fowl additions to our usual sea fare, enabled us to live high for some time; and our monkeys affording a source of amusement, time passed speedily and pleasantly. These little creatures soon became expert in running about the rigging; a suit of sailor's clothes was made for them, and their antics in this attire were most ludicrous. They became much attached to one of the boatsteerers, and followed him, in fine weather, to the masthead. One day he observed them run in company to the extreme end of the maintopgallant yard-arm, when one, with a mischievous grin, pushed the other off; but though the poor fellow fell on deck, he escaped with slight injury.

With a fine breeze, we steered a southerly course, along the West coast of New Holland, until we arrived on our old cruising-ground. The weather here, although a few weeks previously we had found it uncomfortably warm, after our visit to so much lower latitudes, felt quite chilly, and woolen shirts, stockings, and underclothes—articles of apparel to which we had long been strangers — were hunted up from out of the way nooks and corners of chests, and donned. We here saw the ship Stephania, of New Bedford, making a passage for Angiers, whence her course went homeward. She was leaking badly, and her crew grumbled at the oppressive labor of pumping in the existing hot weather. She had considerable right whale oil, taken off the Island of Desolation, which island was described by her crew as a miserable place for cruising — cold weather, with heavy gales, prevailing there almost all the time. A few days previous to our meeting her, they had been fast to a large sperm whale, which crushed a boat in its huge jaws, seriously injuring the captain's hand at the time.

CHAPTER VI.

FINDING, after a short stay, that the ground was deserted both by ships and whales, we pursued our course to the southward, intending to double Cape Leuwin, thence to the eastward, and cruise in the Great Australian Bight. Anticipating heavy weather in those latitudes, our foretopgallant mast was sent down, and the mizzen topmast housed; and no sooner were we thus far prepared than we caught a heavy gale that exceeded in violence anything of the kind we had experienced during the preceding part of the voyage. It lasted eight or nine days, and as there was an ugly sea running, the ship was almost continually drenched the whole extent of her decks. One night whilst lying-to in the gale, when its violence was at its height, a heavy sea broke over the vessel, carrying away part of the starboard bulwarks, and filling the bow boat on the larboard side. The davits of the boat were crushed by the weight of the water, and the boat broke down amidships. The decks were deluged, and it was necessary to knock out a part of the lee bulwarks to allow the water to escape. The third officer, who headed the watch, called the first mate, who, on coming on deck, hurriedly ran over the members of the watch, when missing one, whose look-out he heard it was, and supposing him to have been on the forecastle at the time the sea was shipped, he gave him up for lost. To ascertain, he cried aloud his name at the top of his voice, but the gale prevented it from being heard a short distance from the speaker. He then despatched a person into each top, who sang out for him without result. After all had decided that he was overboard, without hope of relief, he was found snugly ensconced in the starboard boat, totally unaware of the apprehensions entertained for his safety.

On the 6th and 7th of August we fell in with the barques Aladdin and Lady Emma, and the brig Jane, all of Hobartown, carrying the English flag. These were the first whalers we had seen carrying other than our own glorious banner. We gammoned them, and found them but indifferent craft — their rigging poor, and scarce any discipline existing aboard of them; their slouching arrangements contrasting unfavorably with our own neat and tidy appearance. Their crews are composed principally of convicts who have served out their terms of sentence, and ticket-of-relief men: with such material it is scarcely possible to form a good crew. Their officers and captains were, in many cases, from the same class of society; and on board one of the barques the master was so ignorant as to be compelled to carry a navigator, who directed all the movements of the ship, except when they were whaling. A few Yankees were amongst them—in every case deserters from American whalers. The residue of their crews contained representatives from all parts of the world—black, yellow and brown; Portuguese, New Zealanders, Kanackas from all of the South Sea Islands, and Negroes. Aboard some of these ships the forecastle is partitioned into two apartments, in one of which the blacks, and in the other the whites reside — neither party encroaching on the other. These ships usually fit out for fifteen months, but generally return within the year; their forecastles look desolate, from the fact that none of the crew bring chests to sea with them; their stock of clothes consisting, in many instances, only of the suit they wear upon their backs. Their bedding, too, from lack of attention to their outfit, is very scant, and is therefore insufficient in such cool weather as prevails in the Bight at this season of the year. They were disposed to grumble, and exceeded the usual modicum of growling accorded to the sailor. They envied us our positions, and were very desirous of effecting an exchange; some went so far as to ask to be concealed when their boat left our ship. They represented that their ships were leaky, and the officers ignorant; and inveighed in unmeasured terms against their rations, describing them as scant and unwholesome. These must not be considered as fair specimens of the Hobartown shipping, as afterward we saw vessels in which, although their management could not compare with ours, their crews were at least contented, and their vessels and rigging presented a much better appearance to a seaman's eye.

On board these ships grog is allowed; by some, daily; others, semi- and tri-weekly; and when we informed them that we sailed on the total abstinence principle, they expressed much astonishment at the fact, and wondered how we got along without liquor.

Several New Zealanders in the respective crews of these vessels attracted my attention, from the tattooing on their bodies. The figures on the face and breast were not near so disgusting, as from previous description I had imagined them to be.

Quite a pleasant incident occurred on board our vessel, during this evening. One of the crew of the brig Jane came into our forecastle, and inquired whether there were any natives of Patterson, New Jersey, present. Two of our crew, belonging to that city, presented themselves; and, after some inquiries, one of them proved to be the play- and school-mate of the stranger. They had not met since their childhood, and their meeting now caused much feeling on each side. Both had followed the sea for years, and been self-exiled as it were from their native land. When a stripling, the one aboard of us had joined the volunteers in General Scott's army, then in Mexico. After participating in the struggle until peace was declared, he returned to the United States, spent his pay, and then shipped aboard a whaler bound to the Arctic ocean. Having been forty months at sea, he came back, and again spent his earnings just as foolishly as he had done before; and, being compelled by necessity to return to the ocean for support, he shipped aboard a merchant vessel bound for Liverpool. He next made various voyages to different parts of Europe and the West Indies, experiencing perilous vicissitudes; when, finally, he embarked on board our old craft. His schoolmate had joined a New Bedford whaler; which, after being a year from home, touched at a port on the eastern coast of New Zealand, where he deserted, and engaged for a time in the lumber trade; in which, he told me, he would have done well, if he had left liquor alone. From this he proceeded to trade with the natives, and was finally adopted by them; but their mode of life being distasteful to him, he engaged in the coasting-trade, was cast away, and carried into Hobartown, where he at length joined the brig Jane. Both these men possessed talents above mediocrity. They were good seamen, and their qualifications would have rendered them good citizens also, had not a roving, restless spirit of adventure led them to throw away their time rambling over the world.

These ships pursue the blackfish with almost as much eagerness as they do the whale, and their manœuverings for this small game often deceived us. The crews receive a large proportion of the vessels' earnings; but they get only forty pounds sterling per ton for their oil, no matter what price it brings in the market; so that, although the lays are shorter, the actual remuneration is about equal to ours. The only advantage they possess over us is in the shortness of the voyage: during the whole continuance of it, however, they allow no liberty, and only touch at insignificant ports for vegetables.

On the 22d we sighted sperm whales. Lowering away the waist boat, we went on to the fish — the boatsteerer darted; but the irons struck the head, and did not penetrate. The whales started to the windward, and we saw no more of them — getting nothing but fisherman's luck for our pains.

On the 25th we were informed of the probable loss of the ship Twilight, of New Bedford: it being supposed that she had foundered at sea. The report was originated by the captain of the barque Draco. It appears that the two vessels sailed from King George's Sound in company; and, experiencing an exceedingly heavy gale, they agreed to lie by each other during the night, either party, if desirous of running before the gale, agreeing to fire a rocket or show a light. No such signal was seen from the Draco; and next morning, on the Twilight's not being discernible, the conclusion was arrived at that she was lost. We were agreeably surprised, a few weeks after, by a sight of the missing ship. Her captain had before been informed of the report; and, on our running across his stern, to our captain's hail he replied, that his ship was the Nonsuch of New Bedford.

About this time, I was much amused by an original method, which our captain instituted, to stop pugilistic encounters between the boys. On the evening previous, a Portuguese boy and a New Bedford youngster engaged in a game of fisticuffs, resulting in black eyes and skinned noses to both the participants. The captain, on making inquiry the next morning, discovered enough to justify him in punishing them. For this purpose he tied their left hands firmly together, and placed reef-points in their right hands. (These points are manilla ropes, three feet long, whipped at both ends, and about three-fourths of an inch in diameter — a formidable weapon in a strong hand.) Then, after getting them in position, he instructed them to lay their points on each other's backs. The Bedford boy refusing to do this, the captain took the point in his own hand, and gave him a cut, which operated like fire amidst dry wood. At it they went; and, both being game, they continued the infliction of the points for half an hour, when they were stopped by the old man. One of them was then sent to sit astride the extreme end of the flying jib-boom, and the other to occupy a similar position on the spanker-boom. The other ships' officers said, merrily, that old Sherman was trimming ship to beat them.

On the same day, by the ship Alexander, belonging to the same owners as our own barque, I received letters from home; and although nine months old, they were heartily welcome. None but the wanderer from home and friends knows, or can imagine, the joy and comfort imparted by good news from home. Such events are the oases in our desert. Newspapers were also sent to me; and I read them completely through, advertisements and all, with a degree of attention I had never before bestowed on a printed sheet. Others were not so fortunate as myself, and gave vent to their disappointment in bitter terms.

The Alexander had been whaling in higher latitudes than we were — she having visited Desolation and New Zealand. Her present captain came out as first officer; for, the original captain being taken sick, had returned to the United States from one of the Cape De Verde Islands, and his mate succeeded him in command. Her crew described their first captain as having been a trump; relating, with great glee, that on the cook's serving them up beans badly cooked, they complained to him; and, discovering their complaint to be well founded, he forced the cook to eat the whole mess — giving him nothing else to eat until he had completed the task. Ever afterwards, they said, their victuals were nicely prepared. Off the western coast of New Zealand they had seen sperm whales more than sixty times; but, for some reason or other, they had not been very successful in capturing them — having taken but five hundred barrels of oil from the time they left home. This ship then purposed returning, and was anxious for us to accompany her.

Whilst we were in the Bight, the barque Australasian Packet captured a sperm whale. The weather was boisterous, and they did not succeed in getting him alongside until after dark. The boat that was running the line to the ship was struck by the vessel, and stoven: two of her crew clung to the boat, and escaped; the others were drowned. The whale was allowed to go adrift, and was picked up on the following day by the ship Hunter, of New Bedford. By this sad disaster the crew of the Packet were intimidated, and refused to do any more whaling; therefore the captain was forced to return with her to Hobartown.

On the 10th of October we gammoned the barque Rodman, of New Bedford, twelve months out, with twelve hundred barrels of oil. She was by far the most successful ship we encountered. Much of her oil was taken off Desolation; and her crew, like that of the Stephania, represented that whaling-ground as a perfect purgatory. They said that the weather was so intensely cold, that it was necessary to envelop the person in three or four thicknesses of warm woolen clothing when going in the boats. This practice cost one of their crew his life; for the boat in which he was being stoven, from the heaviness of his clothing when saturated he was unable to swim, though he knew how, and he perished — his boatmates having as much as they could do to save themselves. They had also been into Shark's Bay, in pursuit of humpbacks, and lost an anchor there; the captain had also there rigged a bomb-gun, so as to discharge a harpoon, but on putting it into operation shattered his hand.

Doing nothing in the Bight, and being assured of the scarcity of sperm whales on its grounds, we took our departure for the westward. We had counted largely on this season's operations — forgetting the old maxim of not reckoning chickens before they are hatched. We saw sperm whales but once during the season, and then failed to make a capture. We were, without palliation, skunked: our whole additions being a porpoise and cowfish. The latter fish is of the same species as the porpoise, only differing from it in size, it being considerably larger; its flesh is coarser and not so good eating.

During our cruise we were continually in sight of some one or more islands of the Récherché Archipelago. These islands are uninhabited and almost barren — the only green appearance being a stunted brushwood. Around these islands the seal is found in great numbers, and small craft resort to them for the purpose of capturing these sea-dogs. Several of the ships lowered their boats, which went in, and stated that they caught numbers of fine fish.

Steering to the westward we sighted Bald Island and Baldhead, and cruised in their neighborhood for several weeks, seeing sperm whales once, but, after a hard day's chase, giving up the pursuit as futile. One Sunday, at daybreak, the order was passed forward to loose the flying-jib. One of the hands laying out on the boom for the purpose, the foot rope parted, and he was precipitated into the sea. We had had blustering weather for a few days previous, and a heavy swell was on at the time of the catastrophe. No one saw him fall; but one of the crew, imagining, as he thought, that he heard a gurgling sound in the water, looked over the bow, and saw at a glance what had happened. The alarm being instantly given, the cry of "Man overboard," resounded throughout the ship; and, without waiting to dress, the whole crew, fore and aft, made their appearance on deck. In a moment the wheel was put hard down, and the mainyard hauled aback. The first officer sprang into the larboard boat, in his night dress, and cut the gripes; the tackles were let go by the run, and the moment she touched the water she was manned by a crew, who, with strong arms and brave hearts, lustily pulled for their hapless companion. Fortunately, he was a strong swimmer, and, although the weather was cold and he enveloped in the heaviest of sea clothing, with his coat on, also, he found but little difficulty in keeping afloat. In a short time the fourth mate, who was in the head of the boat, grasped him and hauled him aboard. The word was instantly given that he was saved. No cheers followed this agreeable announcement; but a deep-drawn sigh of satisfaction expressed the relief such intelligence afforded. In eight minutes from the time the order was given to loose the sail, we had him safe and snug aboard the ship. He was so weak as to be unable to clamber from the boat up the side. On stepping from the rail to the deck, he was welcomed as one restored from the dead, and, after many assurances that he was all right, except a slight weakness, the excitement began to subside. None but those who have experienced it, can imagine the effect produced by the cry of "Man overboard," on every hearer; and to us, who had lived for more than a year together, seeing and conversing with each other every hour in the day, all depending on the same fabric for shelter against the storm and wave, it came with a ten-fold force — as none knew whose turn it next might be. Nothing serious resulted from the ducking; a slight cold, that soon yielded to simple treatment, being the only affection.

On the 20th we stood in with a fair wind, passed Baldhead, entered Frenchman's Bay, and came to anchor at 7 o'clock in the evening; having taken a pilot when opposite to Baldhead. A few hours after the James Allen made her appearance. We found at anchor the barque Wavelett, of New Bedford. The ensuing morning all three ships weighed their anchors and passed through a narrow passage which connects the bay with the sound. The Wavelett and our barque came to anchor in good shape, but the James Allen, in trying to imitate us, ran aground. After a few hours she floated clear. At anchor in King George's Sound, we found an old hulk, with only her lower masts standing, was moored stem and stern, and used for the reception of coals for the steamships that every month touch there. This harbor is beautiful and safe, it being protected from almost all winds. About a mile from where we lay is the town of Albany, a settlement containing about one hundred houses, and five hundred inhabitants. The tenements are principally of frame, with thatched roofs. Their occupants are of the same class as those of Vasse. At times, it is said, this place presents quite a business-like appearance; but when we visited it, everything like trade seemed stagnant. This was represented to be caused by the non-arrival of the steamers; the government having withdrawn them to use as transports for troops to the Crimea.

For the first three or four days we were visited by heavy rain squalls, which preventing much work being executed, we whiled away the time, between squalls, in angling—the water being alive with fish—salmon, herring, mackarel, and whitings, rewarding the fisherman's toil.

We had little trouble here to procure water—a large tank being walled in, from which we procured an abundant supply. The only difficulty we experienced was from the extreme coldness of the water while rafting it.

On the 27th our liberty commenced. On going ashore and walking up the beach, we found, on passing the custom-house, a notice, signed by the captains of the different ships in the harbor, notifying all persons, that in the event of trusting any of their men, it would be on their own responsibility, as no debts of our contracting would be paid by the said captains. This was unusual to us, as we had never before been posted in port; but it may have been necessary, as the sailor, when ashore, thinks of nothing but present enjoyment. When he is half seas over, he will borrow money, or buy anything on credit from persons foolish or roguish enough to trust him, and when he gets at sea, will tell with great satisfaction how nicely he bilked the land-lubbers; but in ninety-nine cases out of the hundred the landsman has the best of the bargain, seldom letting Jack Tar weather him.

The first move of our fellows was to take possession of an English bar-room, strike up Yankee Doodle, and break down in a genuine fore-and-after. There are five of these public houses in this settlement; one, however, was chiefly patronized by the ships' crews, from the fact of a pretty bar-maid presiding over the spirits; and, as she was the only creditable-looking specimen of marriageable femininity in the place, she was surrounded by admirers. She met all with a cheerful smile, and was ever pleasant to both officers and sailors, always granting them a kiss of her fair cheek, when ready to sail; while her character, from a certain dignity about the girl, was unimpeachable.

Of course, the facilities for obtaining liquor being so abundant, there was the usual quantity of drinking; but, without prejudice, I feel justified in saying, that, of the three crews, ours conducted themselves best, and at sun-down returned in a creditable manner. Old Jack, however, got astray, and was not to be found at night when the boat came off. The next day one of the crew found him, with a bottle of grog, close by a small dam on the outskirts of the town. After being thoroughly awakened by a hearty shaking he took up his line of march, which, by the way, was a very crooked one, for the beach, singing, with great energy —

"The sailor loves his bottle, O!"

One morning, on going ashore, we found that the Wavelett's crew were not on liberty. News soon transpired that there had been trouble aboard of her, and that part of her crew were in irons. Their captain left the town and went aboard, and found that they refused to do duty unless liberty was allowed to them. After some quibbling he consented, and they came ashore. Five of her men deserted, three of them getting clear; but the other two were traced by the natives, and apprehended by the police. One also was caught who bolted from the Allen.

Whilst in this port we had very little, in fact, scarce any, fresh meat. The reason assigned was its scarcity; but the Wavelett's crew were all the time well supplied, and I cannot reconcile the two circumstances. *We* certainly needed it, having been from home fifteen months, and having had it in but one port. Few potatoes either were to be had here, and in lieu of them we carried to sea ruta baga turnips, which were mostly eaten by the pigs. To make amends for the absence of fresh meat, a supply of fish was contracted for with an American—a deserter from a whaler, years since, who has married and squatted down here, where he sustains himself by fishing and boating. These fish, in appearance and taste were very much like those known as porgies at home; they were well enough occasionally, but a continual fish diet, than which I know of nothing more tiresome, soon clogged our appetites, and the supply, in consequence, far exceeded the demand. I well remember our second mate's remark on this occasion — that it would take two men and a boy to haul off his shirt, as he had eaten so many fish that the bones stuck through his skin.

From this time up to November the 5th, we were

windbound in this dull place—the entrance being so narrow that it is impossible to gain egress without a fair wind. On the 3d, the hermaphrodite brig Louisa came in from Adelaide. During these days of inaction, to kill time, some would fish; others go ashore in search of clams, or raking for oysters; some gunning, some sailing, and others in search of shells; the latter generally returning wearied, and with but few of the bivalves.

On the morning of November the 5th, Norman Kinwood, a native of Manchester, New Hampshire, was discharged at his own request, from inability to do duty; he having been sick and off duty almost the whole time since we left home, with chronic rheumatism—at times confined to his berth for weeks together. All were sorry to part with him, but thought it better for him to be ashore when unwell, than to be confined to the narrow limits of a forecastle. For a few days he was much missed, although a very reserved man; still, it was one familiar face gone, and we felt that our little circle had been broken in upon. We afterwards learned that he remained at Albany several months, and then took passage in a schooner for Melbourne, since which nothing has been heard from him. We shipped a new man in his place, and at $9\frac{1}{2}$ o'clock on November the 5th, took the pilot aboard, hove up our anchors, and in a heavy squall stood out of the sound, coming to anchor in Frenchman's Bay. The Allen and Wavelett soon after followed. At 5 o'clock we hove up, a second time were under weigh, and with a stiff breeze stood out to sea, steering to the southward until we were in latitude 40°, where we expected to see plenty of right whales: and we did see them, too, and that was all the good they done us, as we would sight them from the ship, but the moment a boat was lowered they absquatulated in as secret and effectual a manner as a defaulting bank clerk. Finding we could do nothing with these shy gentlemen, we steered north-west for Cape Leuwin, hoping to see sperm whales, to recompense us for six months' time thrown away. On the passage we gammoned with the barque Lady MacIntosh, of London. She last sailed from Adelaide, having carried railroad iron to that port for the purpose of constructing a railway to Melbourne, which, when finished, will be the first work of the kind on the island. She was then bound to the East Indies for a cargo of teak-wood. It is not usual for merchant ships to lose time in visiting; but in this case both ships were becalmed within a few miles of each other, and she setting her signal our captain went aboard.

From the date of leaving King George's Sound, until the 11th of January, 1857, little transpired worthy of record, except the capture of half-a-dozen blackfish, and the usual amount of gammoning with other whaleships — some of which had done better, others worse, than ourselves. During the whole of this time we could not catch a glimpse of a sperm whale; and whilst ships in our immediate neighborhood could see and capture them, we were doing nothing. We double-manned our mastheads, made more sail, and passed over a greater space every day than heretofore, but all to no purpose; the whales were still beyond our vision. Meantime our crew began to get discouraged, almost a year having elapsed since we had taken any oil, and, consequently, since a single penny had been earned by any of us. Some took it very easily, but they were those to whom whaling was distasteful; others chafed with impatience; but, finally, all of us settled down into the belief that we had about all the oil we should get this voyage. The captain kept his spirits up, and was continually foretelling better luck. Our time, during this interval, was got rid of in various ways. In warm weather, the watches on deck, as well as those below, were for the most part slept away; in cold weather, walking fore and aft the deck, with hands thrust deep into breeches pockets, seemed the only occupation any of us had. There was no work to be done, in fact, but to break out our provender from the ship's hold and consume it.

On the 11th, at 4 o'clock in the afternoon, we squared our yards and steered for the land. At $9\frac{1}{2}$ the following morning we let go our anchor in Bunbury Bay, opposite to, and about a mile distant from, the town of Bunbury. This little town is the neatest that I have seen on the coast; and, although the class of population, to a great extent, is similar to that in Vasse and the Sound, still there are many reside in it who are worthy, respected, hospitable, and intelligent. Ours was the first ship that had been in the harbor for years, and our captain received the title of "the opener of the port." At one time it was a place of great resort for American whale-ships, but several having, by some means, been driven ashore and lost, it became unpopular, and was superseded by Vasse. The high price of provisions and generally disobliging character of the inhabitants in the latter place, induced our captain to visit Bunbury as an experiment, which proved successful in the highest degree. We were eagerly welcomed on going ashore, and cordially invited into the settlers' houses. The schools were allowed a holiday, that the children might visit the ship. These youngsters, on seeing us, from the shore, engaged aloft (all the ship's crew being at work in the rigging), tarring down, &c., deemed us monkeys, and could not be convinced to the contrary until they came aboard and had a survey of us. This was rather disparaging to some thirty young men, belonging to the smartest nation in the world, to be compared to brutes; but our occupation originated the impression, and one of the little fellows observed, on coming aboard, "If they aint monkeys, they climb about just like them;" and being convinced that he had gained a point, strutted off in triumph.

The country, hereabouts, presents a fertile appearance, contrasting favorably with the sandy soil in other portions of the colony that we have visited. Provisions were very plentiful here, too, and we were enabled to procure a sufficiency of excellent onions, potatoes, cabbages, and turnips. Part of the onions and cabbages were pickled and stowed away until our fresh supply should be exhausted. Excellent fruit was to be had ashore, comprising apples, peaches, melons, and pears; some of the peaches were delicious, and could be purchased at a moderate price.

Many of the natives here presented a better appearance than any I had before seen, being clothed with European garments, and clean, they lost half of their hideousness, and appeared immeasurably superior to their brethren of the bush, with whom, however, they seemed to be on terms of the utmost equality. I was informed by a resident, that several of the females had been transformed into excellent house-servants; but that they could not depend on retaining them, from their unconquerable predilection for a bush life.

On the outskirts of the town is the barrack, where a company of infantry is stationed, to whom, in a measure, the general good order prevailing is due — their presence intimidating peace-breakers. These red-coat gentry, stationed in a town in time of peace, and enforcing the strictest discipline, appear rather strange to an American; but the state of society renders them a necessary evil, and companies of them are distributed throughout these colonies.

Within a circuit of a few miles there are a number of excellent farms, on which neat buildings are erected for dwellings and dairy purposes. The principal products of these farms are potatoes, onions, cabbages, and the various garden vegetables, wheat, rye, and oats. Their wheat is good and sweet, but dark. Their oats, as they acknowledge themselves, scarcely deserve the name. They informed me that they raised three crops of potatoes during the year. Indian corn, too, is cultivated, but not to any extent. These farms are surrounded by the ordinary post and rail fence, made of the native mahogany—as it never requires renewing on account of decay. The raspberry-jam, a wood resembling in smell the berry of that name, and susceptible of a beautiful polish, is found abundantly in the neighborhood: this is a handsome wood, and when recently fractured or sawn, the odor is delightful. Vessels arrive and depart from here at stated intervals, carrying lumber to Adelaide; they only take the mahogany, which is used for sleepers to the railway in process of construction there. These crafts carry passengers, whom, for the passage of about fifteen hundred miles, they charge the extortionate price of ten pounds a head; but there is no competition, and, therefore, they have it all their own way. The crafts are small, mostly rigged as brigs of about one hundred and twenty-five tons measurement.

As in all other settlements on this coast, the rumsellers drive a thriving trade, although here there are not so many of them, there being but two depots for the sale of spirits in the town. One of them holds forth in a neat brick building, which, they told me, cost two thousand pounds sterling to erect. At home the same description of building would have cost about one hundred pounds, or five hundred dollars. As everybody here drinks, they think it hospitable to greet the stranger with "What will you take?" and consequently our fellows, many of whom never rejected such offers, were alive for fun — and I will guarantee that the denizens of Bunbury will, for many a day, remember the skylarking of the Pacific's crew. One, after getting pretty well elevated, took our two Portuguese up to the school, and insisted on the preceptor's entering their names on his list of pupils.

During my visit ashore I went through the town from beginning to end, and by invitation entered most of the houses. In the garden of one I was shown a young kangaroo, leaping and gambolling about in the most graceful and easy manner. I also saw several collections of birds: the cockatoo and whistling twenty-eight being the most noteworthy. The cockatoo varies from the East India variety in the color of its crest, which is white; and, after some tuition, they talk very fluently, as I was assured by one who, with great facility asked what my name was. Not seeing the bird at the time, I turned round to my companion to answer his inquiry, as I thought, when a repetition of the question from a different direction soon satisfied me as to its author. On my hesitating to answer, the bird curtly informed me that he would tell his mistress. As I did not wish to incur my fair hostess' displeasure, she having furnished me with a most excellent repast, I hastened to satisfy him.

The twenty-eight is a beautiful bird, resembling the parrot. What it derives its name from I cannot imagine, as there is, whether in a wild or domestic state, nothing in its note that to my ear resembles the sound of the words "twenty-eight." The prevailing color of its plumage is green, elegantly variegated about the head and tail with yellow, red, and black feathers. These birds are easily taught to whistle a tune. Their natural note is pleasing, and somewhat resembling that of the cuckoo. They can be taught also to talk, and several in our possession far exceeded in this respect any parrot I ever saw. When taught they are highly valued by the settlers, and almost every family has one or more of them. They exist in great numbers in the bush of the vicinity, and are preferable to the cockatoo, because they are free from his tricks — he being as mischievous as a monkey, when allowed to traverse the house.

A river runs from the town up into the interior. On following its windings, I found it too shallow for craft of the lightest draught. Thousands of fowls skim over its surface: the shag, the swan, gulls, and the monster pelican — all gathering their living from its waters. In the rainy season it becomes a formidable stream, rushing violently over its bed, and carrying away all loose objects that lie along its course. In this river, too, I saw the natives spearing fish, an art in which they displayed considerable skill. Wading in the water, and patiently watching until the prey swam near them, they would expertly strike in their spears and transfix it. I saw one of them thus encounter a shark, piercing him through and through, until he despatched the monster. During the whole conflict he displayed extreme adroitness and activity in keeping out of the way of the infuriated creature, when with gnashing jaws it turned upon its antagonist. Whenever they capture a shark they eat it.

Small cutters are continually arriving and departing from and for Freemantle, Vasse, King George's Sound, and Adelaide. These cutters are sloop-rigged, and vary in size from ten to twenty-five tons. They are built of mahogany wood in the colony, and are represented as safe and convenient crafts; but only the largest of them venture to cross the Bight to Adelaide, and that too at the favorable season of the year. Their freight consists of produce and goods for the various storekeepers in the settlements.

The people of these colonies generally profess the faith of the Church of England; and in Vasse, the Sound, and Bunbury, Episcopalian chapels are erected;

but in none of these places do the inhabitants display a church-going spirit. During the hours of divine service the publicans close their dens, but always manage to supply their customers with the ardent on the sly. They consider the closing of their houses very unjust; and one of them, in inveighing against the tyranny of the laws, gave this as an instance: He mentioned that the government had prohibited card-playing, or any other game of chance or pleasure—even going so far as to forbid bowling-saloons; and that they were led to pass the act by a quarrel arising from a game of cards played for pastime at a public house in Vasse, in which one of the players was killed. Speaking of bowling-saloons, or skittles, as they are called here, reminds me that we heard, previous to our visit to Vasse, that there was a fine bowling-alley there. Congratulating ourselves on this fact, we counted on a game at tenpins as not the least of our anticipated pleasures; but, lo, and behold! when we visited it, we found a floor of mahogany boards, some two feet wide and twelve long. The pins were of the most outlandish shape, and could scarcely be made to retain an upright position, even when held. The balls were nearer oval than round, and as rough on their surface as a cocoa-nut with the hull on. There were only two of these; and when you had discharged them, you were constrained to walk to the farther end of the alley, and carry them back for another trial. After vainly endeavoring for a few minutes to make the balls roll in a straight line, we gave the attempt up as hopeless, and left the skittle-ground, thoroughly convinced of its demerits.

The first time we visited Bunbury there were no wells whence ships could procure water; so we held Geographe Bay in abeyance, knowing that we would have a hundred barrels to drag through its sandy road. After a week's stay we hove short, set our ensign, and were boarded by the police, who here act as custom-house officials. They searched the ship fore and aft, above and below, as they thought — although we might have had a score of the prisoners stowed away, if we had been so disposed; as it was, we had one forward, stowed in the forepeak, of whom they saw no trace. We carried him to Vasse, and set him ashore. Their mode of search was to get into the hatchway, and insert the native spears in the interstices between the casks. They reviewed the ship's company, in order to satisfy themselves no interlopers were there, and then delivered up the ship's papers and departed. We then set sail, and, after twelve hours' beating against a light headwind, we let go our anchor off the town of Vasse, where we procured water. Here we had several quarters of fresh beef — in Bunbury we had one whole sheep.

On the 20th, the ship Twilight came in and informed us that the barque Mars, with numerous letters for us, was on the eve of making this port. The next morning she made her appearance, and her stock of letters had not been over-stated, the majority of our crew, myself amongst the number, receiving letters that had been written only six months previous; and, as all of us had good news, and plenty of newspapers, we were more pleasantly employed than we should have been had we just captured a large whale.

On the same day our second officer, Mr. E——, left us, and went ashore; the reason he assigned being his unwillingness to encounter the cold weather on the coast of New Zealand, whither we were bound. He was a man of a most amiable disposition, had a superior intellect, and was thoroughly acquainted with his profession — both as sailor and whaleman. He had gained the respect and confidence of every man aboard, and never had had occasion all the time we were together to chide any of the crew, and as his chest went over the side into the boat, all felt that we had lost a friend. This was the second withdrawal of members of our original crew from the ship. Mr. E.'s intention was to remain ashore until some whaler should arrive in need of an officer; in which case his well-known ability would easily procure him a berth. When ready to sail, the captain brought an American aboard who had been in these colonies for some years, and was slightly related to the captain's lady. He was taken into the cabin as fourth mate; the former fourth officer receiving the position of third mate, and the former third the second mate's berth. All being in readiness, we hove up our ground-tackle, and with a fresh breeze on our quarter we bade adieu to Vasse.

CHAPTER VII.

EARLY on the morning of January 26th, we spoke and gammoned the barque La Belle Anna, from Melbourne to Mauritius. Through the kindness of her captain, who accommodatingly delayed until we had prepared them, we sent letters home *via* the Mauritius, which were duly received. On the same day we captured a shark twelve feet long. The capture of this fish is effected more in a spirit of mischief than from any good resulting from it; the sailor deeming him his natural enemy, and delighting in putting him to the severest torture. Their tenacity of life is remarkable. I have seen a red-hot iron run directly through the heart of one of the species, and still he turned and bit at the iron, grasping its seething surface between his huge jaws and craunching it, and, vexed at its non-impressibility, lashing his tail with rage. I have also seen them flayed, and still practising as many contortions as an eel; if you cut their heads half off, they swim away; and if you should open the body and allow the entrails to drop out, the creature seizes them in his jaws and tears them in his agony. The skin is used as sand-paper, it being covered with prickles. The backbone is articulated in very small divisions, which enables it to turn with so much celerity through the water. These joints, which are about an inch in diameter, and half an inch thick, are collected and strung on an iron rod, and, when finished, make an odd, though not ill-looking, cane. Few seamen eat shark; but some months after the capture of the above-mentioned one, I saw a person who considered their flesh a dainty. He was captain of a Colonial whaler, and took every possible means of gratifying this strange appetite. I never saw its flesh cook, but from those that have, I learn that no amount of cooking changes its appearance; as, after a day's boiling, it appears as raw as ever.

On the 28th we sent up studding-sails and began a passage for New Zealand. The next morning, at daybreak, whilst carrying all sail, we sighted sperm whales. After a short delay, we lowered for them. The second mate fastened to a large one, fired a bomb-lance into him, and had his boat capsized. The crew were picked up and brought to the ship, also the boat, which was found uninjured. The first and third mates continued in pursuit of the whales, and, after a short interval, the latter fastened to the same whale. The fourth mate approached the fish, and in giving him a lance, got his boat on to the whale's flukes, and stove. The boat was towed to the ship; whilst hoisting her aboard, she broke in two amidships, was condemned as useless, and broken up for firewood. In the evening we had the whale alongside. The following morning we began to cut, being surrounded by thousands of sharks. The boatsteerer, who went down on to the whale to hook on, was seized by a shark, who caught him by the back of the heel. Fortunately, the man who attended the monkey-rope attached to the boatsteerer, saw the movement of the shark and dragged him on deck. The wound inflicted was severe but not dangerous. Sharks around a whale, generally, are contented with what they pick up from his carcass, and to the plenitude of this kind of food for their ravenous appetites, the boatsteerer owes his safety. In this case the sufferer was barefooted, and his flesh being covered with spermaceti, probably the shark thought it a dainty piece of blubber.

The barque Columbus also captured a large whale on this same day. In 1855, this barque visited Vasse and carried away a prisoner, agreeing to place him aboard some merchant ship, on the first opportunity. This was accordingly done, for which the captain received, it was said, a large sum of money — the criminal being well-provided with funds. Whilst we lay in Vasse, it leaked out, somehow or other, that the government intended seizing the vessel on her next entry into a colonial port. When we saw her we gave her the news, and it was timely, too, as they were just going in to discharge men, whom they had engaged in Vasse the preceding year.

The ground that we were now on is off Cape Chatham. There we remained until the middle of February, when, with as much sail set as the old ship would stagger under, and a westerly gale on the quarter, we resumed our passage for New Zealand, which had been interrupted by the appearance of sperm whales. The passage had but little to mark it, except that we went in the course of it through the northern borders of the Antarctic Ocean. On the 22d (Washington's birthday) we entered the South Pacific, and after a spanking run of fourteen days, we sighted land and a

sail at one and the same time. The sail we knew to
be a whaler, from her boats and davits, and a successful
one, too, by the smoke arising from her try-
works — she being evidently engaged in trying-out
blubber. On running across her stern and speaking
each other, both captains answered to the question
of "What ship is that?" "The Pacific." One, however,
belonged to New Bedford, the other to Hobartown. The preceding week she captured two whales.
She reported that she had been cruising to the southward
on the Sullender ground, in company with the
ships James Allen and Alexander, and the barque
Wavelett — that all three of these vessels had been
extremely successful in capturing whales, but that
the Wavelett, when last seen, was on a lee shore,
with a large whale in tow, which eventually she cast
adrift. Her position was such that the captain and
officers of the Pacific unite in thinking it impossible
for her to have escaped from the peril, and should
she have gone ashore, the rugged and precipitous
coast in the vicinity of Mason's Bay, where she was
last seen, augurs the destruction of vessel and crew.
We made up our minds from this report that the
Wavelett and her crew, who but a short time before
had been enjoying themselves with us in King
George's Sound, had gone to Davy Jones's locker;
but five months afterward we were agreeably surprised
on picking up a paper published in the Bay
of Islands, to find her reported as lying in port there
with considerable increase in her stock of oil.

One of those continued and heavy squalls common
to the coast set in on the next day. They are
foretold by the rapid falling of the mercury, and

by the wind at first blowing from the south-west with the greatest intensity from eight to twelve hours, and then, shifting to the opposite point of the compass, we would have a second edition of about the same duration; the north-easterly gusts being always accompanied with torrents of rain, unequalled in violence by any I ever saw elsewhere. This weather would sometimes last for weeks without an interval of a pleasant day, and then be followed by a thick mist, which enveloped everything for five or six days more; thus precluding the possibility of whaling or the performance of other duties. Some idea of this miserable weather may be formed, when I state that during the four months we continued on the coast we were hove-to for fifty-eight days, and at least half as many more we were prevented from whaling by the density of the fog. Whenever our barometer foretold such weather, we shortened sail, until we had nothing spread but a close-reefed main topsail, main spencer, and foretopmast staysail: with this canvass we generally managed to sweat it out; although on two occasions we found even this sail too much, and were compelled to clew up the main topsail, and heave the ship to under the main spencer. On another occasion we heard a clap, like the discharge of a gun, and, hurrying forward, we found our foretopmast staysail blown into shreds.

Of course, little was to be done whilst Boreas was giving vent to his wrath in this turbulent manner. During the watches on deck it was really as much as one could do to look out for himself. Then there was the rigging to keep in repair, preventer-topsail braces to shift and reeve, besides taking in and putting out the boats: with these, in themselves trifling jobs, the watch on deck generally became thoroughly soaked before it was their turn to go below; and then an anxious period was spent in awaiting a gleam of sunshine to dry their clothes. The weather being cold, to use their own expression, "water was wet"; and being in the line of a sea coming aboard was neither safe nor comfortable. We passed the time away, however, sleeping day after day about sixteen hours out of twenty-four.

On the commencement of the gale above referred to, we saw a colonial schooner, belonging to Jacob's River, New Zealand, square her yards and run for Mary's Bay: her captain, on the approach of a gale, usually running into one of the many safe and pleasant harbors on the coast, remaining until its violence has ceased, and then popping out and cruising during the continuance of good weather. This schooner, Eliza, is manned by New Zealanders — her captain and mate are of the half-caste. They are a manly people, without much intelligence, but make excellent sailors and whalemen. The Otago, another schooner, whose mode of conduct corresponds with that of the Eliza, and also belongs to the same place, has a Maurii crew, with an English captain and mate. Some months after this I had considerable intercourse with these very pleasant people; and shall speak of them more fully as I progress with my journal.

Some days subsequently we ran in towards the land, and found that the same storm which had so liberally besprinkled us with rain had whitened the mountain caps with snow. We ran close in: there being bold water to the very base of the rocks, capable of floating the largest line-of-battle ship. The coast is irregular and rocky, possessing no beach, and only in the bays, which are numerous and safe, affording facilities for boat landing. The whole face of the mountains, which in some cases exceed a mile in height, is covered with tall trees. One of these eminences, when seen from the sea, presents an appearance precisely like a saddle, and hence was named Saddle Mount; and this was our landmark for four months: cruising towards and from it — at times going within a few miles, and seldom in clear weather being out of sight of it. It can be seen from the masthead a distance of one hundred and twenty miles, as we proved by experience.

On this ground, in company with us, there were about a dozen English ships from Sydney and Hobartown. After the lapse of a few weeks, the ships Alexander and James Allen made their appearance. Both these ships had run into Stewart's Island for vegetables, and whilst there they had lost several men by desertion. From their description, there is little or no settlement on the island, the country being covered with the ordinary brush, and therefore presenting scarcely any invitation to a sojourner. The men who left the ships were put to a hard shift to sustain themselves. Several of them managed to reach Otago, a town in the vicinity, where they obtained employment; several left in small crafts for other ports on the coast; and one, (from whom I obtained the knowledge of their adventures,) after in vain trying to get along ashore, shipped in the colonial whaling schooner Otago, where I saw him. He gave a ludicrous description of their ups and downs. In the first place, he and another took to the bush for concealment; and, not venturing to show themselves, they remained concealed till night. It was intensely cold, and they were obliged to lie on each other to keep warm. The under place being preferable, and each wanting to secure it, almost a quarrel was occasioned thereby between them. As soon as their ship had departed, they came out from their hiding place, but could find no one to relieve their necessities, nor could they get employment. They finally joined the natives, who fed and clothed them. Becoming tired of this kind of life, they eagerly caught at the offer of a berth aboard a whaler. This poor fellow, my informant, was almost destitute, and had sent to us for clothing, of which a bundle was collected for him. He was a German, with a very thick head, and although the captain of the schooner was disposed to push him forward, he found little ground for cultivation. He made him steward of the craft; but he soon destroyed all the crockery ware, and was so negligent that the captain and mate were compelled to carry their knives and forks to bed with them, in order to find them when wanted.

One of the men belonging to the James Allen adopted a novel plan to get away from the ship. He was a middle-aged man, who had participated in numerous whaling-voyages. On the Allen he held a boatsteerer's berth, but from dislike on the part of his captain, he was broken, and sent into the forecastle. In his many voyages, he had mastered the language of the Sandwich Islanders, which is intelligible to the native New Zealander, and *vice versa.* On the night that he determined to desert, he procured the paunch of a blackfish, which is readily found on board a whaler—it being well adapted for making drugs; in it he stowed his clothes, and firmly securing the aperture, he had an air-tight bag, with which he succeeded in reaching the shore in safety. Having a good deal of Yankee shrewdness, and being able to tinker a little, as well as to converse intelligibly, he managed to get into employment, and was doing quite well when last heard from.

On the last day of March our mastheadsman sung out, that there were boats whaling ahead. We stood towards them, and, in the course of an hour, found that the James Allen's boats were fast to a large sperm whale. We kept on running, and sighted more whales. We lowered away our boats at about 3 o'clock in the afternoon; but at $4\frac{1}{2}$ o'clock we called them aboard, and stood out to sea. The boats were again lowered at 5 o'clock; and the third mate, after half an hour's chase, struck a noble whale, his boatsteerer giving him both irons clear to the socket. Scarcely, however, had the second harpoon left his hand when the boat was struck twice in succession by the whale's flukes. The blows were struck between the bow and amidship thwarts, knocking a large hole completely through her. She soon filled, and capsized. The crew swam to her, and got upon her bottom; but, there being a heavy swell on, she continued to roll over and over, the crew following her as best they could. Several times they regained their position on her; but just as the other boats approached the scene of disaster, to give them aid, they discovered that one of their number was missing. At the same instant the third mate cried out, that some one had hold of his legs, and urged haste on the part of the approaching boat. Being a strong swimmer, he managed to keep himself afloat, notwithstanding the drowning man's clutch, until they had caught hold of him from the boat; but then he instantly exclaimed, "He has let go!" The boatsteerer of the larboard boat dove in, but could see nothing of him; and his boatmates were forced to return aboard, leaving him at rest in the sea, over which he had voyaged for years. Upon the boat's arriving at the ship, the captain hailed it; and, fearing the worst, asked if any one was lost. On being answered that John was drowned, he appeared much affected, and wept like a child. The lost man was a German, named John Walter, belonging to Hamburg. He was of an amiable disposition, and had endeared himself by his good qualities to all on board. He was every inch a sailor, having spent a number of years in the American merchant-service, wherein, strange to say, he had several times narrowly escaped drowning. On our first visit to Vasse, he was also barely saved from a similar fate. It is customary, just previous to leaving port, to roll the boats over and over in the water, for the purpose of cleansing them from the sand that is collected in them by beaching; which is usually done, amid much merriment, by several men stripping and going into the water for the purpose of conducting the operation. On the day to which I have reference, John Walter was seated in a boat, when orders were given to roll her. He remained in her; and the officer, supposing that he could swim, but did not care to take off his clothes, ordered the boat-plugs to be drawn out; whereupon she filled, and rolled over. From his frantic struggles, we then discovered his inability to support himself. The alarm was instantly given; and a boat alongside, belonging to the barque Monmouth, of Cold Spring, was cast loose, and soon had him aboard, totally exhausted. Now, however, after these hairbreadth escapes, as if fate had such a death in store for him, he met a watery grave in the broad South Pacific Ocean. Well may his life be said to have been one of fearful vicissitudes. But he had not always been alone in his imminent perils; for in one case, whilst pursuing the hazardous duties of his arduous profession, he found himself in the middle of the Atlantic, aboard a ship fearfully leaking. The cargo, which was salt, having got into the pump-wells, prevented their being used; and it was only by the most strenuous exertions, that they were enabled to retrace their course, and run their ship ashore in the harbor of Cadiz.

And now our little circle was broken into by the King of Terrors! Sailing under the same flag — every day in contact with each other — depending on the same planks for protection from the wind and wave, — in the course of the two years that we had been upon the ocean, warm friendships had sprung up, and "shipmate" was only another name for "brother." This accident — one to which we all felt ourselves liable — excited expressions of feeling, that one would scarcely believe could emanate from the speakers: men in our line of life seldom making an undue display of emotion. Every good quality and trait inherent to the deceased was rehearsed; and in conclusion, all hoped that poor John was in a better home above; and, if any one on board our ship had a prospect of a bright hereafter, surely he, the least offender of us all against the Divine law, would be the one.

On the following morning we ran down and spoke the Allen. They were cutting in their whale; and the cheerful note of their merry chaunt, as they worked the windlass, contrasted strongly with our own bitter feelings and heavy hearts.

The captain gave directions to have all the lost man's property gathered together, which was done; and, a few days after, the whole ship's company was mustered aft, on the quarter-deck, and all his effects were disposed of by auction, the captain acting as auctioneer. Every one bought something — each wishing to secure a memento of the deceased; and as the bidding was spirited, much more than the intrinsic value was realized for each article. This is a rule of the sea, but whether a maritime law or not, I do not know: the money produced by such sale being handed over to the friends of the deceased, if they can be found; but if unable to do so, it is usually given to the Seamen's Friend Society.

After this event, we remained in the locality several weeks. Sometimes a boat was lowered, and sent into one of the bays a fishing, which always returned with a number of the finny tribe of different varieties — cod, trumpeter, blue, white, and red fish. The last fish, of a red color and covered with fins, was known to the whalemen on the coast as the devil-fish, and another variety is known as the groper. It often equals the porpoise in size. All these fish are excellent eating, and are eagerly welcomed by a person who for months has had no fresh provision. I one day caught a fish of a bright-red color. On hauling him up, he extended three feelers from each side of the jaw, and two beautiful wings from his sides; these wings were bordered with alternate stripes of red and blue, that rivalled in color the tints of the rainbow. They were said to be called the garnet by the natives. The wings I preserved. They are unlike those of the flying-fish, being circular, and much thicker and stronger. The fish was about five inches long.

There are plenty of cray or craw fish, and several varieties of eels, in these bays. The latter are the most disgusting creatures that I ever saw. On being caught, they expel from their loathsome bodies a substance resembling milk. The Mauriis eat them; and when we were in Milford Haven Bay the schooner Eliza's crew, who were then trying out a sperm whale, considered them as a delicacy, with no other preparation than immersing them in the boiling-hot oil. The crayfish belongs to the lobster family — its claws are somewhat similar, only lacking the pincer-like appendage. It is of a bright-red color, and is most luxurious eating. It is plentiful, and easily caught with a net, or hook and line.

Whilst in these bays fishing, the fresh green look of the vegetation, and sweet singing of the birds, made us long for a return to a life ashore. The sailor, if compelled to remain at sea, in all cases prefers to be far from land, with nothing to meet his gaze but sky and ocean — land in sight continually recalling home memories, long dwelling upon which is painful. Another reason, too, why Jack hates land, when he cannot enjoy a ramble upon it is, that he attributes to it, and not without reason, either, a miasmatic influence; and, whilst in its vicinity, every ache or pain is attributed to its vicinage, and he consoles himself by saying, "I will soon be all right, when we leave this infernal land and get outside."

I cannot refrain from remarking on the character of the shipping on this ground. At this time there were some fifteen vessels cruising within an area of a hundred miles — three of us Yankees, nine from Hobartown, two from New Zealand, and a brig from Sydney. At daylight all might be seen busily engaged in hoisting their topsails and spreading their canvass; during the day using their best endeavors to get over as much ground as possible. At sundown, sail was shortened aboard of each. The schooner Otago, at the sunset hour, in fair weather, presented a strange appearance; always at such times and in such cases, taking in every rag and laying under bare poles—the captain assigning as a reason that it saved his sails. This craft originally came out from New London, Connecticut, as a tender to a whaler; here she was sold, and during six months of the year was employed conveying cattle and wool to Sydney, and the balance in whaling. The Eliza was a craft of much more aristocratic pretensions; she was a neat and tidy little schooner, and had been originally constructed as a yacht for Sir John Franklin, when he was governor of Van Diemen's Land. After the daring explorer of the frozen North had removed from the Australian colonies, the Government employed her as a revenue cutter; but now she had fallen from her high estate and was employed as a blubber-hunter. But with far greater claims to pretension, although possessing a much more homely exterior, the old Prince Regent pursued her course in the same humble pursuit; she had been built as a yacht for George IV., the profligate, who for years was prince regent of the British empire. Unlike her royal master, she still survives with sound timbers, and is a staunch sea-worthy ship, though of a rather *outre* model. Two of the Hobartown whalers were clippers, built in Baltimore; on one of them, the Isabel, I saw the American coat of arms in full emblazon. These clippers, if they were only built stronger, would be excellent sperm whalers — being small, light, good sailers, and easy to work.

Several of the barques on the ground were built in Hobartown, from the Hobartown model; they had long heads on them, but their sterns, and run aft, were of a fashion of fifty years since, and, although so recently built, our old barkey would sail away from them as fast as they could come on.

From this time, until the middle of May, we remained in the same locality, experiencing a succession of tremendous gales, from the north-east and south-west, attended by heavy squalls that made the old ship ring again. In the interval between their recurrence, we saw sperm whales two or three times; on one occasion getting to them just in time to see the barque Runimede's boats lying by the side of a dead whale. On another, we lowered away and arrived at the scene of operation in season to see the Sapphire's boats capture four. Our mate fastened to a whale some distance from any of her boats, but it proved to be one that was already wounded by them; so nothing was left for us but to cut our line. The irons that our boatsteerer hove into the whale were recovered when they cut him in. With these irons they fastened to, and saved, no less than four large whales—a fifth they struck, but he sounded and carried off all their line. The irons were of the variety known as the "toggel," and are an American improvement: the captain of the Sapphire was so thoroughly impressed with their value that he repeatedly solicited our captain for more of them. Another improvement that the American whaleman possesses, is the iron rowlock, in which the oar works with little or no difficulty. Other nations use the primitive thole-pin, consisting of pins of hard wood inserted in holes bored in the boat's gunwale—the least crabbing of the oar being destruction to them.

These colonial gentlemen are fair whalemen, but do not possess the energetic, go-ahead spirit of their American cotemporaries. They work very carefully, and seldom expose their boats or themselves to much danger; for instance, they never sail on to whales, always taking the mast down when arriving in their vicinity. I remember hearing the captain of the ship Pacific remark that he had been whaling, man and boy, for thirty-five years, during which time he had never sailed on to a whale, and never had the boat stove in which he was. On the contrary, the Yankee whaleman, with or without sail, danger or no danger, is bound to strike the whale, if possible, and for this reason they are preferred, even in Hobartown, "because," to use their own expression, "they will risk more to capture whales." Several of the captains and officers of these ships were Americans; and great inducements are held out by Hobartown owners in the whaling trade, to induce Americans to embark in their employ.

On the 17th of May, the weather appearing threatening, we signalized the schooner Eliza, and under the pilotage of her captain, who came aboard of us, we kept off for Milford Haven Bay, intending to lay there during the continuance of the gale, and in the meantime to supply ourselves with wood and water, quantities of which can be had *ad libitum* in its vicinity. After beating about with light winds, and considerable towing with the boats, we contrived to drop our anchor at 8 o'clock in the evening, in sixteen fathoms of water, about a ship's length from the shore. Lines were then run from the stern and secured to the rocks, so that we soon had her snugly moored stem and stern. The schooner Eliza was, latterly, very successful; having captured two whales, one of which she lost through stress of weather— the other, when tried out, furnished sufficient oil to fill about sixty barrels, and her captain informed me would reimburse the owners for all outlay on the vessel — provisions being very cheap in this part of the world. Never did I see better meat, or sweeter flour, than the specimens of each this schooner had aboard; both were the produce of New Zealand, and the meat, having been but a short time salted, was much better than ours. As in port anybody is at liberty to board a whaler and get his dinner, we often availed ourselves of the privilege, as did they in boarding us; the molasses aboard of our ship being the center of attraction to them; also the biscuit, which to them is a rarity — they only using their flour baked into soft bread. All lived alike, fore and aft. Little discipline prevailed; the captain was called Tom, and the mate Bill. The shipkeeper and steward were men interested in the vessel, both old English men-of-war's men, who had early settled on the island, and reared families— having married native women. From these men I learned that a marriage between two of the half-caste was always barren, never begetting offspring; but a half-caste man or woman intermarrying with the whites or native New Zealanders, were remarkable for their number of children. I was much pleased with these Mauriis; they were intelligent, courageous, and sprightly. Their songs, delivered with all the gusto of a half-civilized nature, possessed great interest. In their war songs they become imbued with the spirit of their music, and perform most curious antics, attended by horrid contortions of features. Their love songs, too, were accompanied by numerous gestures, one of them taking the lead, and the others joining in the chorus. These love songs were said, by those acquainted with their language, to consist of all that was licentious and disgusting; but to us who did not understand a word of them, it made very little difference. They also performed a pantomime, which, from its ridiculousness, excited our risibilities to prolonged laughter, to their great satisfaction.

The half-caste consider themselves a peg above the native, and take good care to let strangers know the distinction. They are a large, well-built race, and make excellent oarsmen; they are much addicted to the use of spirits; they lament much their inability to read and write, stating, in palliation of their ignorance, that when they were children there were no schools where they could receive an education, but that the rising generation, by the exertions of the missionaries, enjoyed the privilege of attending schools.

From us these people obtained tobacco, and captain, mate, and crew engaged in a game at all-fours for it. They played good humoredly, but appeared to be wholly wrapt up in the game. I asked the captain how he managed to preserve subordination where he allowed so much familiarity. He was a powerful, brawny figure, and a smile passed over his features at my question; extending his bared arm, corrugated with sinews, he said, "I play this fellow right and left amongst them, whenever they make too much noise." The English part of the vessel's crew professed great contempt for these savages, as they called them; but a good understanding appeared to exist between the parties.

On the morning subsequent to mooring our ship, all hands were called at daylight, and we had an opportunity to discern the features and characteristics of the harbor. It proved to be a snug, but not a large bay, encased by mountains, whose caps were white with snow. The sides of these cliffs were covered with noble trees of various descriptions; principal among which is the famed iron-wood, remarkable for its weight and durability. Several species of pine are also to be found. Scarce any beach exists, the shores being covered with huge boulders of many tons weight, evidently displaced by some great revulsion of nature. Few shells of any beauty are found on the shore — the mutton fish, warrener, and limpet, being the only conchological varieties that I saw.

Whilst here, half-a-dozen of our men were in the forest cutting fire-wood, while others were engaged in procuring water. Nothing was required in the latter case but to scoop a hole in the pebbles on the beach, and allow the snow-water, as it descended from the mountains, to run into it; then bail out with buckets and fill casks. Neither was there any trouble in rafting or towing it; our contiguity to the shore being such that it was only necessary to run a small tow-line from the ship, attach it to the raft, and haul it alongside, hand over hand. We also broke out our meat and coopered it, and then our hard work was finished.

We experienced several continuous and heavy rain storms, accompanied by violent squalls; as these would pass over, the rainbow, by which they were always followed, reflecting on and illuminating the green sides and white caps of the hills, presented to our admiring eyes, a grand, imposing and beautiful sight. I know of nothing that I ever saw that more fully impressed my mind with the omnipotence of the Creator than did this splendid work; and I have found myself again and again aroused from my admiration to answer the self-imposed question, "Could any man, after gazing upon such an appearance, candidly feel himself an atheist;" and, after arguing the matter pro and con, could find no excuse for such unbelief.

It is usual in port, during the night, to stand what is called the "anchor watch," consisting of two men; the members of the crew, fore and aft, participating in it. In this port, which was considered so out of the way as to present no inducements for desertion, to allow the officers the whole of the night undisturbed, the watches were all imposed upon the boat-steerers and foremast hands. On the night of the 22d, the watches were set as usual. Everything was quiet until morning, when the whole of us were aroused by the first officer awaking, and finding nobody on deck, and the starboard boat gone, which had been allowed to remain alongside. On mustering all hands, five of the foremast men were discovered to be amongst the missing. Their names were Joseph Riley, of Patterson, New Jersey; Charles W. Baylis, of Rochester, New York; Harvey W. Miller, of Weymark, Weymouth County, Pennsylvania; John Roberts, an Englishman, and David Jones, a Welshman. The three former had sailed from the United States with us; the two latter were British convicts — Roberts, whom we shipped in Vasse, and Jones, who had joined the ship at King George's Sound. They had taken the boat, furnished with oars and sails, and all the other furniture belonging to her; also a tub of tow-line and the ship's spy-glass; and from the appearance of our bread and harness casks, had liberally supplied themselves with provisions. The absence of any officer on deck afforded them time to safely convey their clothes and bedding off; and so equipped, they left us, in an obscure bay, hundreds of miles from any settlement, on a stormy coast, in an open whale-boat. No one ever expected to hear aught of them afterwards; but as my narrative progresses, a recountal of their adventures will be elicited: for the present we will leave them and return to our barque. On discovering the loss of his men the captain stormed; but finding that the whole procedure had been carried on with the utmost secresy, and that few, if any, of those remaining, were cognizant of more than the mere desertion of the men, he allowed it to drop, and little was said about them thereafter, until circumstances obtruded them on his notice. It will be observed that Kedge Anchor has at length managed to get away, on this, his third attempt, having endeavored to get clear from us in Vasse, and Balli, and now, in the most unpromising place of all, has succeeded. He was the possessor of two or three English sovereigns; and this circumstance must have caused the others to enlist him in the enterprize, as they knew his uselessness too well to count on his being of service to them.

On the afternoon of the 23d, the barques Isabella and Lady Emma anchored in the bay, and, soon after, the schooner Otago—making, in all, five of us moored in this shelter. The Otago reported having spoken the James Allen. She had taken three hundred barrels of oil, including the whale we saw her capture, during the present month. The captain of the Otago also reported having fallen in with the lower mast of a vessel of about three hundred tons, evidently carried away in a gale from some ship. They managed to get it in tow, but the line parting, they took no further trouble with it. This circumstance elicited our fears of a terrible misfortune to one of the whalers on the ground, and whether American or English we were unable to surmise. We have never to this time been able to discover to whom it belonged, though it certainly had not belonged to any one of the whale-ships we had been in company with, as we saw them all afterward.

The Lady Emma, a few days since, put into Open Bay, where three of her men deserted. In the vicinity of this bay there is a settlement containing eight Mauriis. This is the only settlement on the coast, from Jacob's River to Cook's Straits — Milford Haven being no exception to the rule, as no white or civilized natives exist in its whereabouts. Some of the wild natives have been seen here. During a former voyage, part of the crew of the barque Runimede, whilst cutting wood, were driven to the beach by these savages.

The next day, being Sunday and so stormy that we could not enjoy ourselves ashore, a number of us spent it aboard the Eliza. We were the more easily induced to do this from the fact of her having a French cook, who left the Alexander at Stewart's Island and joined the Eliza. He was discharged from the Alexander, and the oil belonging to him was rolled ashore. Here he professed to be very happy; and, as he was thoroughly master of his business, he was much esteemed by those whom he catered for. I was much surprised at the palatable, and even luxurious, taste of the salt-beef, after having been manipulated by him, compared to that which had undergone the same operation by the hands of our own cook. Although I may have been prejudiced, or the superiority of the viands had rendered my appetite fastidious on that particular day, yet certainly, the fare was such as not to have been laughed at, even at the table of a first-class hotel. There were wild ducks, wild pigeons, wood-hens, noble fish from the bay, excellent corned-beef, and, to crown all, a noble plum-duff; and we did good justice to the repast. At supper we drank, as a beverage, a decoction of a New Zealand plant, which is used throughout the island instead of tea. It possesses an aromatic taste, and the little I partook of enlisted me in its favor; but how a continued use of it would answer, I am at a loss to say. The Frenchman said that he had used it for several months, and preferred it, for his own consumption, to tea produced in China. As he was a Parisian, and a restaurateur into the bargain, I do not see that I could quote better individual authority.

On the 25th we lowered away two boats, and manned them with the starboard watch, bound up the river, or sound, as the Mauriis call it — bent on a day's recreation. Guns, ammunition, and fishing-tackle, were provided — also a good stock of eatables. After ten miles' pulling, we arrived at the head of the river, where we landed, and built a fire. Previous to our trip to this locality, our curiosity had been excited by the description of a falls, which, according to the account, rivalled Niagara in magnitude. The Mauriis stated, that it fell from a height of nine hundred feet, in an immense volume; and I fancied, previous to having seen it, that I should have to chronicle in my log-book the existence of the greatest falls in the world in this out-of-the-way corner. I went, and saw it. Its height was about three hundred feet — it first falling from the summit of a high mount into a basin about a hundred feet below, and then descending into the river. Its appearance was handsome; but, having been prepared from hearsay to see something momentous, I must confess that I was disappointed, and under the influence of chagrin did not appreciate it as fully as it deserved. On our way up the river we saw numerous minor falls, descending hundreds of feet from the summits of the cliffs. The river was alive with porpoises and cowfish; whilst ducks, gulls, and pigeons, skimmed over its surface. Those of the party who were provided with fire-arms penetrated into the bush. Soon the crack of their pieces announced their success in finding game. As the sun indicated the hour of noon, one by one they straggled in to the fire, more or less successful, according to their expertness in handling their guns. Their game comprised ducks, pigeons, and woodhens, besides several varieties we knew no name for. The ducks were about of the same size and appearance as the wild ducks of the Northern States. The pigeons were like our wild pigeons. The woodhens resemble in appearance a pullet of the common barnyard breed. They do not fly, but run with excessive swiftness, dodging here, there, and everywhere, in a manner to puzzle any one. They are attracted by fire, and a number of them came around ours. If not startled, they displayed little fear, approaching within a short distance of us with the utmost indifference. These birds can be easily domesticated; and aboard the schooner they had several running about in their hold, in company with other fowls. All the birds mentioned, when dressed and cooked, were palatable and appetizing.

Whilst on this island myself and another were left ashore, the rest having gone to the main with the boats. Through an oversight, they took the water-keg along with them, leaving us unprovided with water. We immediately searched for a spring, or some other depository of the priceless liquid, but it was in vain. As we had but a short time before been freely eating of salt junk, our thirst became intolerable, so that we even went so far as to drink of the water of the river, which was salt and brackish. After we had thus suffered for several hours, one of the boats returned, and supplied our want. Never before in my life did I taste so grateful and sweet a draught as I imbibed at that time from the most ordinary of boat-piggins. This was the nearest approach to deprivation of water for any length of time that I ever experienced. If any person should wish to be pestered with a gnawing, unquenched thirst, let him follow our example by eating about a pound of salt meat, and then sitting for hours on an island where no water is to be found, except such as will have a tendency to aggravate his thirst.

After the arrival of the English ships, our nights were passed in an excess of mirth. The rainy weather preventing any amount of work being performed during daytime, their listlessly lolling about the ship made the men feel prime for sport at night; and as none of our ship's company, since the desertion of our men, were allowed to leave her after twilight, by common consent our barque became the rendezvous for all; so that, about half an hour after supper, whole boats' crews would come aboard. One night I counted seventy men in our forecastle. Each vessel contributed its singers, and the choral performances were really a diverting medley. The cook of the schooner, being French, sang the Marseillaise for us; a German sang the Fatherland; a Portuguese, I know not what, but, like all the others, he was loudly applauded for his performance; the Mauriis, Sandwich and Navigators' Islanders, all sang their respective songs; whilst English, Irish, Scotch, and Americans, also gave vent to their national melodies—Rule Britannia, Erin go Bragh, Scots wha hae wi' Wallace bled, and the Star-spangled Banner, or Hail Columbia, followed each other — one song being as good as another, so that it had a tune to it. Amongst the Lady Emma's crew were four excellent singers, who had practised together, and performed very creditably; so that we were not without good singers. Instead of spirituous drink, we indulged in a beverage, known as switchell, concocted of molasses, vinegar, and water, with the addition of a little ground ginger. At a late hour we separated, without being muddled, as is usual in many, in fact most, assemblages of the like character amongst people who profess more morality than the sailor. On these occasions all was mirth and jollification: discipline, for the time-being, was set aside, and the utmost good-feeling pervaded the company.

On the last Sunday we lay in the haven, all hands from each ship went ashore, numbering about one hundred and thirty souls. We provided ourselves from our ship with potatoes, biscuit, a piece of salt pork, and a saucepan filled with molasses. We soon had a rousing fire going; and the Mauriis were immediately on the *qui vive* for the collecting of mutton-fish, warreners, and limpets, which they quickly detected, although to our unpractised eyes there was no appearance of shellfish. These creatures they detached from the rocks, not without exerting considerable force, as they adhere with tenacity. The mutton-fish is quite large, weighing from four to eight ounces. The warrener is smaller, and inhabits a cone-shaped shell. The shell of the mutton-fish, which is similar in shape to that of the clam, is single, having a number of holes in the anterior part, through which the animal breathes; the lower part of its body presenting the appearance of a large leathern sucker. The limpet has a three-sided shell, and is much smaller than either of the others. All these shells are of an inferior pearl; useless, on account of its frangible construction, for manfacturing any of the various articles for which the true pearl shell is used. These shellfish, after being captured, are torn by the natives from their habitations, and eaten, alive and kicking, with apparent epicurean relish. This practise of devouring the struggling animal, at first, seemed revolting to me; but upon reflection I remembered the cool indifference with which we dispose of the bivalves, which possess feeling equally with the mutton-fish, but have not the same energetic way of displaying it.

One of our party volunteering to act as cook, after sufficient of these fish were procured and deprived of their shells, contrived to make us an excellent dinner—we doing justice to a chowder prepared from these creatures, beside having them raw, roasted,

15*

and in the shell. The molasses was converted into candy and handed over to the Mauriis, who, until they had disposed of it within their capacious maws, had neither eyes nor ears for anything else. Our dinner ended, we wended our way up the bay. This was a task of no little difficulty, the beach being covered with huge masses of granite, worn smooth by the percolation of water; these were to be ascended, descended, and occasionally circumnavigated, so that several hours were devoted to perambulating but a short distance. Our object was to collect specimens of the green stone, which is washed down from the mountains, and, by the continual friction of the water, assumes a circular and polished shape. This stone is used for ornamental purposes, in the decoration of their persons, by the Chinese and Mauriis — they using it for ear-rings, necklaces, and nose pendants. Half way up to the summit of the mountain that frowns above our barque, as she lies at anchor, there is a quarry of this substance, which I should venture to call serpentine, but for its extreme obtusity. I said that there was a quarry, but I have only the authority of the Mauriis for my assertion; I went to the spot, and, from observation, decided that if it had been worked, it must have been at some time beyond the recollection of any of my informants. This bay, twenty years ago, was the rendezvous of a sealing party, who successfully operated in their business, living ashore until the rainy season approached, when they boarded their crafts and sailed for home. A whaling company, also, had a try-works ashore, where many a fine jacket of blubber has been converted into oil; as these men might have, occasionally, found time hanging heavy on their hands, to them may be attributed the working of the mountain, carrying such specimens as they pleased to their homes, for gifts or sale to the various tribes along the coast. The seals becoming scarcer every year, and the increase of whale-ships rendering the capture of the fish less a matter of certainty than formerly, the bay fisheries were deserted, and ever since it has been resigned to its original inhabitants, except when some old and barnacled whale-ship touches at it, or the schooners of the Maurii run in for protection from the weather. Nothing illustrated to me the slight influence exerted by man here, more strongly, than the fact of the smaller birds (those, from their size, too insignificant for the attention of the gunner), viewing man without the slightest fear, flying around and around one, and alighting on the person, as if desirous of forming an acquaintance; having had no experience of the refinement of cruelty inherent to man, they do not fear him. I do not wonder at the sealers and whalemen deserting this vicinity when they found that their game had left, as there is nothing either inviting or enticing to induce a stay on these shores. The ground can never be made serviceable for cultivation, as it is broken and uneven to an extreme degree; scarcely a foot square can be found without a variation in the grade of its surface.

We remained in this bay seventeen days, every succeeding twenty-four hours seeing some new creature, or meeting with some novel adventure. One day a gust of wind would come rushing down the mountains, and carry away our stern moorings, from the intense strain thrown upon them by the ship's swinging. Another day all were interested by the capture of a female shark, from whose body were taken seventeen small sharks. These creatures were put in the deck tub, where they swam around with surprising celerity. They were each about six inches long, without teeth, but betraying their origin by snapping at anything they could reach with their toothless gums.

I cannot take leave of Milford Haven Bay without stating my conviction of its superiority to any port that I had previously visited, with the exception of Balli. This was the opinion of all, and often afterwards, when we were on the eve of making an insignificant port on the Australian coast, have I heard it said, "I wish we were going ashore in Milford Haven; because there you can see something." You can procure no liquor there, whilst here nothing new is to be seen, and rum stares you in the face at every footstep.

On the 2d of June the Isabella hove up her anchor and stood out of the bay. She soon lost the breeze, and was endangered by her proximity to some reefs at the mouth; but a few hours subsequently she was enabled to resume her course. We, and the rest of the shipping, taking advantage of the same breeze, squared our yards, and were soon merrily bowling out to sea, far from the abode of sand flies, and mosquitoes, which had no mercy on us whilst in the bay.

CHAPTER VIII.

On the 7th, after having, during the preceding week, seen and lowered for whales several times, our masthead'sman sung out that the James Allen's boats were whaling. She was some distance from us; but we lowered away, and arrived in time to find they had turned up a large whale. This was the fifth she had taken within the past eight weeks, making her three hundred and seventy-five barrels of oil. Our boats returned to the ship empty handed; and, as is usual when another ship has been successful, we all indulged in a regular growl at the hardness of our luck, complaining that we could capture nothing, whilst others were filling their ships. But, to view the matter impartially, we were having returned to us a Roland for the Oliver we presented to them whilst on the Shark's Bay Ground; in that vicinity the success being all on our side. The next day, as if our bearishness had been productive of good effect, at daylight we sighted sperm whales. We lowered away three boats; the desertion of our men in the bay, rendering it impossible for us to lower four boats and leave a sufficient number aboard to work the ship in case of need. Directly after lowering, the first and third mates struck large whales; after remaining fast for a short time, the irons belonging to the larboard boat drew—the boatsteerer had had a long dart, and struck the fish in his small, where there was not sufficient blubber for the iron to take firm hold. The other fish, to which the starboard boat was attached, was going at the rate of I do not know how many knots an hour, breaching, curvetting — now with his head out of water, and, again, with his flukes reared high in the air, presenting all sorts of resistance that characterize the right or sperm whale — snapping his huge jaws together, and lashing the water, left and right, with his flukes. For a time he kept running along at a rate that deterred the other boats from approaching him; but, finally, the chief mate managed to get a line from the bow boat, which was taken in tow. The whale continued running for some time after; when he halted for a moment, the mate, watching his opportunity, hauled his boat on to him, and, with a well-aimed lance, stopped his running forever. We soon afterwards got him alongside. He was a noble specimen of the cachalot, exceeding in size any one we had previously taken. On account of the heavy weather incident to this coast, we took time by the forelock, and cut him in that same night. It was calm and the moon was at its full, whilst scarcely a ripple disturbed the surface of the ocean, so that we had an excellent time. At midnight nearly all was on deck. The following morning we hove in the junk, and bailed the case — the immense weight of the latter preventing us from hoisting it aboard. This whale yielded us one hundred and ten barrels of oil.

It will be seen that whales are plenty off the coast of New Zealand, and the query may be raised, why are not more captured? But seeing whales is not taking them, and killing them is not securing them; as may be exemplified by the case of the Prince Regent: whilst near us, she captured two large whales, but lost them both from the severity of the weather. The Flying Childers, too, lost the greater part of another. The James Allen, however, was more fortunate. One day, after having by the most strenuous exertions succeeded in getting in a whale which they had taken the previous day, sperm whales came up close to the ship. The mate wanted to lower; but the captain, deeming the weather so boisterous as to make such a proceeding injudicious, refused his consent. The mate then went below, charged his gun, and fired a bomb-lance into the whale with such effect, that on rising again he discharged blood from his spout-holes, appeared bewildered, and attempted to grasp the sides of the ship with his jaws. By this time all hands were thoroughly excited; and on the spur of the moment, although the experiment was a hazardous one, a boat was lowered away, which, though stoven by coming into contact with the fish, yet managed to save him.

I will here take occasion to relate another fish-story, which emanated from the James Allen. Her boats had been down for several hours, and when lying still, awaiting the re-appearance of a school of sperm whales that had sounded, a strange fish, in size between the grampus and whale, rushed by them with open jaws. He kept on for a short distance, then about-ship, and returned. Both jaws were furnished with sharp, wicked-looking grinders. Deeming discretion the better part of valor, they gave his fishship a wide berth He did not, they said, appear to be in pursuit of them, but kept on his way, unmolesting, and unmolested.

On the 25th we lowered for blackfish, and captured six, which yielded us ten barrels of oil. These fish, like the whales on this coast, are fatter than they are elsewhere, and average larger. Two days afterwards we gammoned with the barque Emily Downing, of Hobartown. She reported, that on the day we were blackfishing she had sighted two schools of sperm whales. Swinging only three boats, the captain and second mate went in pursuit of one school, and the mate of the other. The last seen of the mate's boat he was close to the whales, and his boatsteerer standing up, preparatory to darting, when a thick fog enveloped everything. The two boats in company proceeded to regain the ship, which they did with much difficulty; and had not those on board kept up a continual ringing of their ship's bell to guide them, the probabilities are, that they would have fared no better than the mate and his crew, who had neither been seen nor heard of since. Conjectures were rife as to their probable fate: some surmising that the boat had been stoven, and all hands lost; others thought that, as the mate was a prudent man, of much experience, and well knew the locality of the land, he would most likely direct his boat straightway to it, and lose no time in searching for their ship. The latter were right, as was proved on the 30th, when the Downing and we were in company, lying under short sail, — a fresh breeze blowing, with a heavy sea in attendance — our mastheadsman apprised us, that there were several sails off our weather-beam, squared in, and standing directly for us — coming down before the half gale like race-horses. We at first thought that they were whaling; but as they neared us, and we saw that they all had their colors flying, we at once suspected the true reason for their manœuvring. In a short time, the barque Isabella ran across our stern, spoke us, and informed us of the safety of the missing ones; and that all, though weak and exhausted, were as well as circumstances would permit. This was glorious news, and was received with hearty cheers. Later in the afternoon we learned that the poor fellows had been five days in their boat, with nothing to eat, except half-a-dozen biscuits, an albatross that they had killed by darting a lance into it, and a piece of squid that they managed to pick up. The latter, they said, was not very recent; but, in their necessity, it was to them tall eating, and they were disposed to grumble at the quantity, rather than the quality of their food. They said that they had made for the land immediately on finding that they had lost their ship, but had not succeeded in reaching it until Sunday. As they approached it, they fortunately discovered the ship James Allen close-to. They made for her — told their story — were taken on board, and everything that could be afforded for their comfort was plentifully supplied to them. They were much emaciated by their long fast and exposure; but under the genial influence of good victuals and their present position, they were gradually recovering their wonted hardy condition. The James Allen, being in the course of a few days bound off the ground to Hobartown, handed over the missing ones to the barque Isabella, who placed them aboard their own vessel. Their shipmates — as did all the members of the fleet — expressed the greatest joy and satisfaction at the recovery of these poor fellows; for we could all sympathize with them in their forlorn situation, inasmuch as we were at any time liable to meet with a like accident whilst engaged in our present pursuit.

Among the vessels that ran down to us was the ship Gœthe, of Bremen, Captain Austin. This was the first German whaler that we had seen during our voyage. She had been cruising for right whales off the islands of St. Paul and Desolation, and had taken nine hundred barrels of oil — two hundred of which she disposed of in Hobartown. In that port, which she had recently left, she lost a number of her men by desertion. Her captain, officers, and three-fourths of her boatsteerers, were Americans; and, although most of her foremastmen were Germans, all duty was carried on in English. She is a Bremen-built ship, of about six hundred tons, and well-looking — originally a packet between Bremen and New York, from which line of trade she was not removed any too soon, for she is the dullest sailer I ever saw. She carried (independent of her whaling-tackle, which was American,) an assorted cargo of German fancy-goods — accordeons, flutinas, drums, violins, flutes, &c. — also tobacco and schnapps; which she disposed of, either in the various ports she touched at, or to the ships she met with in want of such articles; and as there is no duty on the high seas upon these goods, I have no doubt that a considerable amount will be realized by her owners.

From this date until the 11th of July we experienced a succession of heavy gales, with a very slight proportion of moderate weather; and we observed that the squid was floating on the surface in great quantities. The entire absence of whales and black-fish caused us to conclude that some disease had affected the squid, causing it to die and appear on the surface, and also rendering it unpalatable to the fish. Deeming it of little use to remain longer, we bade adieu to New Zealand; and, with square yards and a fair, though light wind, we stood away from it. Its high cliffs were discernable the next day, when by computation we were one hundred and twenty miles distant. And now, that we had left its snow-capped mountains, its heavy gales, dense fogs, and cold, inhospitable climate, behind us, we rejoiced in the prospect of warmer and pleasanter cruising-grounds; leaving no regrets, but all glad to get away: the four months we had passed off its shores being a series of unpleasant days, that would have dissatisfied less mercurial persons than sailors.

On account of the prevalent westerly winds, we were forced to run several degrees to the northward. On our passage to Hobartown we crossed the middle ground (which is midway between New Zealand and New Holland). This is a famous ground for sperm whales, and did not, in this case, belie its reputation— we seeing a school, whilst crossing it. We lowered for, but scared them, much to our discontent. We made no stay here, but steered directly for Van Dieman's Land; and on the 21st were becalmed in sight of it. The next evening we took a pilot aboard, and the following morning passed the Iron

Pot light, and entered the Derwent river. This is a noble stream, two and a half miles wide, and navigable for one hundred. The country on both sides of the river appeared fertile, and it being the proper season of the year, in this latitude, for the husbandman to break the ground and plant his seeds, the agriculturists of the section were to be seen intent on such employment. Some of our crew, whilst closely watching these busy laborers, thought of their earlier youth, when, like them, they followed a kind father or elder brother in their occupations around their farms at home, and on contrasting their present rough and boisterous calling with the more peaceful and quiet one they were formerly engaged in, they were rather disposed to think the farmer had the best of it; and several expressed a willingness to exchange conditions with them. They may have been sincere, but I doubt it; as those who have been employed in agricultural pursuits, after once becoming identified with whaling by the performance of a voyage, although they may inveigh against its hardships and discomforts, rarely fail to go again. Why this is; is easily deduced. In the first place, in their old calling, there is too much work for them after leading the lazy, rollicking sailor's life aboard a whaleship, where the regulations of the service allow him four or five hours sleep (without whales are in sight) in the daytime. A man has little inclination to labor from sun to sun. Again, in rural localities, there is a degree of wonder and interest attaching to a sailor, that makes him feel flattered by the special attention displayed towards him; and, after spinning all his marvellous yarns to an admiring audience, he feels it incumbent upon him to keep up the character by again embarking, with the prospect of returning in the possession of new stories and songs.

Going up the Derwent we saw many fine farms, with neat and commodious tenements upon them. The river itself was studded by small craft, engaged in carrying produce to the city of Hobartown. A part of them possess the curious cognomen of "she oakers;" these are a distinctive class from the others, and are employed in the conveyance of the she oak, prepared for fuel, to market. On nearing the town, we discovered the James Allen at anchor, and found, beside her, twenty or thirty vessels — all sailing under the English flag, except a Dutch brig, and we two Yankees. At 3 o'clock P. M. we came to anchor within a short distance of the town, or rather the city.

No sooner was our ground-tackle down than boats were alongside containing prostitutes, who here, as elsewhere, claim Jack Tar as their especial property. They boarded us, extended invitations to all, when they came ashore, to call upon them; and with the most unblushing assurance, indulged in libidinous promises of the advantages possessed by their establishments over all others, and vaunting their superiority over anything of the kind in the city. Some of these frail ones delighted in most euphonious names, one was Double-Jointed Polly, another, Slippery Liz, another, Polly, the Jumper, and other equally select and high-sounding appellations, which they seemed proud enough of.

Directly we were secure, the mate of the James

Allen boarded us, and informed us of the total loss of the barque Henry H. Crapo, of Dartmouth, Massachusetts, with the destruction of all the crew, fore and aft, excepting the captain and a Sandwich Islander, who were picked up by an English steamship, after thirty-six hours immersion in the ocean. It appears that whilst off the Cape of Good Hope, she was struck aback by a heavy squall that tripped her up. The two persons saved sprang to cut away the rigging, to save her and give her opportunity to right again, when they were washed overboard. Coming in contact with part of a whale-boat, and a cutting-stage with lanyards attached, they constructed a raft, on which they were saved. At the time of the accident one watch was aloft furling the foretopsail. This craft previously bore the reputation of being tricky, having, according to the account of those who had been in her, several times before been on her beam ends. All her crew were known to us, and we had seen them, but a few months previous, rejoicing in the prospect of a speedy arrival at home.

On the 23d and 24th we were busily occupied in breaking out and getting ashore our right whale oil. After getting it all in casks, we launched it overboard, and, with four boats fully manned, the crews of all joining in a rattling, heaving song, we towed the casks along before the city front, attracting hundreds of the citizens to the wharves to witness the method of the Yankees at work. They seemed to be satisfied by their scrutiny, that we were the smartest nation in all creation. I heard one of them say, "They are a bloody smart set of young fellows, and no bloody mistake;" and, indeed, to judge from the appearance of the specimens of the two races here exhibited, the denizens of the city presented a worn, dissipated aspect, whilst our boys, fresh from the sea, with cheerful countenances and sprightly motion, looked capable of any amount of exertion. Directly opposite where we lay was the Government barracks, and the presence of the red-coated sentries, with their periodical cry of "All's well" resounding through the air, strangely jarred on an American ear. Speaking in terms easily understood of monarchical governments and their hirelings, this town is indeed little else but a collection of people under martial subjection; the character of the inhabitants, and their antecedents, rendering them subjects of peculiar care to the British government; and to ensure their good behavior, a regiment of these scarlet-coated gentry, who have seen actual service, are permanently stationed here. By their presence, rather than any work they are called upon to perform, these people are intimidated into decorum. Sentries are stationed before the governor's house and the various public buildings, and a nightly patrol is placed near the water. They are continually to be seen walking about the streets accompanied by the handsomest females in the place. This seems a peculiar privilege of the soldier — no matter where you go, you will always see him with a pretty girl; his continual presence on one station giving him an immense advantage over the sailor; and then, too, the color of his coat is so much more gay than the modest blue, that, in the eyes of the lass that loves display, Jack stands no chance against his hereditary rival.

Just above the town there is an eminence, mounted with heavy artillery, which commands the harbor. It is laid out with taste; but, being little versed in military science, I can neither vouch for, nor detract from its effectiveness. It is a favorite resort for the citizens, and is often the theatre of prize-fights, which take place, not only between the male, but also the female part of creation. During our stay, two courtezans fought for a pound a side, and battled away for some fifteen or twenty rounds, when the police arrived at the scene of combat, and conveyed the participators and a number of the spectators to the lock-up. The police force is well organized and effective, and patrol the streets night and day. In conjunction with the soldiers, they are the guardians of the public peace; and one would think that, being coadjutors, friendly relations existed between them; but, on the contrary, many and bloody battles occur. The soldier hates the policeman, and the policeman fears the soldier. If the policeman detects the soldier in any little peccadillo, he without more ado arrests him, if he be alone, and there is no prospect of falling in with any of his captive's comrades; but, woe betide him! if in an unguarded moment he has counted without his host — they flock around him with wondrous alacrity, take off their belts, and with these effective weapons soon beat off the police with their staves, and decamp in triumph.

During the three days we lay here, before going ashore on liberty, numbers of young women visited both ships, professedly for the purpose of obtaining washing; but, no matter how respectable or tidy they looked, their vulgar breeding would display itself before they left. Two of them got into a fracas on board the James Allen; and, after indulging in every expletive in and out of the Billingsgate vocabulary, were about settling their difficulty pugilistically, but were restrained by the mate's peremptorily ordering them into their boat. On their showing some reluctance at starting, he threatened them that they should never again come aboard, unless they obeyed. This had the desired effect, and they went away, to settle the matter ashore.

A short time previous to our arrival, the water-police for the suppression of smuggling had been abolished; and, scarcely was our anchor down, when the watermen came aboard, to bargain for tobacco and other contraband articles.

Hobartown, from the water, does not present a striking appearance. Apart from the military and the public buildings, there are but few objects of interest to the beholder, excepting several churches, and a huge windmill, perched on a tower, where corn is ground. The town is scattered, or rather the buildings are — which amounts to the same thing, — over a considerable area. Its population is variously estimated, from fifteen to sixty thousand; I having been assured by at least a dozen respectable, intelligent citizens, that both these numbers were correct. In the absence of a certified copy of the census, I will establish a mean between the two, and estimate it at less than forty thousand. Its streets are laid out at right-angles with each other: the foot-path is paved with flags, and the carriage-way macadamized. The city is lighted with gas, the works for which were imported from England. Several of the streets present a business-like and animated appearance; particularly Murray and Liverpool streets, which contain the business-marts — the latter, like Chatham street, New York, or South street, Philadelphia, (both of which thoroughfares I have mentioned before,) being the place of business for pawnbrokers, Jews, old-clothes-dealers, haberdashers, &c. At almost every step a groggery stares you in the face, and a glance within will assure you that they do not lack patronage. It is not unusual to see a husband and his wife, whose dress and appearance betoken an acquaintance with better circles, standing at the bar, and partaking from the hands of the rumseller of the beverage that intoxicates. I know of nothing that more disgusted me, during my whole absence from home, than witnessing two females, each with an infant in her arms, settling some domestic concerns, and ratifying the settlement with a nobbler.

But here I have been describing Hobartown, when as yet I have not been ashore. The last date I gave was I believe the 25th, and the 26th being Sunday, on the day succeeding it, which was liberty day, all were busily employed in washing, barbarizing, and attempting to change our semi-barbaric appearance into a more civilized one; so as to be enabled to make some pretension to being ladies' men, and enter the lists for feminine favor with the landlubbers ashore. After beautifying our persons as much as our means would permit, long togs and other clothing, that had been stowed away in the corners of donkeys for many months, were ferreted out; and, when we had donned them, we presented a pretty creditable appearance. Thus unusually attired, and feeling something like fish out of water, we jumped into the boat, and started for the shore.

On once more arriving among houses, streets, and marts for business, after a two-years' exile from them, thoughts of my own happy home rushed up in my memory, and bitterly did I deplore my foolishness in having left it; but soon, in the contemplation of new objects, I cheered up, and began my peregrinations through the city, with a determination to criticize everything impartially, whether English or colonial.

The most prominent objects, were the very conspicuous signs of the different groggeries, among which I noticed one, on the corner of two streets, with large letters, to the effect that it was the General Washington House; and a few steps further on was the Virginia House: fully attesting that some wandering Yankee, who still retained his American bias, (and where is there a son of our native land — no matter how long he has been absent — that does not retain it?) had squatted here, and christened these two sinks. Amongst other names, I also noticed, the Marquis of Waterford, the Garrick's Head, Handsome Bar-Maid, White Swan, Inkermann Arms, &c. Many of these were houses of ill-fame or assignation.

Before going ashore, our captain, in a short, but pithy address, strongly recommended to us the necessity of avoiding the allurements of the various shipping-agents located here. Seamen were scarce, and these harpies, ever on the look-out for American seamen — more particularly whalemen, to whom, in order to secure them, they will at any time give the post of boatsteerer — made many offers to induce our men to desert. The captain mentioned the fact, that no American whaler had ever made this port without losing a part of her crew, and urged us to be an exception to the rule. He then stated, that there was not a man or boy in his ship, whom he wanted to part with; and wound up his address by warning us particularly against a worthy, whose sobriquet was Peg-legged Johnson. What his real name was, I do not know. He had a wooden leg, and a brilliant reputation, all over the Indian and South Pacific oceans, for stowing away seamen who deserted from their vessels; and then, on the offer of a reward by their captains, returning them. The captain's advice was well timed, and had a good effect. It was otherwise with the James Allen's crew, as will be disclosed as I proceed.

Some six months previous a number of our ship's company had instituted a temperance pledge, which had ten signers, none of whom deviated from it, and, indeed, I did not see a single case of inebriety amongst our crew during our stay in Hobartown. I mention this as a sort of salvo to the general intemperate reputation of seafaring men.

Going through the streets, I was much surprised at the number and variety of the occupations of the hawkers crying their wares. Here one was calling at the top of his voice "Long, strong, and three yards long, all for a two-pence;" he had shoe-strings for sale. Another was vending hot sevilloys, a compound resembling a sausage; whilst another, with a bell in hand, was lauding the superiority of his establishment for the purchase and sale of second-hand clothing; and a multitude of others were striving to vociferate louder than their competitors their claims to the attention of purchasers of oysters, oranges, nuts, &c. Besides these notorieties, in every street there was an unusual number of blind beggars. I for a time kept handing a small sum to each of these mendicants; but soon gave up charity, as I found that it was deleterious to the state of my exchequer; money being worth twenty-five cents advance on the dollar here, and therefore a commodity not very liberally forked over by our captain. On stating my suspicions that some of these people were impostors, I was assured to the contrary; my informant saying that the climate was hurtful to the eyes—a film, somewhat resembling the cataract, covering and destroying the sight—a disease easily remedied by the knife of a skilful optician. The government supplies an asylum for these unfortunates, but many of them prefer strolling about the streets, to confinement in such an institution. Many of them are attended by dogs, who lead them about with precision.

Soon after I went ashore I came in contact with a young American, who had been located in the city for several years. Of course, our being from the same State, betrayed us in a review of the place of our birth, into a friendly intimacy. I asked him his opinion of Hobartown, and shall never forget his answer; it was, that "lewdness filled the streets, licentiousness the houses, and profanity the air." Although not prepared to endorse his sentiments in toto, I must confess that he was not very wide of the mark; and, whilst I have him in remembrance, I may as well review the opportunities offered by this part of Australia to induce young men to emigrate to its shores. The state of society, makes those engaged in business here, whenever they find a young man coming to their neighborhood with the character of an honest man, anxious to secure his services, and offer him a good recompense for them. During my stay on the coast, I, in several cases, had such offers tendered me; and, although in a pecuniary point of view they were advantageous, I have never once regretted not accepting. In nine cases out of ten, where young Americans have taken up their residence here, they have, however repugnant the habit may have at first appeared to them, contracted a taste for alcohol, and not having, like these people, been accustomed to imbibe it from childhood, soon became sots. Hence the reluctance of captains of whaleships to discharge on the coast any of their crew in whom they take an interest; well knowing that among such companions moral or intellectual improvement is out of the question.

As the lower class of the population, more particularly the female portion, consider the sailor fair game, our ship was continually the scene of their visits. Although we were at first quite pleased, and felt enlivened by the presence of the fairer part of creation aboard our floating home, we shortly discovered that we were only favored with their company from interested motives; and, therefore, after several visits had passed, but little more attention was paid to them, except by the idlers, who were glad to have any object to assist them in whiling away their time.

Great attention was paid by these dames to the younger members of our crew, whom they hoped, on account of their inexperience, easily to dupe; but it was only on one occasion, (the eve of our sailing,) that any encouragement was extended to induce them to prolong their visit aboard our ship. On that evening—fancying that we had some stray shillings in the corners of our pockets, and wishing to relieve us of an article that would be of no use to us when at sea—they came off to the number of a score; and as their blandishments could produce no ill effect, (for none of us wanted to go ashore again at Hobartown,) our accordeon-player was pressed into service, the quarter-deck cleared away, and all hands indulged in dancing—officers, men, and visitors taking a part. The presence of the officers, and respect for the old ship, restrained those whose buoyancy of spirit would otherwise have led them to run riot.

After being tired out with dancing, singing was substituted; and, take it all in all, it was about as merry an evening as could well be passed. All parties, before entering into these gayeties, had been pledged to decorum; and, as there were no intoxicating liquors, by an indulgence in which any one might be led to forget his or her sense of propriety, nothing was said or done that could have called a blush to the most modest cheek: a circumstance, the more remarkable, when the motley character of the assemblage is remembered.

There are several establishments in the city, professedly theaters, but really houses of questionable character, where dancing, in which all the audience indulge, is by far the greatest part of the performance.

One of these houses my curiosity led me to enter. Having paid over my shilling to the door-tender, I was ushered into a small amphitheater. On its stage sat five performers, whose faces were blackened with burned cork. They were attempting to give delineations of Ethiopian characteristics; but, although the audience seemed delighted with the performance, their brogue smacked more of the Paddy or Sandy than of that of the Virginia Darkie.

It is to be deplored that such establishments so often entrap the unwary sailor; who, on his liberty-day, bent upon amusement, his mind unoccupied, and in possession of funds sufficient to make him an object of attraction to the harpies who conduct them, is led to enter, and, ere he is aware, (unless he has a spirit that is proof against temptation,) they lead him from one folly to another, until he becomes helplessly intoxicated, and then he is an easy prey to whoever wishes to plunder him. Strange it is, that, with the victims of such sharks continually before his eyes in every seaport he visits, he should still persist in entering such places. He certainly does not do it blindly, but with a culpable recklessness, that is almost inexcusable. He will not stop to consider what may be the consequences of the first steps he takes in the path of sin. He is never deterred from his evil course by viewing the wreck of his fortune; for, when utterly impoverished by his heedless career on land, he again returns to his favorite element, upon whose broad expanse, or in whose mighty deeps, he sanguinely expects to regain all his treasure. He scorns to reflect upon the vile arts by which he has been debarred from the field of fair sailing ashore, nor regards the foul atmosphere of the brothel as more to be shunned than the spray. So, at sea, he thinks not of danger, when the storm king in his wrath is sweeping over the surface of the ocean, but goes aloft unfaltering, although surrounded by the elemental war.

The Hobartown market is abundantly furnished with most excellent meat—the beef I never saw surpassed, and the mutton is excellent. The principal part of the beeves consumed here are brought from Port Phillip in small craft known as "bullockers," and, despite their uncomfortable passage across the straits, land in excellent condition. We had plenty of such provender whilst we lay here — the cook, or steward, having orders to get abundant supplies each morning, except Sundays — and we did it justice. Although a seaman sighs for fresh meat, after a long cruise, when he has enjoyed it for several days his appetite becomes surfeited, and he gladly hunts up salt junk, and partakes of it with a relish. The consumption for the first and second days is treble that of the succeeding three. A vessel, several years ago, touched at a port on the western coast of South America, for a reason not assigned. There was no fresh meat furnished to the crew, in lieu of it poultry was substituted, which, for a short time, was partaken of with relish; but one day the captain was surprised at seeing his men come aft and complain of their chicken diet, asserting that they had had too much of it, and could not work upon it. Salt junk was served out in its place, and the difficulty settled. This is not an isolated case of the kind; I have read elsewhere, I think in one of J. Fennimore Cooper's works, that the Scotch garrisons originally stationed on the various outposts of Great Britain, on the lakes, were accustomed to complain when an over supply of venison or salmon was meted out to them; these articles, to us luxuries, being so plentiful near their abode, and so often partaken of as to lose their novelty. At the present writing I have been but a few months without fresh provisions, and so long a dissertation on the coveted food, has conjured up to my imagination, visions of fresh and juicy meat, vegetables in profusion, and amongst other delicacies, last, though not least, a buckwheat or Johnny cake; neither would a piece of bread and cheese be out of the way, or any other of the little et ceteras grateful to the appetite, that the poorest person ashore can command at will, but which the wanderer on the sea must deny himself when engaged in a long voyage; the owners generally considering salt junk and hard bread as the staffs of life at sea.

Daily, whilst here, some one or more of the crew of the James Allen would cut stick, and defy the most strenuous efforts of the authorities to recapture them. Finally the crew was reduced to but a moiety of her usual number. They were restricted to the day ashore, at night being required to return aboard their ship; those who violated this restriction were confined altogether to the vessel, and those allowed to go ashore were put by their captain under the surveillance of the police, and if found ashore at nightfall, were placed in the lock-up. Our captain, to secure us from molestation, furnished us with passes to the effect that, by his permission our liberty extended for twenty-four hours; but as our men behaved themselves in the most decorous manner, they were never interfered with; and I do not remember having heard of a single instance where they were required to show their passes.

This passport system was a feature worthy of the worst despotism of the Old World. Here were we, a body of Americans, visiting an English harbor, after a long confinement aboard ship at sea, debarred from enjoying our rambles on shore with perfect freedom, and feeling ourselves liable at any moment to be stopped by the police, and have our passports demanded. And why? Forsooth, was this done, beause several of the James Allen's crew — disgusted either with whaling, the sea, or the harshness of the discipline aboard that ship — chose to remain ashore? To be sure, they had all signed the ship's articles, and agreed to remain as part of her crew during the continuance of her voyage, and by leaving her here they violated the letter of their agreement; but when it is remembered, that the greater proportion of those now deserting, at the time of joining the vessel and registering their names, were minors — totally ignorant of what their duties and hardships might be — their offence appears to be merely venial. And, again, the captain is also bound by these articles and by the maritime laws of the United States; and, if he has observed those laws in letter and spirit, he will be entitled to sympathy, should his men desert him. But, unfortunately, as soon as a ship is outside of land, and away from the jurisdiction of our courts, the captain is too apt to consider himself as the law and all its officers. He is, emphatically, when on the high seas, himself the judge and jury; from his decision there is no appeal, and to his fiat the seamen under his command must submit. Now, should he be guilty of gross personal abuse, or otherwise injure any of his men, or by a system of petty annoyances, render a situation under him unpleasant and uncomfortable, who will say that the party so injured or offended may not withdraw from the ship? The captain, however, will not let him go. What, then, shall he do? Life is a burden to him whilst under the espionage of his tormentor. His remedy, the superficial observer at once would say, would be to throw himself and his complaints on the consideration of the American consul, and demand justice. I will merely relate a case that happened at the American Consular Agent's Office in Hobartown, (the agent, by the way, was not an American,) to wit:

At Flores we received aboard a Portuguese, without an agreement. He remained with us, as one of the crew, up to the time of our arrival at Hobartown, and had become a pretty good seaman. One liberty-day, as he was going ashore, the captain said to him he wished that he would accompany him to the consul's office, and have his name put upon the ship's articles. The Portuguese assented; but, previous to this, the shipping agents of the town had conferred with him, and, discovering that he was not bound to the ship, had offered him a seaman's wages to sail in their employ; consequently, he imbibed a notion of the real value of his services, and when taken to the consul's office and offered a landsman's lay by the captain, he demanded a greater proportion of the vessel's earnings — one commensurate with his services. His remonstrance was answered by a box on the ear; and he was taken to the wharf, put in a boatman's charge, and conveyed to our vessel; from which time he was not allowed to go ashore again whilst we remained in the harbor.

It may be seen, from the result in this instance, that men have but little encouragement to apply to the consul. What, then, shall they do? The English courts will not receive an American seaman's complaints — stating that they have no jurisdiction in such a case; but, at the same time, they will grant to the captain of a vessel warrants for the arrest and detention of any of his crew who may desert.

Thus, both these avenues to justice and right are in a measure closed against the sailor; but, even were they open, I doubt whether Jack would resort to them. Taught by experience, as well as from the prejudice of ignorance, he cherishes a strong antipathy toward both the law and its executors; for which reason, he does not care to prefer a complaint in a court of justice, but would rather forswear its promised shelter, and take the seemingly shorter and easier method offered by desertion, to gain a release from tyranny or exemption from unbearable wrongs. In adopting the latter course, however, it not unfrequently happens, that, instead of having improved his condition, he finds, to use a homely adage, that he has jumped out of the frying-pan into the fire.

But I must resume my narrative, and speak of the colonists, among whom there is a generation now rising who have been born on the island. They are known as Van Diemanians or Tasmanians. The males are large, fine-looking fellows, and the females generally possess some beauty and intelligence.

This city having considerable whaling trade, there is a corresponding interest taken in everything pertaining to that pursuit. For instance, all the boats that ply about the city front, large or small, are in the form of a whale-boat. Regattas are held, under the patronage of the colonial government, at which various prizes are distributed to the victorious crews of the successful boats: and now for a word about these boats. During the voyage we had two of them, one of which was purchased from the Flying Childers, when we were off the coast of New Zealand, in exchange for tobacco — the other we procured in Hobartown. The former had taken a prize at the regatta; and, therefore, I think we may be said to have had fair specimens of the manufacture. These boats are longer, sharper, higher, and heavier than ours; they are built of hard wood — there being no wood in this country comparable to our cedar for the construction of whale-boats. Being heavier, they are of course more difficult to pull, and, although higher and sharper, some peculiarity in the model renders them so wet and uncomfortable, that, to use the words of those who had often got wet jackets whilst in them, "They do not ride a sea, but pass right through it." One advantage they possess in the polished smoothness of their surface, which enables them to glide through the water with scarcely any perceptible noise, and approach the whale before he has an inkling of its whereabouts. Many of these Hobartown vessels totally discard boats manufactured by the artizans of that town, whilst others vastly prefer them to the American boat. From experience, I should say that the latter craft, viewed in every light, is superior; and, again, it has the advantage of being two-thirds cheaper — the Hobartown boat costing from thirty to fifty pounds, and the American fifteen or twenty at the most.

We had but little trouble in procuring water, for, if so disposed, a ship can have it brought alongside; but if not, all that is necessary is, as we did, to tow a raft of casks to the dock, fill them from a hose, and then convey them back to the ship. The water is of an excellent quality, and keeps sweet a long time.

As liberty was given every day, and the watches were ashore alternately, the privilege of remaining ashore during the night was extended to each individual. For the convenience of those who were disposed to return aboard, a boat was sent in at sundown; but it seldom brought off any of the liberty-men. It was manned by the watch on duty; so that three-fourths of the ship's company might be ashore every night. The boat generally returned before midnight; and it was customary for the crew that manned it to sing a jolly heaving-song at the top of their voices — all joining in the chorus; and the nights being still and serene, the effect produced was rather startling through the silent harbor.

On the 5th of August all hands were aboard — liberty having been discontinued — all preparations made for sailing, and no intercourse allowed with the shore. Many of our crew wished to provide themselves with little articles for sea-use; but the captain, having all on board, determined to keep them there, and took the execution of all their little commissions upon himself. There was, however, no need of this precaution, in order to confine us on board our ship; for, throughout the entire day, we did not fail to have many opportunities to desert, if any of us had felt so disposed, and had availed ourselves of the watermen's boats, which were continually arriving at, and departing from the ship.

In referring to the account of what transpired aboard the ship on the last night of our stay in the harbor of Hobartown, it may, perhaps, be said by the strict moralist, that too much latitude of correct moral principle was allowed by admitting female visitors, whose reputation, at least, if not their real character, was that of the lowest grade; inasmuch as by their participation in the gay hilarities of that evening encouragement was given to the idea, that their guilty course of life was no hindrance to the realization of lawful and innocent pleasure. Now, considering the fact that so many youngsters were comprised in our crew — "young bloods," of keen susceptibilities for sport, whom the license of an hour might probably transform into "fast young men,"— we must acknowledge the apparent justness of this objection. But, on the other hand, let us consider the relation in which the captain of a ship stands to his men: it is not one which authorizes or requires him to assume the care and rod of a parent, or teacher of morals; but is one which demands a disciplne that can secure their willing, hearty, and effective service. Moreover, it is impossible fully to control the inclinations of a boy, who likely has always had his own way at home, and has been sent to sea on account of a too free indulgence of self-will. I say that it is absolutely impossible to govern such a stripling, (after his parents have failed, while he was surrounded by the influences of home,) when separated fifteen thousand miles from his native country, and after two years of forecastle life, during which, being continually in the society of sailors, boys grow to be men in opinion and ideas, and expect to be treated as such when ashore. As to the expediency of somewhat relaxing the rigid rules of moral discipline, we may be satisfied by a mere contrast of the position of our own with the crew of the James Allen at the same moment. On board the latter, the men had been hectored and thwarted, and consequently more than one-half had deserted — leaving the void to be filled up with green hands,—and those who remained were sullen, dissatisfied, and discontented; whilst our own crew were all aboard their ship, both cheery and ready to go to sea. The fact of all the hands that were brought into this port again going out in the ship, of their own accord, is unprecedented in the annals of the arrival and departure of American whalers; for, commonly, such vessels lose a half or two-thirds of their crews. A few months ago, the ship Hunter, of New Bedford, touched here, and lost a number of her men — several of whom are now acting as policemen. Our non-success in capturing whales gave good cause for apprehending that we should meet with a like loss, and our not doing so may be attributed to the general good treatment which characterized our ship throughout her voyage. Although not a paradise, still she was as good as the best of whalers. No overt act of cruelty or brutality had been exercised on any one of our crew; and therefore they were now all satisfied again to go afloat in her.

In the morning three new men came aboard: two of them were ordinary seamen, or as such they represented themselves — one having steered a boat, and the other having been a year before the mast in a colonial vessel. If these were fair specimens of colonial seamen, the poorest must indeed be very low; for none of them knew the compass, or the rigging, or how to furl a square sail. The whole three were Irishmen, of the class that are banished from their country for their country's good.

CHAPTER IX.

At 8 o'clock on the morning of the 6th we hove up our anchor, got under weigh, and, with a fair wind, stood down the river — leaving Hobartown in the distance — bound on another long cruise to the westward.

But before I take leave of Hobartown, I must acknowledge the general welcome and hospitality with which we were greeted and treated by its inhabitants, who seemed very desirous to add their contributions to make our time whilst in their harbor pass pleasantly. The mere fact of our being Americans was a passport to their good opinion. Although, when we are absent, they jeer at our national peculiarities, and lay great stress upon "guess" and "calculate," yet they are all suavity when in our company. Away from home the whole of our people are known as Yankees, whether hailing from the northern, southern, eastern, or western section of our Union. Being an American, as far as my experience goes, is indeed a passport to civility amongst the inhabitants of all these penal colonies. Though the greater part of these people have been banished from Europe for their violation of the laws of their native country, nevertheless, they still consider themselves to be the injured party, and view England as a great oppressor, by whose peculiar societary organization her subjects are urged on to evil; and therefore they say, as such, they have neither regard nor respect for her. I noticed that the military band were continually playing, God save the Queen; but I saw nothing of that affection for the sovereign, which the English papers are forever rehearsing, as being an inherent principle in the British composition. Respect for her virtues, as a woman, they readily yield; but these people have a vague idea of republicanism, that will eventually cost Great Britain her Australian colonies; although self-government among such a people will undoubtedly be productive of little else than anarchy and disorder. The discordant elements composing the population need a thorough alterative, ere they can hope to form a government in any way resembling our Union of the West; and from my own impressions, drawn from an observation of both the higher and lower classes of society, I should say that it would require all the abattoirs of Paris, — which extend, I forget how many miles, and render it the most thoroughly drained city in the world, — as an outlet for the moral corruption of this country.

And now I must touch briefly on Van Dieman's Land business-operations. Yankee cuteness in bargaining has became a proverb, but I doubt whether the sharpest of the speculators from the land of wooden nutmegs could outdo the sharpers found here. Long before we passed the Iron Pot light, a boat, containing a couple of speculators, came alongside, and her passengers jumped aboard of us. (One of their names, by the way, was Smart, and he sustained the aptitude of his cognomen to the best of his ability.) We purchased a boat of them, which, after we were outside, was found to be much worn, and the crevices filled with putty and neatly painted, so as to defy detection. The potatoes, bought for first-rate, were very ordinary; and the salt-meat, ten tierces of which had been bought for corned beef— being represented as having been but a short time out of pickle — was fairly white with an encrustation of salt, which no amount of soaking would remove: being ten times more saline than that which we had brought from home twenty-four months previously. This meat, when opened, was not, like ours, of a rich red and yellow hue, but of a sickly pink and white, which may have been owing to the absence of saltpetre in the pickle. It was quite fat; but the fat was like suet, and eatable only whilst warm; wanting the rich, pleasant taste of the fat on our own meat. The epicure may laugh at my expression of "rich taste," applied to a piece of salt-junk; but let him do, as I have done, after hours of fatiguing night-duty — when his system is almost prostrated from exposure to wind and weather — go down to his messpan, get a piece of fat beef, a cake of hard bread, and a raw onion, (if he is fortunate enough to possess the latter,) and then go on deck, and munch it, then, I think, he will find the taste of it rich, grateful and pleasant.

Before I go farther, I must relate a New Zealand adventure, which escaped my notice whilst writing of that delectable coast, and as it is one of the few incidents of my voyage with which a woman is connected, it would not be just for me to omit it: it was as follows. One night whilst we lay in Milford

Haven Bay, one of the owners of the schooner Eliza approached me very mysteriously, and asked the privilege of a few minutes conversation with me. Of course I acquiesced, wondering at the motive for his request. I was soon enlightened. He stated that in the settlement where he lived, at Jacob's River Bluff, at the extremity of the middle island, their former physician, who for many years had practised in the vicinity, had died, and they, therefore, were without medical attention. Having heard my shipmates call me Doctor, and discovering, upon inquiry, that I had dabbled somewhat in physic at home, he made up his mind that I was an expert practitioner, and the idea entered his head to secure me as a resident at the Bluff. He stated the matter to me, assuring me of a remunerative practice, and, as a further inducement offered me one of his daughters as a wife. He represented her as a beautiful half-caste girl — and I found, upon inquiry, that he did her but justice. I was both amused and surprised at the ardor with which he urged the matter, and did not give him a final answer, wishing to draw him out. The old fellow thought that he had me safe, when I deemed it time to put a stop to it, and informed him that my engagements to the owners of our ship were of so urgent a nature that I could not leave without the captain's full consent. He assured me that there would be no difficulty about that, if I would but give *my* consent to the matter; he would stow me away so that no one would be able to find me, and at the end of their cruise carry me to the Bluff. Of course I could not consent to this, although every time he renewed his solicitations, he enjoined on me to remember the gal. I certainly should have liked to have formed an acquaintance with her, but I had too many ties at home to forget and forsake my country. This old fellow was an English man-of-war's man who had deserted from his ship in the early days of the settlement of the island, and marrying a native woman, had reared a family of handsome and interesting children. His code of morals was not of the highest standard, neither was his sense of duty as a parent, or he would not have wished to dispose of his daughter so summarily without her consent; but then he may have been fully acquainted with her wishes, and I was assured that these girls consider it as a great honor to secure an American husband. In proof of this I will relate the adventures of a townsman of mine. He sailed from New Bedford in a whaler, deserted at Bravo, one of the Cape De Verde Islands, contracted some sort of a marriage with one of the Portuguese girls there, became tired of her, and shipped aboard a second New Bedford ship bound to the South Seas. She cruised off New Zealand, and then proceeded to the Australian Bight. Whilst in these latitudes, this young man fell from the maintop into the waist boat, and displaced his ribs. A few days after the accident we fell in with her, and I went aboard and set them. We saw no more of the ship or him for a long time, when one day, whilst we were gammoning with the Colonial ship Pacific, I was surprised at seeing the self-same individual step aboard from her boat, well and hearty, having perfectly recovered from his injury. He told me that being weak for some time after he was hurt, his captain had left him ashore at Stewart's

Island, with sufficient for all his wants, promising to call at a certain time. The ship not making her appearance at the stated period, and being perfectly recovered, he became weary of inactivity, and on the Pacific's touching at the island, he joined her, throwing away several hundred dollars which were his proportion of his former ships (the Alexander) earnings. The Alexander touched at the island a few weeks after, but found the bird flown, to the captain's regret, as the missing individual was one of his most useful men. He continued in the Pacific for five or six months, and on her touching a second time at the island, deserted from her and married the girl whom the cooper was desirous that I should mate with. Thus this youngster, scarce arrived at manhood, had, in the course of two years, left his home, and been a member of three ships, married twice, and at the last account of him was snugly anchored in an out of the way nook in the South Pacific, thousands of miles from his kindred, who know nothing of his whereabouts, neither are they likely to, without, amongst his other freaks, he should attempt that of returning home. Thus it is, a free life on the salt water certainly engenders this unsettled, roving tendency. A sailor considering himself at home in every clime; well-knowing that however little employment there may be for other professions, the ways of commerce will always supply him with a berth sufficient to provide for all his wants. The better the seaman, generally, the more wild and reckless are his frolics; never learning wisdom, or staying his rollicking career, until the blue waves of old ocean close over his sinking form, or he is hove down in some foreign hospital, a prey to disease brought on by his own imprudence. His life ebbs out, amongst strangers, when, if at home, his sick couch would be surrounded by kind friends, or, perhaps, a fond mother or sister, who, at the dictates of affection, would minister to his dying wants, and smooth his dreary passage with all the comforts procurable by affection.

But I must resume the legitimate course of my log, which was interrupted, I believe, as we were making our way down the Derwent. By night we were outside and beating up for the Southwest Cape. There, on Sunday the 9th, we sighted sperm whales. We lowered away, and in about an hour had one snugly moored alongside. The following day we cut him in despite a gale of wind; fortunately, saving the whale. On the following Wednesday we saw another school of whales, but, after chasing all day, gave up the pursuit as hopeless. As soon as we were done boiling, the James Allen hove in sight, having left Hobartown several days after we sailed. They informed us that after we left, her cooper, and one of her boatsteerers deserted, having been enticed away by the smiles of some of Hobartown's syrens. They also stated that the Prince Regent had arrived, and brought news of our missing boat's crew. That, a few days after our leaving the coast of New Zealand, they came alongside the Prince Regent and begged for provisions and some water, saying that they had been lying in a bay a short distance South of Milford Haven, waiting for our departure from the coast. Those who saw them said that they were emaciated and woe-begone to a painful degree. The captain of the Prince Regent, who, both with his own countrymen and strangers, bears the unenviable notoriety of being a niggard, refused to give them a single thing. They left him and went alongside a Maurii schooner, where their wants were supplied — the semi-civilized man, who is sneered at by his more polished cotemporary, displaying the most humanity. Afterward they were seen to go into Open Bay, take aboard several men who had deserted from the Lady Emma, and direct their boat to the northward, where we will leave them, until, in the due course of the narrative, their further exploits are developed.

On the 15th the sun arose amid a pretty fresh gale of wind. Directly after breakfast we sighted sperm whales. The weather looked rather dubious; but we wanted oil very bad—so down went our boats and after them. They were slightly to windward of us, and it was impossible to force our boats to the weather, in the teeth of both sea and wind, so, at 10 o'clock, the boats returned aboard. At 11 we tried it again; at 12 again returned, ate dinner, and, not at all discouraged by the two preceding failures, at two o'clock dropped our boats a third time, after having beat up with the ship to windward of the school. The third attempt proved successful, and, fortunately, the fish struck ran but very little, and was easily disposed of. Some idea may be formed of the hardships of the whaleman's life, from a recountal of this day's work. During the whole time that the boats were down, the rain descended in torrents, and the sea was so rugged that it was only by incessant bailing that the boats were kept from swamping. Added to this, the weather was quite cool, and the wind was at such a height that double-reefed topsails were all the ship would bear; yet, despite all this, the brave fellows, when they came aboard, although chilled through and wet to the skin, made light of the difficulties, and stated their willingness and even eagerness to encounter the same hardships again for another whale. The wind continuing, we had a troublesome job the next day in getting him aboard. The following Wednesday, as if fortune was determined to make us some reparation for the former sparsity of her favors, we again saw whales, captured one and got him all aboard the same day — making over two hundred barrels of sperm oil taken by us in ten days. The James Allen was in sight of us when we captured the last two, and had the same chance; her miscarrying, therefore, can be attributed only to the fact of her boats' crews being unaccustomed to boat duty, and unable to compete with ours — her old crew being pretty nearly all gone, and her boats now manned by men who never saw a whale before. I think that this should be a sufficient inducement for whaling captains to treat their crews well, so as to retain them, when, at the end of two years, they make a good port, they may not have an inefficient, almost helpless crew, instead of able hands to do their behests.

The next Sunday, unlike the two preceding ones, was a day of rest — on one of the former being engaged in whaling, and on the next in cutting-in. Being a fine day we gammoned with the James Allen; whilst so employed, we noticed a brig to leeward with her colors set at the mizzen-peak. At first, little attention was paid to her; but the colors continuing set, we squared our yards and ran off to her. She proved to be the brig Julia, of Hobartown, five months out, with twenty-eight tons of sperm oil. Her reason for showing her colors was, that she had on board a boat's crew, who, with two other boats' crews, now ashore in the vicinity, belonging to the brig Maid of Erin, of Hobartown, separated from their vessel, having lowered for whales just at nightfall, and lost sight of the brig in their eagerness to capture whales. There was no one aboard the Maid of Erin, except a few inexperienced hands, and the boat's crew expressed their apprehensions of some casualty to her, should it come on to blow. What the result was I never learned, as a short time afterward we left the cape, proceeding northward to Kangaroo Island. Seeing no whales, we changed our course to the westward, passing the Recherche Islands, and having a fine view of Pollock's Reef — a dangerous line of rocks, a long distance from the main land, extending for several miles, over which the sea roars and tumbles in huge broken masses, impressing the beholder with a sense of danger as he gazes upon it. Just before reaching this locality we saw right whales, but could get nowhere near them. Soon afterward we gammoned the ship Lapwing, of New Bedford; she brought letters from home for us, but gave them to the Alexander, supposing that we still remained off New Zealand. Whilst gammoning with her, a line of dangerous reefs was sighted close to us, and, during the night and following day, we carried sail to get a wide berth from it, and ran the old ship into a school of sperm whales. We lowered away our boats. The second mate fastened, and the whale sounded, taking out most of his line; the third mate ran down and attached his line to it, just in the nick of time, and saved the whale. The whales in this vicinity plunge and sound deeply, when first struck. Half an hour previous to the second mate's fastening, the first mate struck a fellow that carried off all his line.

About this time a curious malady affected a number of our crew, the seeds of which were sown by exposure to the rains and damp air of the South Pacific. It resembled inflammatory rheumatism, causing excruciating pains in the joints, and resisting all application of medicine. I experienced the affection myself. Having heard of the marvellous efficacy of the oil extracted from the liver of the sun fish, I urged the necessity of procuring some of the article; the captain, coinciding with me, lowered away a boat and captured a sun fish. It was a most curious creature, almost without shape; in weight, I think it would exceed five hundred pounds; it had no scales and no flukes; the after portion of the body appearing as if unfinished; on each side was a long narrow fin. The skin was of a brown color, and as rough as sandpaper. The eye was most beautiful, and the largest and clearest of any creature's that I ever saw. The bones were soft, and on being exposed to the sun gradually melted away. The flesh is prepared with vinegar and makes excellent eating. The oil, extracted from the liver by expression in the sun, is of a reddish color, and fœtid smell. It proved of great service to me—an application to a stiff joint at night rendering it pliant and free from pain in the morning. Long yarns are spun by seafaring men of the wonderful properties of this oil; they assuring me that a too free use of it was always attended by salivation, and enjoining an application of but a small quantity. I used it pretty freely, but experienced no bad effect from it.

On the 5th of October we picked up a spruce plank, about twelve feet in length and three in breadth; it was copper-fastened, and was adjudged to be part of the keel of a large ship.

On the 17th we ran in and anchored in Frenchman's Bay, intending to procure a supply of water. This bay is the introduction to King George's Sound, and is a safe and pleasant harbor. We lay within a mile of the shore, and from a spring close to the beach, procured three hundred barrels of most excellent water. There were no vessels in the bay, but in the sound there was an English barque, the Prince of Wales. She brought out to the sound materials for the erection of two light-houses — one on Point Possession, at the entrance of the sound; the other on Breaksea, at the mouth of Frenchman's Bay. These have long been needed on the coast, and their advent will be a matter of congratulation to the navigator in these seas. The crew of this vessel refused to proceed in her, alleging as a reason her immoderate leakage, asserting that she was unsafe and unseaworthy. The crew, including the second mate, on the complaint of the captain, were arrested by the authorities, and kept in durance vile until such time as the vessel should leave the port. This probation had now continued for months, and as the crew were determined not to embark in her, a new crew was shipped, and, on the arrival of orders from England, she sailed for some port in the West

Indies. At her departure her former hands were released.

The next day after anchoring was Sunday, and all hands were bound for a run ashore. The bay presented little attraction, but the green appearance of the vegetation was enough to induce us to have a nearer look at it. On landing we found the country covered with the prevailing bush, and as it was in many places dry and inflammable as tinder, we ignited it, and had a rousing fire coursing up the hills like a demon in pursuit of prey. Having tired ourselves with this amusement, we ran along the beach with the intention of shaking the scurvy out of our bones; and as we progressed, saw numbers of mutton-fish, crabs, and limpets. We gathered a sufficient quantity of these shell-fish, roasted them, and had a fresh mess. Proceeding along the beach, over an uneven ridge of boulders, after a walk of about eight miles, we came to the whale fishery. Here we found about a dozen men, who were engaged in a warfare against the humpback and right whales that resort to the bay. They had taken, during the season, two of the former and one of the latter species, yielding them one hundred and seventy barrels of oil; they desired us to set no more bush afire, stating that the smoke or glare of the flames intimidated the whales from entering the bay. From these people we learned that the ships Alexander and James Allen had touched here but a short time previous, and that whilst here both ships had lost men by desertion, and that these men were now knocking about the town, unable to procure employment. The James Allen also lost an anchor here, in about the same spot in which she broke her windlass whilst getting under weigh last year. From all accounts her Hobartown crew had been anything but orderly and obedient, so that the captain was glad to be rid of them. Amongst the men at the fishery there were several Americans who had been in this section of the world for years; they did not like the country, and, if we had wanted men, would gladly have engaged and gone home with us.

It is the law of the English government, that no fishing shall be carried on within three miles of the coast of colonies. This law is a dead letter in the Indian Ocean, excepting where their fisheries exist; and I am sure that, had whales made their appearance in this bay whilst we were present, our boats would have been down amongst them. The men at the fishery strongly urged their exclusive right to this privilege; but, at the same time, they informed us that, a few weeks previous, the ship Congress, of New Bedford, had taken a humpback whilst lying where we now were; for, having no casks at the fishery, they were necessitated to buy some from the ship, and because of this favor, they had agreed not to interfere with their prize.

Returning from the fishery, we took a short cut through the bush, which is lower here than any I have seen elsewhere in Australia — no tree or shrub appearing that was over eight feet in height. Amidst the general desolation, beautiful flowers of various descriptions and colors sprung up; forming a strange contrast, and appearing as if Nature, to make amends for the general loneliness and negligence displayed, had caused these gay flowers to flourish here, and truly, as the poet says,

> "To waste their sweetness on the desert air."

On our way down, we continually passed little mounds, shaped like beehives, and constructed of dried grass and sand, arranged to a nicety. At first I was at a loss to tell the true character of these nests; but, on knocking the top off of one of them with my stick, I saw myriads of ants — it being a granary for these insects. On being disturbed, they rushed hither and thither in search of the violator of their domicile, and on discovering him, they ran up his clothing, and bestowed no very gentle bites upon his legs and body. They are much larger than our ants; and, unlike ours, instead of excavating a place of retreat, they build it upon the surface of the earth.

We also saw and destroyed (without knowing what we were killing) several iguanas — little creatures of the lizard species, that abound here in great numbers. They are said to be a fierce enemy of the serpent tribe, and to engage in long and severe contests with his snakeship, and always gain the victory—running, when bitten by him, to a certain herb that acts as a specific. When we were at Hobartown, I was told of a man, named Underwood, who possessed a sure and speedy antidote for the bite of any snake. The government had offered him a large price for his secret, but he refused to divulge it on any terms. He was a convict of the lowest grade, and represented that he first discovered the antidote by observing the iguana running to, and eating it, after having been bitten by his foe. This remedy, which is vegetable, he states to be very common. Its infallibility is implicitly believed in by the residents; and, from their account, even a stranger cannot refuse credence to its worth, after listening to a recital of the many satisfactory tests it has been subjected to by the faculty.

Whilst we were engaged ashore, those who chose to remain on board the ship passed the time in angling. Amongst other specimens of what had been caught, was one known as the snapper, each weighing from twenty to thirty-five pounds. They had scales, and were of a reddish color. Another, known as the groper, from its swimming close to the bottom, weighs from fifty to one hundred and fifty pounds. It has scales on its body, and is black in color. Both these fish have ivory teeth, from a quarter to three-quarters of an inch in length, and of the same shape as those of the sperm whale. Both are good eating, salted or fresh. They require a strong line and stout arm to secure them. Beside these members of the finny tribe, there are also to be found here others of less note: the mackerel, herring, benita, salmon, and whitings — existing in great numbers. We caught and salted a barrel of them; but, from an excess of salt, they were unpalatable, and we were forced to heave them overboard when we got outside.

On returning to the beach to go aboard, we discovered that one of our party was missing. It proved to be a New Bedford boy, who, although his name was John, had been 'yclept Barney, from the first day of our sailing. He was a good-natured fellow, who did not care what name he answered to, and became more accustomed to his alias than to his true cognomen. A call for John would pass unnoticed, when one for Barney would secure his attention in double-quick time. Having no taste for whaling, and being desirous of getting home speedily, he had donned several suits of clothes, and determined to run for it. He separated himself from the rest of the party soon after going ashore, and started directly for the town of Albany, where he arrived at midnight; but finding those who had left the ships before mentioned in a sad predicament — destitute and wretched — he changed his mind, and gave himself up to the captain, who was about instituting a search, and offering a reward for his apprehension. Two days afterward he was aboard the ship again.

On the 21st we had all our work done, but were unable to get to sea, being wind-bound by a heavy easterly gale. The mouth of the bay being narrow, precluded the possibility of our beating out. The gale gradually increased; but our ground-tackle was good, and, with both anchors down, we rode it out. On the afternoon of this day the steamship Simla made her appearance. She is a noble vessel, of twenty-five hundred tons burden — three hundred and sixty-five feet in length. Just before approaching the sound she took the pilot aboard, and under his guidance proceeded in. Here she came to anchor alongside the Larkin, in order to receive her coal — this being, after leaving Melbourne, the first station for fuel for the line of steamships to which she belongs. They remain here for twenty-four hours, and bring hither and convey hence the mail to and from the Swan River colony. On the morning after the Simla's arrival her mails were opened, and hardly an idea can be formed of our surprise on seeing the following announcement in a copy of the Melbourne Weekly Herald:—

"Supposed Loss of the Whaling Barque Pacific, of New Bedford, U. S.

"The following letter appeared in the Nelson Examiner of the 16th ult.:

"'*To the Editor of the Nelson Examiner.*

"'SIR:—I regret to inform you, that there is too much reason to believe that the whaling barque Pacific, of New Bedford, U. S., foundered on the western coast of this Island, on the night of the 21st of May last. As the readiest means of communicating the news to those who are interested in the fate of the vessel and crew, I send you a copy of the deposition of one of the known survivors, which is fully corroborated by the statements of the rest. I have ascertained that the Pacific belonged to the firm of Swift & Perry, of New Bedford; that she had on board three hundred and fifty barrels of oil when she was supposed to have foundered. The names of her officers were: John W. Sherman, master; John Hood, chief mate; John Dexter, second mate; Clarke Allen, third mate. The names of the men who landed on the western coast were: Theodore Jerome, David Jones, William Charles Baylis, Joseph Riley, William Anderson, William Owen, Harvey William Miller, David Ling.

"'Yours, etc.

"'H. G. GOULAND, *Resident Magistrate.*
"'COLLINGWOOD, September 10th, 1857.

"'(*Deposition above referred to.*)

"'Theodore Jerome, being sworn, said: I am a seaman, and belonged to barque Pacific, of New Bedford; Sherman, master. The barque Pacific belonged to Swift & Perry, of New Bedford. She was a whaler, of three hundred and fifty tons burden. She left New Bedford last June was a twelvemonth. The last port we left was Bunbury, in New Holland. We put in there for supplies, and left in January last. The vessel leaked considerably when we left New Bedford, but in Bunbury she was caulked.

"'We made the coast of New Zealand early in February last. We were whaling off the coast. Shortly after making the coast of New Zealand we experienced several gales of wind, which, according to the captain's opinion, increased the leakage considerably.

"'On the night of the 21st of May the leakage increased considerably, and the pumps were kept constantly going till near midnight. The carpenter reported the condition of the vessel to be dangerous, and the captain thought it advisable to abandon her. He called all hands aft, and stated the condition of the vessel to them, and advised them to be orderly, and to get in their respective boats without confusion. He turned to Mr. Hood, the chief officer, and told him to put the vessel before the wind, to make it easier for the boats to get away from the ship's side. The captain ordered Mr. Allen to clear away the bow-boat, and lower her; at the same time a heavy sea pooped the ship, and swept her fore and aft. The vessel was by this time settling by the stern.

P

There was then an immediate rush for the boats — each man getting in the first that he could. I and others got into the bow-boat. I saw Mr. Allen, the third mate, standing on the rail, giving directions for the lowering of the boat. I never saw him afterwards. The boat that I was in escaped from the ship's side, and we put her before the wind. It was about 11½ o'clock when we were called aft by the captain. It might have been half an hour between that and the time we got clear of the ship's side. At the time we got into the boat there was another boat in the act of lowering — there may have been more, but that is all that I can say positively. We stood in towards the shore; and made the shore, as nearly as I could judge, about 3½ o'clock in the morning. The boat was stoven in landing. We landed between Milford Haven and Open Bay, on the Milford Haven side of Cascade Point. We had been cruising off and on the shore, and had seen land the previous day. We had been into Milford Haven about a fortnight before this, to get water. From cruising off and on, and repeatedly seeing the land, I was sufficiently acquainted with the coast to know where we landed. At break of day we ascended a hill to look for the ship, but saw nothing of her or of the boats. The weather was very hazy, and it rained heavily then and for several days afterwards; and we saw no wreck, either of vessel or boats. My opinion is, that the currents run outward from the shore, and would carry any wreck out to sea. It was blowing a double-reefed topsail breeze when we left the vessel. The vessel appeared to be waterlogged, and was settling by the stern. I think that in all probability the vessel foundered. We remained where we were for one day, and then endeavored to go to the southward; but the bush was so thick, and obstacles so great, that we could not get on in that direction. We then shaped our course in the other direction, towards Open Bay; that is, to the northward of where we landed. We found natives at Open Bay, and remained with them about a fortnight. A native sealing-boat came into Open Bay while we were there, and from one of the crew, that could speak a little English, we got directions that enabled us to make our way along the coast. We left Open Bay, and made the best of our way along the coast to this place, where we arrived yesterday evening. The names of the persons who landed with me were, William Harvey Miller, David Ling, Joseph Riley, W. C. Baylis, William or John Owen, William Anderson, and David Jones. Miller and Ling have not yet arrived. We left Ling, who is a boy about eighteen years old, with the native sealers at Open Bay. The natives told us that the roads were so bad, that he would not be able to travel. Miller's feet were too sore to walk, and he remained behind. We found the road very difficult. We crossed several rivers; among others, the Mewera and Kawatiri — the names we got from the natives. Whenever we met with any natives, they proved very kind to us: they fed us, and gave us food to take on with us — this, with fern, shellfish, and whatever we could get, enabled us to live on the journey. I cannot remember the names of all the persons aboard: but I can of a good many of them; and of the officers, the captain's name was Sherman — I don't know his

Christian name; the chief mate's name was Hood; the second mate's, Dexter; and the third mate's, Allen. There was also an acting fourth mate and boatsteerer, whose name I do not remember. The number of officers and crew was thirty-two. I am inclined to think, that if any of the other boats escaped, and had any of the officers aboard, they would shape their course to the nearest port — that is, Jacob's River.

"'(Signed)
"'THEODORE JEROME.

"'Sworn before me, at Collingwood, the tenth day of September, eighteen hundred and fifty-seven.
"'(Signed)
"'H. G. GOULAND,
"'*Resident Magistrate.*'"

It is almost needless to append, in explanation, that the above is a tissue of falsehoods, fabricated by the deserters from our ship, whilst in the South Pacific. Their story is plausible; and, were a person not aware to the contrary, it would obtain implicit credence. It was concocted by the one named Joseph Riley. He is a native of New Jersey — of Irish extraction. He has been for years in the merchant service; and this, united with a previous voyage whaling, rendered him well acquainted with maritime affairs: hence, he found little difficulty in weaving a yarn that sounded plausible enough, although there is not a particle of truth in the whole account — our old ship never having leaked, during the continuance of the voyage thus far, more than enough to keep her sweet; only requiring to be pumped once a week, and then but for a few minutes. The carpenter is an imaginary personage — we never having possessed one: one was shipped in New Bedford, but ran away before we sailed. The person, who, under the name of Theodore Jerome, made the deposition before the magistrate at Collingwood, is supposed to have been in reality John Roberts, a London cockney, who had been transported to Australia. He had been in the Henry H. Crapo for twelve months, but left her in Vasse, and engaged with us; thus escaping the fate of the crew of that vessel, to live and play a rascal's part in another clime. The true Theodore Jerome is still on board our ship, and justly indignant at the liberties taken with his name. The fact of their assuming it is attributable to their having in their possession an American protection, bearing the name of Theodore Jerome. Roberts is the only one of the party whose description corresponds with that contained in it; and hence we suppose him to be the person who made the affidavit. He is weak-minded, with little intelligence, and totally incapable of giving such an account; except at the instigation of a person like Riley, and afterwards being well drilled, until he was perfected in his part. The other names were real; or, rather, a part were those of our crew, whilst the rest, Owen, Anderson, and Ling, were the names of the deserters from the barque Lady Emma, of Hobartown, whom our fellows took aboard their boat at Open Bay. From their own account, they had pretty rough travelling; but the descriptive part, like the substance of their narrative, may be more romance than reality. But, apart from this, let us candidly judge their culpability. In the first place, no doubt, they were driven to an extremity by hunger and suffering; and, knowing that, as deserters, they would meet with no sympathy, in such emergency they concocted this method to obtain relief for their necessities: but why did they not, if such was their intention, substitute a fictitious name for that of our ship, and avoid particularizing as they did? Secondly, should any amount of personal suffering induce men to embitter for months the whole tenor of the existence of many happy circles, who, on the reception of such fatal news through relatives and friends, without any rebutting information on the subject, would at once set us down as irrecoverably lost?

Here was a pretty kettle of fish — some thirty-two of us consigned to the tender mercies of David Jones, Esq., the hereditary enemy of our profession, with as little remorse as if we were so many kittens; but, fortunately, the same mail that conveyed the papers containing the baleful news, gave us opportunity to send our own missives explanatory of the proceedings; but then our letters from Hobartown, in July, were sufficient evidence of our safety; so that, although it might create some uneasiness, it would be but evanescent.

Some months before we touched at Frenchman's Bay, one of our boatsteerers received a letter from his family, in which was contained the report of a vessel having been seen by a merchantman in the South Atlantic, bottom up. She was evidently a whaler, a barque, and bore on her stern the name of Pacific, New Bedford. This was thought to be us, and thus our old ship was given up to the mercies of that ocean over which she had so gallantly rode for more than half a century, and, as far as I am able to judge, still rides as proudly as in her palmiest days — carrying her spars as jauntily as any of the constructions of shipwrights of the present day.

At 10 o'clock on the morning of the 26th, the gale having moderated and the wind shifted to a favorable quarter, we took our departure from Frenchman's Bay. When directly opposite Baldhead we saw right and humpback whales, bound up the bay. We lowered away, but could get nowhere near them. They saw them from the fishery but met with like success in their attempt to capture one.

CHAPTER X.

WE now directed our ship's head to the westward, and fell in with the barques Cherokee and Pamelia. The former had sailed from home some two years previous; but, mutiny breaking out amongst her crew, she was run into Mauritius, and all the foremast hands discharged. The captain shipped a new crew, and was scarce a whit more fortunate in his selection; as a number of rough alleys, hearing of his reputation as a harsh man, determined to ship with him, in order, as they said, to work him up. At the time they shipped they were informed that they were engaged, not as sailors, but as whalemen. Soon after they got outside, an order was passed from the quarter-deck to make spun yarn, which they refused to do, repeating the terms of their engagement. The captain was forced to succumb, and, consequently, captain and crew were at variance during the remainder of their stay together. A boat's crew from her came aboard our vessel. They were powerful, manly fellows—every one a thorough seaman, competent to perform his duty anywhere. Some months after we gammoned her she touched at Vasse, and set several of the ringleaders ashore.

Aboard the Pamelia we found Mr. Edwards, our former second officer, acting in the same capacity there. Her mate having left at Vasse, and gone home in the Dolphin, her former second mate took his berth, and Mr. Edwards the one left vacant by his promotion. Her crew seemed to us like old friends, and were greeted as such. They had been cruising on this coast ever since our departure, had been very successful, and anticipated a speedy return home. Their third mate had been taken very ill aboard the ship, and they had but a short time previously touched at Vasse for the purpose of leaving him, supposing that he could receive better attention ashore. Soon after they spoke the ship Canton, and were informed of his death. How the report originated I know not; for, in the following January, when we touched at that port, he was alive and well, and had been amusing himself kangaroo hunting.

The Pamelia brought us letters that had been received by mail at Vasse. As I was one of the fortunate ones, I was much gratified at receiving good news from home, and had my mind set at rest regarding the welfare of all my friends for another year.

On the 3d of November we lowered away for blackfish, of which the waist-boat captured one. A breeze springing up, the boats set their sails. The starboard-boat, by the carelessness of her manager, was capsized whilst merrily gliding along in pursuit of the fish, and her occupants, of whom I was one, got a ducking. When the boat went over, I was caught by the backstay that secured the mast, and had some difficulty in disentangling myself under water. The waist boat ran down, picked us up, and put us aboard the ship, where the whole affair was made a subject of laughter: this view always being taken of an accident to a boat where no person is seriously injured.

On Sunday, November the 8th, we sighted sperm whales, and though the weather was foggy and disagreeable, the boats were lowered; but, after being down all the forenoon, we returned at 1 o'clock, and ate dinner. At half past one we dropped boats again, when the waist-boat fastened to an immense whale, which ran very rapidly; but he soon began to spout thick blood, and we counted him as ours. On the appearance of blood, the bow-boat cut her line, and came aboard. The captain, observing that the whale continued on in his course, lowered away, and lanced him also; but still he would not turn up, although incessantly discharging blood from his spout-holes and the various lance-wounds in his body. Night approached, and still the whale kept going ahead. The rain was descending in torrents, whilst not the slightest vestige of a breeze rippled the surface of the water; so the boats, together with their locomotive attachment, were gradually widening their distance from the ship. Directly after nightfall, the captain returned with his boat, leaving directions for the others to keep up good lights in their boat-lanterns; so that we might very easily know their whereabouts. On arriving aboard, the bow-boat was dispatched with refreshments and a couple of bottles of New England rum, to revive those who had been sitting in their boats drenched to the skin; and, surely, if there ever was a moment when men needed an alcoholic stimulus to enable them to withstand exposure, it was on this occasion. Just after the bow-boat left, we lost sight of the light of the boat-lantern in the distance, and did not recover it again until midnight, when we discovered the boats coming toward us, with the dead body of the whale, as we believed, in tow; but were chagrined to find that they had cut from him, which, unavoidable as it was, was far from being pleasant, after the trouble and pains-taking he had caused us. They stated, that they were out of sight of the ship's light; that the whale showed no more signs of exhaustion than at sunset; and, as the weather looked very threatening, there appeared to be no other recourse left them but to return: so, after a consultation, in which all hands were included, the line, not however without many regrets, was severed, and the monster allowed to go on his way, and die alone — his surviving more than a few hours being out of the question.

The bow-boat, after leaving the ship's side, pulled in the direction where the boat-lights had last appeared; but it was not until after they had cut from the fish, that they found the other boats, whose men, from their fatiguing duty and benumbed members, were not just then particularly delighted at the idea of pulling ten or twelve miles back without refreshment: they therefore hailed the arrival of the bow-boat with acclamation. They hove up; and, after having satisfied their appetites, the bottle was passed around, and each indulged in a hearty swig: then, with renewed vigor, they bent to their oars, and regained the vessel.

This unfortunate result would not have occurred had we had the least breeze, to keep anywhere in the neighborhood of the boats; nor, had there been land anywhere within a reasonable distance, the mate, who in no wise lacks energy, would not have cut; but, under the circumstances, he acted with discrimation in withdrawing the boats whilst there was a chance of their doing so with safety. No doubt, had he remained attached to the whale, it would have been as difficult for us to find our boats the succeeding day as it was to find the carcass of the fish, which, despite our utmost endeavors — thoroughly going over the ground — we never afterwards saw.

How it was that this whale sustained life so long, whilst the vital current was swiftly escaping from his system, it is difficult to account for. He was lanced in the same place as other whales we had taken, and which expired in the course of several hours. It was done, too, by men who were no novices, either in handling the lance, or in combating the whale. Not a few shook their heads, mysteriously; and one, in a spirit of confidence, broadly stated to me, that the creature was not a whale, but Lucifer himself, who had assumed this form to puzzle mankind; and hence he accounted for the tenacity of life displayed. This opinion, of course, I could not subscribe to; but I found it futile to attempt to satisfy my superstitious shipmate that all might be produced by natural causes. My opinion being, that the whale was of such a prodigious size, (every man who was in the boats stating him to have been the largest of the cachelot species they had ever seen,) and his vitals were covered with so thick a coat of blubber, that the lances were of insufficient length to deal a mortal wound. This view of the matter, after many arguments, *pro* and *con*, was finally adopted, as being the most probable of any advanced.

After remaining on this ground a sufficient length of time to assure ourselves of the improbability of picking up the wounded whale, we proceeded to the northward, hoping to be more successful off the capes Chatham and Leuwin. Our passage up was unmarked with incident, except the capture of a large shark, and the picking up of a dead grampus of the variety known as the bottle-nose. The shark's capture is worthy of mention merely for the method we adopted to kill him. He was struck and hauled in, and beat over the head with a heavy handspike. The forge being up, and a good fire burning in it, a bar of iron was heated, and run directly through his heart, with but little apparent effect; for he still continued to lash his flukes, and set his jaws upon a piece of pine board, to which he held fast. His head was then cut off, and his skin removed; yet every member of his body still retained the power of motion.

The grampus is a most beautiful fish — the handsomest in form of the many inhabitants of the deep that it has been my fortune to see. On account of their shyness, there is great difficulty in approaching these fish when alive, and consequently very few are taken: even in the whaling career, seldom does a seaman have an opportunity of examining one on deck. The one in our possession was about twenty-five feet long, and as much around the bilge. His skin was smooth, of a shining black color. His head gradually sloped, until it ended in a long pointed jaw, resembling that of the porpoise, but which, unlike that of most other fish in these waters, was not furnished with teeth. No mark, accounting for his death, was found upon the body: doubtless, he died from some disease peculiar to the species. The blubber was several inches thick, which on being tried out yielded three barrels of colorless, inodorous oil.

We remained off Cape Leuwin but a short time. Seeing a large lone sperm whale, we lowered away for him, in company with the boats of the barque Pamelia; but we did not succeed in capturing him. We then, accompanied by said barque, again steered for our old ground to the southward.

On Sunday, December 6th, just as we had arrived in our latitude for cruising, we sighted a large lone sperm whale, at 9½ o'clock in the morning; and by ten — the hour when well-behaved folks in civilized countries are wending their way to church — we were deep in the encounter. He occasioned us but little trouble: the first mate fastening to, and killing him before the other boats could reach the scene of action, though all pulled with a will. At the moment of darting the harpoon, the whale struck the boat with his head, knocking a small hole through her bows, and pitching the boatsteerer, who was standing up, over the prow of his boat upon the top of the whale's elevated huge head; but the imperilled man, with a nimble spring, quickly regained his legitimate position in the boat, where he very probably felt much more comfortable than mounted on such a Pegasus. This was a noble fish, and yielded us over one hundred barrels of sperm oil, valued, at the time we left home, at about sixty dollars a barrel; making, in the aggregate, the snug sum of six thousand dollars. A very creditable day's work: but, then, it has to be divided into so many shares, that those who undergo the peril and discomforts of making the capture come in for the smallest portion of the gain. The ship-owners, sitting at ease in New Bedford, grasp thousands, whilst Jack and his coadjutors can reckon their proportion without very largely intruding on the scores. Thus it is throughout the world: he who does least, is paid best. Intellect overbalances mere physical exertion; and thus it ever will, and ever should do in the promotion of great enterprises.

On the 14th we again met whales, which were not seen until within the ship's length of us. Our boats were lowered away in haste. A moment afterwards, those of the Pamelia, who was not more than a mile distant from us, were also in the water. Our bow-boat fastened ten minutes after striking the water, and in an incredibly short time the whale was dead, and ours. The remaining boats continued in pursuit of the school, and got near enough to enable the boatsteerers to dart, though at long distances, and without producing any other effect than a pricking of the prey, at which they raised up their huge bodies, and with their flukes thrashed the sea all around them into a boisterous foam. Finding it useless to continue the pursuit, the boats came aboard, and the ship's head was put in the direction of the whales. We then proceeded to cut in. The Pamelia, meantime, ran down to us; when, with a disinterestedness uncommon to rival whalemen, our captain informed hers of the direction in which the whales had gone. Not being encumbered, as we were, with a whale in tow, she soon passed us. An hour afterwards we saw her lower away and capture a whale, which, as ours done for us, yielded in the neighborhood of one hundred barrels of oil: the whales of this ground all averaging about the same quantity. They are larger, in general, than I have seen them in lower latitudes, besides being always in better condition than when found in a warmer climate, and their blubber on the application of heat almost wholly dissolving into oil.

On the 19th we again saw the same school. At 5 o'clock in the afternoon the waist-boat fastened, was stoven by the whale's flukes, and her crew obliged to swim for their lives, when they were picked up by the starboard-boat, and carried to the ship. The other boat then went on to the whale, and her boat-steerer darted at him half-a-dozen times in succession, but without effect. Night approaching, we were compelled to desist. Early the next morning we saw a large whale alone—lowered, and the waist-boat fastened. She continued attached for some time, when, her line being nearly run out, the larboard boat's was bent on to it. By mistake, a line that had been exposed to the weather, had been put into the waist-boat, in lieu of her line that was carried off the day before. The mate, finding that his own line was fast running out, attached a drug to it—hoping that by its resistance in the water the whale would be to some extent forced to moderate his soundings. The old line, unable to endure the strain caused by the drug, parted; and away the whale went to windward eyes out, with a speed that, to the chagrin of all, defied pursuit. So, here was the third whale, this season, lost by the one boat. On reviewing this journal, it will be seen in the preceding pages, that a singular fatality has attended all the operations of this boat since we left home. When under the management of Mr. Edwards, (our former second officer, and as good a whaleman as ever stepped into the head of a whaleboat,) she was capsized. Under her present manager, she had her line taken by a whale, off Cape Chatham, where she was also capsized. In the Bight, the whale was only saved by the timely arrival of the bow-boat with its line. The large whale that went off spouting blood, was fastened to from her; the whale of yesterday, that capsized her; and that of to-day, that parted her line — go to make up a catalogue of misfortunes that the annals of whaling-voyages can scarcely equal. And all her disasters — capsizing, losing her whale, losing her line, and being stoven — arose, not from incapacity on the part of her officers, but from a combination of unforeseen circumstances, which it would have been in vain for the most experienced whaleman to guard against.

On the last day of December we experienced the initiation of a gale, which lasted, in incessant violence, until the 6th of January, '58, but doing no injury to us, further than shipping a heavy sea that cleared away our gangway, and deluged our decks, fore and aft, without so much as saying, "By your leave." We kept on one tack, heading constantly to the north and westward.

On the 10th we sighted Baldhead but a short distance off. We stood in for it; and in the evening the captain lowered away, and proceeded, through Frenchman's Bay and the Sound, to the town of Albany: the ship standing off and on, with the cable bent on to the larboard anchor, so as to be ready to let go in case of emergency. In the bay we found at anchor the barque Margaret, of Liverpool, from Adelaide for Mauritius. She had sprung her mizzenmast in the recent severe westerly gale, and, the wind being directly in her teeth, she put in here for shelter. On getting into the sound they found that the Prince of Wales had sailed for Callao, and therefore her crew were at liberty. Most of the hangers-on that had composed part of the population, when we last were here, had departed in the American ship Kensington. This ship had as passengers three hundred Chinamen, who intended landing at some port in these colonies; but, on account of a legislative enactment forbidding the ingress of these people into the country, she had already met with great difficulty in getting rid of them.

A day or two before our arrival, the natives came into the town, with portions of cotton canvass, and numbers of spermaceti candles. They reported that fragments of casks and barrels were strewed around the beach in every direction. The fact of her carrying cotton canvass augurs that the wreck must have been an American vessel, as those of other nations carry hemp almost exclusively. These evidences of shipwreck were found on a part of the coast contiguous to the White Top Rocks, which is justly accounted a most dangerous locality, and has in more than one instance been the theater of similar disasters.

And now I shall touch on another subject, which reflects but little credit on the parties concerned, either as Americans, or as honest men. It is simply this: — At the sound our captain found a letter from the consular agent at Freemantle, directed to the captain of any American whaler who might first touch at the port. The purport of the missive formed a caution to the barque Pamelia's master not to enter any port in the Australian colonies, as her smuggling tobacco on her last visit to Vasse had been divulged, and vessel and cargo thereby forfeited to the crown. The other party concerned, to whom the tobacco had been delivered, and placed aboard the brig Champion, had had his brig seized, and was heavily mulcted beside, for his part in the nefarious transaction. He is a man well to do, and at the time of the smuggling was fulfilling heavy contracts with the English government; supplying them with timber for the construction of the railroad from Adelaide to Melbourne.

This is no unusual method of turning a penny, amongst those who visit this coast; and I have seen more than one instance of it. In some cases, the authorities wink at the fraud committed against the government; and, as the party who is fortunate enough to escape conviction trebles or quadruples the amount of his outlay, the temptation is strong to engage in the illicit traffic.

Beside this budget of shipping news, it was said by the inhabitants of Albany, that gold in considerable quantities had been discovered by shepherds, about one hundred and fifty miles distant in the interior, and that a party was preparing to visit this El Dorado.

At 2 o'clock in the afternoon of the 11th the boat returned; and, bracing forward, we stood to the westward, in hopes of seeing the Pamelia before she went into port; for we knew that it was the intention of her captain to touch at Vasse about the middle of the present month. On our passage we fell in with the barque Eagle, of New Bedford. She was employed in cutting a whale she had taken the day previous, and, as the weather was anything but good, she was having a dirty time. We afterwards learned that she had lost the greater part of the head in the operation. After a short time spent in company with her, and learning that the Pamelia had been seen a few days before, we resumed our course, and the day succeeding spoke her, and communicated the intelligence we had received at Albany. It was timely, too, as they were now bound in, and twenty-four hours' delay might have been productive of serious consequences. On the 18th, her captain, knowing full well that to enter a port in the vicinity would be madness, made himself dependent upon the various ships on the ground to contribute a quota in the supply of water, &c., to enable him to take a short cruise, and reach the Mauritius. In pursuance of this idea, on the same day a raft of casks, in tow of one of the Pamelia's boats, was brought alongside of our vessel, and made fast; then, according to orders, they were hoisted in. Our crew had an inkling of the affair, but said nothing, until they were ordered by the first officer to fill these casks, belonging to another ship, with the water from our own casks, which it had caused us so much labor and trouble to procure, and which would have to be replaced from one of the wells on the coast, under a burning sun, and through scorching sand. Under these circumstances, a flat refusal was accorded to the order; because we did not deem that our engagement obliged us to supply another ship with water, unless she was in absolute distress. All hands aboard, except the first and second officers, united in this view of the case. The mate expostulated, but found it useless. A messenger or spokesman was then dispatched to the captain, who acted with moderation; and the whole matter was amicably adjusted by the captain of the Pamelia complying with our terms; which were, that we should be paid for the trouble we would have in replacing the water. As soon as this was understood, all hands turned to. The casks were filled, rafted, and towed aboard the Pamelia in double-quick time; and our boat returned with money and several boxes of soap as a compensation.

It may seem, to a disinterested reader, that our thus refusing to supply the wants of a countryman, in this far off sea, was niggardly in the extreme. But the master of the Pamelia was unpopular over the whole ocean, and our men were affected with the general opinion respecting him. They alleged that he had came aboard our ship some months before, and remonstrated with our captain against the quantity of provisions he allowed to his crew; stating, at the same time, that he (meaning himself) did not give his men all they wanted: which assertion one would indeed find no difficulty to believe on hearing his crew talk, who represented their fare to be extremely meagre.

This was the nearest approach to insubordination that had thus far occurred amongst us; and which, if our captain and officers had been bullying, threatening men, might have been lashed into a mutiny, that in the eyes of justice they would have been held responsible for: because it was certainly due to every man aboard, that the captain should have stated his intention of furnishing another ship with water, and his reasons for so doing — appealing at the same time to what would be the sense of our own necessities, if placed in such a situation; and then not a man aboard would have raised a dissenting voice, or spoken of remuneration. It is, however, a mistake too often committed by shipowners, shipmasters, and ship's officers, to think that the sailor has neither part nor parcel in the concerns of the ship or voyage, and that the disposal of his time is altogether at the pleasure of his superiors; and thus they conduct themselves toward him, treating him with no more deference than they would accord to a dog aboard the ship; and in this way are sown the first seeds of mutiny, which spring up, bear fruit that come to maturity, and destroy the original causes of their production.

On the 19th we gammoned with a barque belonging to Fairhaven. This circumstance is only worthy of notice from its being the first opportunity we had, since leaving home, of seeing that peculiar creature known amongst seafaring men as the spread eagle; which consists in a human being lashed to the rigging by his wrists, when, as the case may be, he is punished with the lash, made to stand for an immoderate length of time on one leg, or his arms seized at such a height that he can but just rest on the tips of his toes. In the present case the culprit was forced to stand on one leg, shifting at periodical times; and was thus punished for thirty-six hours. He was quite a lad, and his offence was said to be the participating in a fracas in the forecastle. Whether just or unjust, the application of this harsh and cruel punishment recoiled upon the captain, as a few weeks afterward, when several of her crew deserted from her in Bunbury, he could not replace them: notice of this circumstance having got ashore—whether from our crew or hers, I cannot say; but it was all-sufficient to deter any of the men ashore from engaging with her captain, as they answered his proposals to them for that purpose with scorn and insult.

On the 22d we saw sperm whales going off to windward at a tangent. We lowered, but found it useless. Two days afterward we squared away for Bunbury. In the afternoon we doubled Cape Naturaliste at a slashing pace, knocking twelve knots an hour out of the old ship. That night we came to, with our head-yards aback; and the following morning cast anchor off the town. Our first job, after anchoring, was to heave our maintopmast up, and substitute a new fid for the old one. This was but little trouble. On extracting the old fid, we were at a loss to account for the mast having so long remained upright, with such a miserable support: the weight of the topmast having crushed the stout oak fid almost completely through — but a few inches of solid wood remaining to sustain it.

Almost as soon as the boat could convey them to us, fresh beef and vegetables were brought aboard; proving that, when inclined to purchase it, meat was no article of scarcity in this market.

After adjusting our topmast, we went ashore

to fill our casks with fresh water. A well had been constructed since we were here a year ago; the captains of the different whaleships touching at the port having subscribed to a fund for its erection. It was larger and much more convenient than those at Vasse; and, as the distance to the beach was not so great as at that place, we had little fault to find with it, and soon conveyed on board over three hundred barrels of water.

On the 28th the brig Lochinvar arrived from Freemantle, in ballast, for the purpose of loading lumber, and conveying passengers to Adelaide. The lumber consisted altogether of the native mahogany, and was intended for sleepers to the railway there. The passengers were charged ten pounds sterling per head for their passage — a distance of fifteen hundred miles. Rather a contrast to our own cheap steam-conveyances, where comfort to the traveller can be procured at so moderate a rate.

On boarding the Lochinvar we found a former foremast hand, belonging to the Pamelia, acting as her second mate. Her crew consisted of several hands on wages of six pounds sterling per month; the balance was composed of sailors and landsmen, the former of whom were on mere nominal pay — their compensation being but one shilling per month — while the latter were obliged to pay down seven pounds, and agree to assist in loading the brig. These men were actuated in thus shipping, at such a trifling rate, by a desire to get away from this section of the country: they viewing Adelaide and its vicinity as a land of promise.

Soon after the Lochinvar came to anchor a derrick was rigged, a cart conveyed ashore, and they at once proceeded to get off timber — engaging all the unemployed ones in the place (and they were not a few) to assist in the operation. Their plan was, to take one of their boats, which was broad in the beam, and furnished with lockers, containing air-tight cylinders; then they would lash around it, and over it, as much mahogany as she would be buoyant under; and as this wood is extremely heavy, and sinks like a stone, their load was not a large one. Then they would pull off to the brig, where it was soon hove in by the aid of the derricks. One stick escaped from its lashing when alongside the brig, and a boy, who belonged ashore, dove down, and attached a rope to it in four and a half fathoms of water, which is equal to twenty-seven feet; hence this was somewhat of an exploit.

One day when the workmen employed on the beach had lashed the timber to the boat, and had pushed her off—several of them wading a short distance to give her an impetus—two of the men were observed struggling, as if to keep themselves afloat. Both disappeared; but one rose again in an instant, and grasped the boat. The other was not seen for some minutes. On searching, his lifeless body was discovered. He was a good swimmer, and a few strokes would have saved his life; but he had been drinking to excess a short time before the accident, and to this was attributed his inability to help himself. His body was conveyed to the jail, cast into a rude mahogany box, and buried within a few hours afterwards: the climate here forbidding the keeping of a corpse more than twenty-four hours.

Two days' liberty was allowed to each watch, and as, after we left the year previous, two whale-ships, on the recommendation of our captain, had visited the port, our advent created no surprise. Ships and sailors had become familiar sights, and the inhabitants were not as ready to spend their money, or listen to our yarns, as they were on our former visit. In the town things had changed but little — no improvements, no marriages, and no deaths during our absence. Therefore, as there was little either to interest or divert us, a number of our crew who, during the previous visit were enjoying themselves with rational pleasures, in the absence of former novelties, flocked to the groggeries and passed their time there. Apart from the general jokes and antics of seamen, one circumstance only, worthy of note, occurred; that was the mulcting of one of the publicans for allowing two of our men to play cards in his house; their laws prohibiting card playing even for amusement.

On the 1st of February the barque Iowa came in and gave liberty, so that there was quite a number of us ashore for several days; but after that we became tired of listlessly walking through the sand, and preferred remaining aboard the ship.

On the 5th our men proceeded some ten miles up the river to the village of Australind. On our way up we passed several grazing farms stocked with noble cattle. Along the river thousands of birds were to be seen, amongst which our pilot pointed out, as peculiarly worthy of notice, the black and white swan. Arriving at Australind we found ourselves in a beautiful country, excellently cultivated, appearing as an oasis in the sandy district that surrounded it. We had received, or understood that we had received (and certainly such was the gist of the message conveyed to us), an invitation from the proprietor of a handsome garden in the vicinity to visit him, and help him to eat some of his abundant fruit, partake of dinner with him, and generally enjoy ourselves at his expense; he wishing no other return than the pleasure of playing the host to an assemblage of Neptune's sons. This, even to our unsophisticated ears, sounded almost too disinterested for the inhabitants of Australia. Nevertheless, having little else to do, we determined to face the music, providing ourselves with plenty of biscuit in case of disappointment. We landed and went up to milord's house, which proved to be a neat and substantial brick edifice, and, with the assurance of invited guests who had come ten miles to please their host, we approached the door. We found that the individual who was so liberal in his promises was absent, and in his stead his home was garrisoned by a party of women, the young and pretty of whom were kept in the background by the high shoulders and higher cap of an old dame, whom I afterwards understood was a genuine specimen of the English titled lady; but I doubt it — as I have always understood that the matrons of England were distinguished for their hospitality, and this lady certainly possessed no such quality; as, with a vinegar aspect, she informed us of the absence of her spouse, looking at us meanwhile as if she thought us a party of marauders come to storm her vineyard. She indulged in remarks which, without misconstruing, easily made known to us her desire for us to begone; but we were of too turgid a composition to comply with her wishes. We had come for a day's pleasure, and we were bound to have it whether my lady was desirous or not; and we did have it too, for the butler, and several others, finding that we were in no hurry to decamp, to relieve the old lady from the infliction of looking on such barbarians as we, made a virtue of necessity and asked us down into the vineyard. Here the gardener, as if to make amends for the churlishness of the others, took considerable pains to show us over the grounds, and gave us full permission to regale ourselves with as much fruit as we could eat. We took him at his word, and soon were deep in the discussion of splendid grapes, water and musk-melons, mulberries, bananas, and peaches. There were acres of grape vines—the proprietor cultivating them for the manufacture of wines. They were splendid specimens; and as they were a novel dish to us, we were not the most moderate consumers of them, as the skins that strewed our paths testified. The mulberries were larger, but much tarter than ours at home. The bananas were not of so good a flavor or such a size as those we had seen at Balli. The gardener informed me that the banana plant bore the whole year round. The fruit is preceded by a splendid flower resembling the dahlia in color, but treble its size. Besides these fruits the usual garden vegetables were growing, amongst which I noticed the tomato, and, strange to say, the taste of its raw fruit was pleasanter and more refreshing than that of the more valued kinds I had been eating. Deeming this a freak of my palate, I mentioned it to my companions as singular: several of them said that such was precisely the case with them, and they preferred it to the other fruit. After several hours spent in rambling, we returned to the house for the purpose of procuring a draught of water, which was drawn from a well by means of a hydraulic pump, and which, by the way, was the only spot where I procured a good, cool drink of water in New Holland. We were again attacked by the old lady, who, to some extent, apologizing for her brusqueness in the morning, very plainly intimated that, for a suitable return, she could supply us with a repast. Like most sailors, having receptacles capable of and requiring more substantial food than fruit after our exercise, we closed with her very liberal offer, and were soon seated at a table furnished with excellent edibles, bread and butter, milk, jam, and other articles, making together a first rate supper. On our taking leave we gave to each of the underlings who had been attentive to us some tobacco. They informed us that their master had been unavoidably called away from home on business, and stated that had he been present we should have passed a very pleasant day. Giving the gentleman the benefit of this assertion, we took leave of his estate, embarked in our boat, and directed her head towards Bunbury. We reached the ship at nightfall and were pretty well wearied with our jaunt. Those of our shipmates who had remained aboard, had prophesied in the morning the miscarriage of our proposed pleasure; but as we kept our own counsel, they were none the wiser of our experience of old English hospitality, and they expressed some chagrin that they had not formed part of our expedition.

On the following day and night a collation was spread aboard the Iowa, and to it flocked all the wit and beauty of the neighborhood. After they had satisfied their appetites they resorted to our ship. Music was in demand, and the quarter-deck was made a stage on which New Holland's damsels and Yankee whaling officers were vieing in displaying their individual grace and activity as disciples of Terpsichore. The ladies looked very well, and talked equally so, with the exception of a remark one let slip; but then some allowance must be made, as she did not know that any one was listening. Indeed, I hardly know whether I am justified in betraying the failings of the fair sex. However, I was never celebrated either for wisdom or prudence, and I shall not in this case exercise a virtue to which I have no claim; so here it is, and if any attach blame to the lady for it, I can, only answer him or her with the motto of the knights of the garter, "*Honi soit qui mal y pense*," or "Evil be to him who evil thinks." But here is a long dissertation without the conversation, which if any lady reads, I know that her patience will be exhausted, so I needs must proceed with my disclosure. Two ladies who had just sat down to rest themselves after the dance, engaged in conversation, and, in the course of it, one stated that she felt sea-sick. "I feel a little qualmish, too," returned the other, "and I have heard that brandy was good for it. I wish that I had brought a bottle in my pocket. Indeed, I intended to, but forgot it." Remark is needless, and superfluous.

The refreshments at this entertainment were coffee and cake; unlike that at Vasse, where spirituous liquors flowed as freely down male and female throats, as whiskey down an Irishman's gullet at a wake.

On the Thursday following was the anniversary of their annual races, at which prizes are offered by the government to the victor. These prizes are given for the purpose of inducing the settlers to pay attention to the improvement of their stock. To avoid the confusion and irregularity which generally prevailed among the inhabitants on these occasions, and in which our men would be too apt readily to join, we hastened our departure; and, accordingly, on Tuesday, after having had our vessel searched by the government officials, we got under weigh, and stood down the bay towards Vasse. Soon after the Iowa followed our example; and, with a head wind, which forced both of us to beat, we pursued the same direction. We soon weathered our companion, and left her far in the distance. The following morning, at 11 o'clock, we let go our anchor off the town of Vasse, where we found three barques and two ships: all whalers—all carrying the star-spangled banner—all belonging to New Bedford, and all, except one, clippers. Every year the number of old-fashioned ships is decreasing, and wedge-shaped craft taking their place: the whaling-service (a branch of commerce the last to countenance innovation) fast yielding to the march of improvement, and adopting the modern model—a long head, a clean run, and a round stern.

The next day liberty was allowed; and, as there

was a report of a prize-fight to come off during the day, almost everybody that had liberty went ashore. There were seven ships in the harbor, (the Iowa having arrived the preceding evening), and therefore the number going ashore formed quite an army — no less than one hundred and thirty. The prize-fight, however, took place at so early an hour, and at such a distance from the town, that our countrymen were prevented from witnessing it. But the day passed off pleasantly, and with moderation, as far as regarded the imbibition of spirits: no one of the whole motley assemblage, comprising natives of almost every clime, having gone beyond the proper bounds.

During the next week I saw one of the participators in the brutal contest above alluded to. He presented appearances of severe punishment. On stating my surprise that he was at large, when the fact of the fight was so well known to the authorities, I was informed that the law had no power over the combatant, unless he were caught in the act.

Amongst the celebrities in this village are the post-master and school-mistress. The former is as deaf as a post, and it is only by raising the voice to a high pitch that the least intelligence can be communicated to him. My patience was well-nigh exhausted in an attempt to inform him of the miscarriage of several of my letters from home; but he either could not, or would not, be made to understand my complaint, and consequently I received no satisfaction.

The school-mistress, from her position, was of

course a wonder of learning and profundity. Being desirous of a conversation with her, (the more so, because, apart from her implied erudition, she was a pleasant-looking and blooming damsel,) an officer of one of the ships scraped an acquaintance with her. She was in nowise loath to enter into conversation, and in a few minutes both were deep in argument. During the colloquy, the mate had occasion to mention Samson's feat of destroying the harvest of the Philistines by attaching firebrands to the tails of foxes. This, to his surprise, was received as something novel; and the fair questioner expressed a desire to know who Samson was: wishing to be informed whether the scene of his exploits was the United States, and whether he was a native of our country. I need not say that D—— was taken all aback. At first he thought that the lady was making game of him; but the look of childish wonder and simplicity that she wore on her countenance forbade such a conclusion. He was so surprised at her ignorance of Holy Writ, that he did not endeavor to enlighten her, but allowed her fancy to roam free over the subject, and, as soon as he could with credit, took his departure: fully convinced that, whatever were the acquirements of the preceptors of youth, who teach the young idea how to shoot, and wield the scholastic birch in New Holland, they at least had not advanced so far as to make the Bible one of their school-books.

I noticed this strange unacquaintance with Holy Writ in more than one individual in the colony. I have no doubt they can manage to live without it—

as far as their idea of life comprehends "living"; but how they can manage to die happily without it, I cannot conceive.

Another fact I must notice; that is, the great number of males and females living together in couples as man and wife, but whose union has not been sanctioned by a performance of the sacred marriage rite. The men who come out here usually bring their wives along, if they are voluntary emigrants; and if convicts their helpmates occasionally follow them — preferring to share the exile of their husbands rather than spend a lone life in their native home. In the latter case they are allowed to consort together, provided the prisoner by a course of good conduct has merited and received a "ticket of relief." Not unusually when any of these females are removed by death, they are replaced by mistresses, who assume all the privileges of the departed, as well as the maternal government of the children, if there should be any; in which latter relation they in most cases act prudently: for children are here an element of wealth as soon as they arrive at an age at which they are qualified to help themselves — there being plenty for them to do, if only these nominal mothers and their husbands are diposed to teach them to labor.

This state of affairs does not appear to be looked upon by the inhabitants as criminal, neither is it made a matter of scandal — both parties being allowed to enter society without reserve. These are harsh assertions, I am aware; but, ere they were written, their asperity was well digested, both by myself and scores of others, who, not from hearsay, but from observation and unrestricted intercourse among these people, are confident they do not do them injustice. The climate is blamed by them for their predisposition to sensuality; and the law is anything but lenient to the offender in such cases: the violator of a female, when brought before a court of justice, being always punished by death.

CHAPTER XI.

On the 16th of February, after having added three new men to our crew, (two of them Englishmen, the third a Swede,) we hove short, and at 3 P. M. stood out of the bay. On arriving off Cape Naturaliste, some twenty miles from our place of anchorage, we sighted a sail that proved to be the barque Pamelia, which was hovering off this locality, to intercept the barque Eagle, which was to bring her third mate out, and also provisions for her consumption. Esculents she needed very much, as several of her people, the captain amongst the number, were affected by scurvy. We supplied them temporarily, and thus kept off that disease, which occasions so much terror to the seaman. She contemplated returning home in a short time, and several of her crew, whose motives I cannot fathom, not contented with a three-years' sojourn in these waters, exchanged into the ship Lapwing, that had some twenty months more to remain. They must either have had an overweening desire to acquire money, or else there were but few attractions at home to induce them to return.

After leaving the bay, we steered to the southeast, in hopes of picking up a whale or two; but we met only with strong gales of wind, which put whaling out of the question. We then returned to the northward, and had the like success: nothing occurring to vary the sameness, day after day, but a series of heavy tempests, attended by terrific thunder and lightning. One night (the 12th of March) the scene was absolutely appalling — presenting a perfect war of the elements. In the words of an old song (than which I know of no better description):

> "Now the dreadful thunder roaring,
>   Peal on peal contending clash;
> On our heads fierce rain falls pouring,
>   In our eyes blue lightnings flash.
> One wide water all around us,
>   All above us one dark sky;
> Different deaths at once surround us—
>   Hark! what means that dreadful cry."

What the words "that dreadful cry" referred to in the song, the reader must imagine; in our case it was that of a shark. A monster of that species, attracted probably by his instinct, which led him to expect prey on such a night as this, swam around and around the ship; the intense darkness of the night and phosphorescent gleam of the ocean made his huge bulk show out in relief, and appear treble his real size. With a swab trailed astern, we soon got him within darting distance, and hove an iron into his carcass, which stopped his marauding forever. He was an enormous sized one, and required the united strength of half a dozen of us, after he was mortally wounded, to drag him part way from the water.

The storm did us no damage — the lightning ran over our yards and the various ironwork of the ship in a manner to terrify the boldest. The reason assigned for so few cases of injury to ships by lightning, is the number of points presented in her structure for the dispersion of the electricity. One precaution is invariably taken, that is, to remove the pump-spears, and fill their place with swabs, to prevent the iron rods acting as conductors for the electric fluid into the hold of the ship.

There is something terrifying in such a scene, that carries with it a sense of danger to the sturdiest: no matter how many such outbreaks have before been viewed by the beholder, still an indefinable fear will pervade his system. The gale is a feature to which, in his routine of life upon the ocean, the seaman becomes accustomed, and only asks for a short warning to battle with it; but there is something in the lightning that makes one feel completely at its mercy, though we know that in this as in all other perilous situations, we are under the protection of the same wise Creator.

On these grounds we were continually meeting merchantmen bound to and from the various Australian and East Indian ports, and it was a matter of congratulation to us to see that all the swiftest and best of these ships carried our own starry flag, maintaining the pre-eminence of our ship-builders in this far-off sea.

We were now thirty months from home, and as our ship was fitted at the outset to remain from home but forty, this was to be our last cruise; and home was the all-engrossing topic on every tongue, from the captain's to the steerage boys', all uniting in a sincere wish to return, oil or no oil. Our return, which but a short time previous had been commented upon as a vague and distant termination of a protracted voyage, was now viewed as feasible and not very remote; and we felt ourselves considerably elevated by the mere thought, when we gammoned with ships but a short time from home, of the probation they, poor fellows, would have to go through ere they arrived at the degree of experience we had acquired on this coast. The wildest of those of our crew, who had left home on the impulse of the moment, were the most anxious to return, feeling that they had paid dear enough for their whistles.

We were now the longest out of any ship on the coast. It is an old adage, amongst whalemen, that when a year from home, on gammoning with any ship that has sailed subsequent to your own departure, you have the privilege of begging; when two years out, of stealing; and when three years, of stealing and begging too; so that we now had the right of exercising this privilege, in which there is more reality than romance. Fresh provisions are seized upon by the old residenters without ruth, as if they had the best right to them. This is seldom disputed by the owners, who, in the abundance of their sympathy, do not wait to be asked for such things, but press them for acceptance without thought of remuneration; doing as they would be done by, and setting an example worthy of imitation by more polished ones.

During the latter part of February and the month of March, we were occupied in beating around the south-west coast of New Holland, occasionally seeing land or sighting a ship to vary the monotony. Early in April we steered to the northward, the strong south-east trades being greatly in our favor. These winds prevail throughout the year in this vicinity, only interrupted by fierce gales from the north-west, which, though severe throughout their duration, seldom last more than from twelve to sixteen hours. During our passage, as we emerged into the warmer latitudes, shoals of flying-fish, bonita, albacore, and dolphin were continually in sight, skipping hither and thither. The bonita and albacore remaining in attendance upon our journey for months, we occasionally caught them. Their prey being flying-fish, they are easily hooked by cutting from solder or tin a shape resembling the little creature, attaching a hook to the lower part of the solder image, and a line to the upper; the angler then perches himself upon the end of the flying jib-boom, and dangles his tackle to and fro, imitating as nearly as possible the aerial flight of the tiny creature it is intended to represent. The voracious skip-jack, or albacore, as the case may be, ever on the alert for its prey, rushes to the bait, seizes it, and is hooked for his pains. It is a pleasant sight to watch these fish whilst about the ship; their agile movements in pursuit of the flying-fish; their instinct teaching them that these are to be found in the greatest number about the vessel's prow, which, in her onward course, disturbs them in their retreats, and forces them to seek safety in the air, on their descent from which an ever watchful enemy is prepared to meet and devour some of their number. At all times these creatures, apparently with the utmost ease, keep in advance of the ship, leaping from the water and varying their course with the direction of the vessel. As I before said, they are often caught, but are only serviceable for food when cooked with other articles, their flesh being extremely dry and insipid. I have been assured by those who have had experience of it, that long indulgence in eating them, produces scurvy of the most violent type — more than one instance of such a fact being on record.

At noon of April 20th we saw the Abrolhas' Islands, and a reef in their vicinity known as the Turtle Dove, which, from observation, we found considerably out of the position laid down on the chart for it. Immediately on closing with the land we lowered away two boats—one of which went fishing, the other prospecting; at dark both returned, the fishing boat with several barrels of snappers, jew-fish, and gropers; the prospecting party landed on Long Island, and found it a long, narrow strip of coral reef covered with broken shells and fragments of coral cast up by the surf. A few mangroves and stunted bushes comprised the vegetation. Large numbers of birds were present, and on some portions of the island were extensive deposits of guano, though so mixed with coral and fractured portions of shells as to be unfit for the purposes of the agriculturist.

On the following day we again went in, and, carrying the boat across a narrow part of the island, we launched her again in the so-called bay, and proceeded to make soundings, by which we ascertained the feasibility of anchoring here. We also visited Middle Island, where a small mound and a headboard gave notice of the interment of a poor remnant of mortality. The board bore the inscription, "Thomas Williams, deceased April, 1851;" purporting to have been placed there by the captain of a schooner. From a person who knew something of the history of the vicinity, I learned that the deceased had been an American seaman, a colored man, who had left an American whale-ship in Freemantle, years previous; there he had married, joined the schooner and set out as one of a whaling party to the Abrolhas'; but before he had reached the scene of operations, he had fought his last battle, and been conquered by death.

On Middle Island there is a rough house erected, which has remained for many years; as also the ruins of a try works—memorials of a whaling party. The tenement is built of stone, the roof of mahogany, and, no doubt, was formerly quite a substantial building; but the north-westers that howl through the islands have made sad havoc with its fair proportions, and it is no longer tenantable.

At night we braced forward and stood out to the open ocean. On the 29th we gammoned the clipper barque Sunlight, of New Bedford, a beautiful craft, twenty-one months from home, with eight hundred and fifty barrels of oil. Her captain, a namesake of the iron-handed protector of England, was described by his crew as being a fiend incarnate — cursing, beating, and abusing every one under his command; giving them scarcely enough to eat. Poor fellows, they were glad to get hard bread, which we, touched by their relation, gave to them: this they secreted on their persons to carry aboard and make a meal of. The account of their sufferings from this monster almost exceeded belief; but as it was the same story from all grades of the members of the ship's company, and was afterwards corroborated by the crew of another vessel, we were forced to yield credence to the tale.

On May 1st, a few minutes prior to sunset, we saw boats and a ship whaling. On nearing the scene of operations we found it to be the ship Abigail, of New Bedford, which proved to be unsuccessful. The succeeding day we again saw her boats whaling. We lowered away our own, but to no purpose. They, however, made an acquisition in the shape of an eighty barrel whale.

On the 6th we gammoned the ship Congress; she brought from home a budget of letters for us, but had delivered them over to the James Allen, in October last, supposing that the latter would see us first— they are now lost to us entirely. The Congress, it will be remembered, returned to the States since we have been on this coast, full of oil; and in the sixteen months, during which she has been from home this voyage, she has taken sixteen hundred barrels of oil, or nearly double what we have taken in three years. She is commanded by the person who acted as her mate during the last voyage.

On the 9th we saw a barque to leeward, manœuvring for whales, and evidently desirous, from her signals, of attracting our observation. On running down to her we found that she had a whale alongside, and that she was the John A. Robb, of Fair Haven, captain Baker, the same who was cast away in the barque Henry H. Crapo; her whale was a sulphur-bottom, and, as these are seldom captured, much curiosity was manifested to get a sight at him. The head was shaped like an inverted scoop; the fins and flukes resembled much those of the right whale. It has on its ridge a very small fin or hump, which serves to distinguish it from the fin-back; its jaws are furnished with black bone, but so short as to render it of little value as an article of commerce. In color its body is of a light grey, and is much longer, in proportion to its bulk, than any other fish I have seen. The blubber was about four inches thick, corrugated and arranged on the belly in great folds or rolls; it was literally covered by wounds made by the remora or sucking-fish. The whole length was eighty feet, and its yield fifty barrels — the oil commanding the same price as that of the right whale.

It is seldom this variety of the whale is disturbed by the whaleman, its extreme shyness rendering it almost an impossibility to strike it. In this instance it was shot from the ship by a bomb-lance, which, by a great chance, caused a fatal wound, disabling the fish so that he was an easy capture.

The high price of whalebone at home renders the ships on this ground, which have a large supply of it, anxious to get theirs to market ere there is a depression in price, and we being the only ship anticipating a speedy return, we are continually having it offered to us as freight. Amongst these ships is the Richard Mitchell, which narrowly escaped being driven ashore at Bunbury a few weeks ago. She had landed her captain to bargain for provisions, whilst the vessel was standing off and on, when a heavy southerly gale sprang up and stripped her of every inch of canvas. By great exertions they bent new sails, but it was not until after seventy-two hours beating that she was enabled to get an offing that secured her safety.

From this time up to July 4th we saw little and done less, with the single exception of lowering away for a sperm whale on June the 6th, but seeing nothing of him after we had dropped our boats. On the 4th, whilst in company with the Europa, making for the Abrolhas' Islands, we sighted sperm whales, lowered, struck, and killed one. Previous to striking we had hoisted our ensign, which was imitated by the Europa. This signal was a bond of copartnership between the two ships during the day's operations, each being entitled to half the proceeds of the day's capture. The Europa did not fasten, but chased the whales to windward, in which pursuit we lost sight of her; meantime we tried out our whale and stowed it between decks, so that we would have but little trouble in giving her her half of it when we met. After some days we fell in with her, when her captain, with a generosity unusual with his profession, declined taking any part of it, assigning as a reason our long-continued bad luck; saying, that after having taken but one whale in six months, it would be too bad to deprive us of half of that.

The Europa had experienced a hard time of it since we had last seen her, meeting with several of those accidents which the vicissitudes of a seaman's life render him ever liable to — having, in the first place, shipped a sea that went completely over her, and stove the three larboard boats almost beyond repair; then, again, having run close in towards the land in hopes of seeing us, she had been jammed between the Turtle Dove, Abrolhas' and main land, in a gale of wind, when crowding sail to madness was their only hope; but, fortunately, a timely shift of wind enabled them to clear the main land by a hair's breadth, and dispelled all their gloomy fears.

On the 16th both vessels stood in for the Abrolhas' Islands, and at 9 o'clock were snugly anchored amid the cluster, of which, by ascending our tops, twenty-five different islands could be counted. As soon as our ground-tackle was secured, we struck the topsail and topgallant yards and the topgallantmasts, housed our mizzen topmast, and then unbent all the sails, except the spensers: our object being to present as little surface as possible to the action of the wind; thereby rendering our anchorage more secure. The anchorage showed coarse white sand, combined with pulverized coral and shell, which constitutes excellent holding-ground.

Not expecting the humpbacks in before the first of August, we passed the time in making excursions to the various islands of the group. We soon found a novel and exciting sport in the destruction of seals, which exist here in great numbers. These creatures bring forth their young on the land; and, this being the season in which they breed, they could at all times be seen basking in the sun, fast asleep, and quietly enjoying themselves to the full. Our method of attack was to approach as slyly as possible, and deal heavy blows on the tip of the nose, which is the most sensitive portion of their organism. If well aimed, the first blow despatches them; but, on the contrary, if you should deliver it on the shoulders, back, or quarters, it seems to produce no deleterious effect on the animal, which instantly rears upon his hind flippers, and, with a sharp, querulous yelp, displays a set of ivories little inferior to those of the lion; however, it requires hardly any address on the part of the pursuer to avoid him. When the animal once gets into water, no matter how shallow, farther chase becomes hopeless, as it can then propel itself at a powerful rate; but while on land, though its movements are by no means slow, it is no match for a good runner.

A young seal, by the knowing ones said to be about six weeks old, was captured alive, passed into the boat, and carried aboard the ship. It seemed in no wise disconcerted, except at night when a light was placed near its eyes, whereat it became much alarmed. It showed but little timidity when caressed, and evidently considered our dog as one of its own species, so solicitous was it to form an intimacy with him; but puppy fought shy, and avoided companionship with the amphibious creature. From its docility, we anticipated keeping it for a long time; yet during the several days that it was retained, although offered both small and large fish, it would partake of no sustenance, but wandered fore and aft the decks, crying for its dam in a note not unlike that the cow-calf uses on similar occasions. We were at last reluctantly compelled to kill it — stuffing the skin for a memorial. The skins of these, known as the hair-seal variety, are of little value intrinsically; but, being easily tanned, they were very useful to us as chafing-gear for the rigging.

Some of our savants, having either themselves eaten, or having heard of other persons eating, the liver of the seal, assiduously extracted, cleaned, and cooked one. It being a young seal, the dish proved very palatable, in taste much resembling hog's liver. All now became alert to procure a fresh supply of them; but, as it happened, the next seal pitched upon was a patriarch of the gang, whose destroyers were overjoyed indeed at the quantity yielded by their prize, and brought it aboard the ship with the air of conquerors. The cook dressed it; but, lo, and behold! the following day, most of those who had partaken of it were affected by nausea at the stomach and distressing headache — half of the number being unable to leave their berths: consequences, I opine, arising from the indigestibility of the liver, rendered tough by the animal's great age. Since then I have been assured that this is by no means an isolated case of indisposition from the same cause.

In rambling, we found Long Island the most inviting of the group. It was scantily furnished with several varieties of low shrubs; amongst which were the native Australian gooseberry and a species of wild oats. There are also on the island several thickets of the mangrove, which, from the peculiar growth of the trees, though of only a moderate height, are almost impenetrable. This tree affords excellent fuel, and we took advantage of this by cutting and carrying away some eight or ten cords of it for firewood. Its fracture is of a light yellowish color, and the heart of it is decayed, but I cannot say whether this is owing to the bad quality of the soil, or is a natural characteristic of the wood. It is very heavy. The leaf is small, and eagerly sought for by the rabbits, which abound on the island. Several pairs of these little creatures were placed here years ago, and they have increased until their number is legion. Had they a supply of fresh water, they would in a short time become so much more numerous as to consume all the herbage within their reach. We seldom visited the island without bringing away half-a-dozen of them. Occasionally, in running our arms into the burrows for rabbits, we would take hold of a disgusting iguana, or get a handful of small eggs, deposited by a very diminutive variety of gull, that burrows in the ground, and there hatches its young. The whole island is excavated by these little diggers. Their eggs, almost double the size of a pigeon-egg, have a white shell, and are very excellent eating. The larger gulls lay an egg superior in size to those of our domestic hens, which are mottled, and food fit for an epicure. The shag, another variety, lays a pink egg, of goodly size, which is also equally palatable. These birds would lay on the bare ground; and, on our robbing their depositories, they would move to another island, and repeat the process. This they did four or five times, and at last either gave up in despair, or lit upon some place secure from our depredations; for we were unable to procure a further supply.

On Long Island we saw several osprey-nests, in one of which were eggs; in another, the half-fledged young of the species. The eggs were about the size of a goose-egg; but, as we had reason to think they were addled, we had no opportunity of testing their fitness for the table.

During the whole of one day we observed immense flocks of birds flying in the direction of this island, and on visiting it found the clumps of mangroves literally swarming with small birds about the size of a blackbird, busily engaged in building nests from the kelp which is thrown up by the surf. They seemed to take but little notice of us. We held a consultation, and finally decided that they were fit to be eaten, and, in pursuance of this resolution, began bagging them. This we found but little trouble; all that was necessary being to ascend one of the mangrove trees, and, as the birds wheeled around in circles to more nearly examine our, to them, strange appearance, knock them down left and right. In this way but very few minutes elapsed before we had sufficient for our purposes — two hundred and fifty of the little feathered bipeds being a mess for the ship's company; and all united in deciding that they made an exceedingly savory stew. We repeated the operation often after having been initiated into their good qualities. Some idea may be formed of the number consumed, when I state that the feathers, which were saved by old Jack, weighed twenty pounds; the old salt in his green old age being determined to have a soft bed to repose his weather-worn limbs upon. To this end he had been collecting feathers during the greater part of the voyage— albatrosses, monimokes, ducks, pigeons, hawks, and whale birds, contributing each their quota to his store.

I cannot take leave of this subject without attempting to give some idea of the immense numbers of the birds. I had read of the innumerable flocks of wild pigeons which frequent our Western States, and I had seen at sea immense flocks of various birds migrating to other countries, but I had never formed an estimate that came within many removes of the actual number I here saw. I can indeed liken them to nothing else, as regards number, than a swarm of bees; their bodies obscuring the sun's light when they passed overhead, and a stone thrown at random never failing to meet a mark.

The conchological specimens found on these islands are varied but inelegant; they comprise both descriptions of the nautilus — the true and paper varieties being found in abundance. These shells externally possess but little beauty, but on being sawn apart in a lateral direction, they present a handsome pearly arrangement contained in an air-tight apartment in the base of the shell. A small variety of the cowrie, too, is abundant. There are also periwinkles, scollops, and oysters, all three of which are excellent eating, and, therefore, were in great request with us.

Crabs are also found in great numbers, and can be had for the trouble of picking up; so that we made shift to fare pretty well during our stay here.

One of the islands to which we made several excursions, was known as Dead Man's Island, from the fact that an encounter between the members of the crew of a Spanish ship, which was wrecked on the reef in the seventeenth century, resulted in the death of several of their number. The circumstances are these: the crew, after their vessel was stranded, made for this island, having saved provisions and other articles, amongst which was a chest of treasure. A dispute arising regarding the ownership of this treasure, from words they proceeded to blows and bloodshed, and some of them were sacrificed to their avaricious spirit. After the battle the defeated party were banished to another island, and the cause of strife was deposited for greater security on Square Island, where, tradition says, it still remains; and many have been induced by the rumor, incited by love of gain or adventure, to toil in hopes of its *éclaircissement.* To this day human bones are to be seen on the surface, and had there been as good evidence of the treasure as of the struggle, no doubt our Yankee inquisitiveness and acquisitiveness would have induced some of us to have made search for it.

I can imagine no more inhospitable locality for a ship's company to be cast away than amongst these islands. They would be unable to find any material to erect a covering for protection from the weather, unless some portions of their vessel were cast ashore—the islands themselves supplying nothing of the kind. To be sure they might manage to eke out a subsistence from the birds and fish which are so abundant at certain periods of the year; but they would be unable to exist without water in the summer season, when, for months, no rain falls. The only place where we found any fresh water was on Middle Island; and it was a mere deposit of rain, in a well dug by the whaling party who formerly made it the scene of their fishing operations.

On the 27th of July we sent off two boats from each ship to erect a look-out on an island several miles to seaward of the ship. Whilst the boats were thus engaged the crews saw humpback whales, but forebore to meddle with them, supposing them to be the pioneers of the school said to frequent these islands, and wishing to do nothing at this early date to scare them from the haunts. On their return to the ship with this cheering intelligence, all was bustle and activity. The blubber-room was cleared out, useless casks were sent ashore, and every preparation was made to carry on whaling with the utmost spirit; but alas! for the vanity and frailty of human expectations, these were the sole and only representatives of their species that we had a sight at during our five weeks' sojourn amongst the Abrolhas'. Things thus remained in *statu quo* until the 14th, when, as we began to send up spars and make preparations for our departure, the luminous idea struck somebody of sending one or more boats over to Champion Bay, to ascertain whether whales had been seen on the coast, and whether the Port Gregory whaling company had accomplished anything during the present season. In pursuance of this resolution a boat from each ship, provisioned for a week, was despatched to the main, under the conduct of the mates of the respective vessels. We started at 1 o'clock P. M. with a fair wind, and at nine the same evening made the main land, in the vicinity of a headland known as the Wizard's Peak. In the opinion of our fourth mate, who had been here previously, we were too far to the northward, and, as the line of breakers presented no point where we could land, in pursuance of his suggestion we kept off to the southward, and continued running until midnight, when we anchored in fifteen fathoms of water, and endeavored to get some sleep; one of our number standing watch all through the night. At daybreak we resumed our course to the southward until about 3 o'clock in the afternoon, when we became convinced of the incapacity of our pilot, and thought it advisable to retrace our course to the northward; the wind being ahead, we had to pull in the teeth of wind and sea. At dark we again came to anchor in fourteen fathoms of water, and passed the night in the same manner as the preceding one. At daylight, seeing nothing of the entrance, the feasibility of a return to the ship was mooted, but as our supply of water had dwindled to a gallon in both boats, we were loath to adopt this measure, except as a dernier resort; but the wind, fortunately for us, having hauled during the night, we set sail, and at nine o'clock in the morning discovered the wished for haven within a few miles of the peak we had sighted the first night— a very fortunate conclusion to our misadventure. On reflection, we could now see the dangers of our late situation. Had a gale come on from the westward we could not possibly have escaped being driven on shore; and if it had come from the eastward, even provided our boats had not been swamped, we were without a supply of water, and must have perished from thirst before we could have reached the ship.

On our landing at Champion Bay we were met upon the beach by the three magistrates of the settlement, and a large proportion of the inhabitants, who anxiously inquired if we had been wrecked. On our answering in the negative, they inquired where we were from. On our again answering, the barques Pacific and Europa, at the Abrolhas' Islands, they evidently regarded us with suspicion—thinking that we were either mutineers or deserters, who had fabricated this story for our own purposes; and I believe that, had they dared, or even had they thought themselves the strongest party, they would have clapped us all in limbo, until assured of the truth of the story we told. We heard whisperings as to our physical ability. The boats' crews being picked men, they said, were a very rugged-looking set of fellows; and the fact of each man being provided with his belt and sheath-knife seemed a recommendation to their respect. Then, again, had there been any difficulty, the penal population, who are largely in the majority, would have readily joined the strangers, in hopes of being delivered by them from their penal servitude.

Our first queries were, as to whether whales had been seen in any numbers on the coast the present season. They stated, that, from some unknown cause, the whales' food was not so plenty as it is during most years at this period. The meducæ, which exist in great quantities, or rather numbers, generally by their volume gave to the water a yellowish hue, but at present scarcely any indication of their existence was perceptible; therefore, although the whales had appeared as usual, they made but a short stay. The Port Gregory fishery had been fortunate enough, during their brief visit, to capture five of them — making quite a profitable season's business. They took their last whale some weeks since — about the same time that we saw whales at the Abrolhas'; and I am persuaded that we were too late for the season.

On our informing them that there were no whales at the Abrolhas' Islands, they professed much surprise, and would scarcely give credence to our intelligence; stating that, for years, every vessel which had passed these islands had borne testimony to the immense number of whales that frequented the waters around them.

Having now progressed up towards the settlement, we found it neatly situated, although the buildings, which number about sixty, were much scattered. The herbage appears luxuriant, and the soil fertile. Many of the settlers own immense flocks of sheep and herds of bullocks; but they deprecate the system of raising stock with a view to a pecuniary return: for in the immediate vicinity of the settlement there grew, I was assured, no less than sixteen varieties of vegetable poisons, which the cattle browse, and are soon afterwards affected by spasms that result in death.

A short distance from the settlement there is an extensive copper-mine, which is the means of affording employment to most of the inhabitants. The ore is said to be very rich, and is exported to England, whence several vessels were daily expected for freights of it. This article affords their only means of commerce with foreign countries: their supplies and wool coming through, and being shipped from, Freemantle, to and from which city cutters continually ply.

The wind being unfavorable for us to return to the ship, we made up our minds to enjoy life ashore, for a day or two, as well as circumstances would allow. So, in accordance with the decree of the clerk of the weather, we took up our quarters at the only public house in the place, and were soon deep in the discussion of a dinner, consisting for the most part of fresh mutton. We had brought with us several hams, which the habitues of the house preferred to the fresh meat. We therefore had them boiled, to their as well as our own satifaction; for while they were engaged with the bacon, we were enabled to appropriate to our ourselves the lion's share of the other edibles, which — as our appetites had been sharpened by between sixty and seventy hours' exposure to the bracing sea-breeze, with a spice of hard pulling — we were fully competent to dispose of.

Not feeling in the mood to cruise around much during the afternoon, the greater part of us remained about the house, wondering, from the sparsity of the landlord's visitors, how he managed to eke out a living; but, as soon as night approached, we were convinced that he lacked not for customers, who now one after another dropped in to have a look at us, and imbibe the potations he had to dispense.

One thing is greatly in favor of this colony; that is, the government has as yet refused to grant a license for the sale of spirits in less quantities than a gallon; and, as a gallon costs two pounds sterling, (equivalent to nine dollars and eighty-eight cents of our money,) the ardent is not within the reach of everybody. During the time we remained in the place, I did not see a glass of spirits drank. Malt-liquors, comprising porter, ale, and beer, were however swallowed without regard to quality or quantity.

Here, as well as everywhere else that I have visited in these colonies, the males and females alike frequent the tap-room. They were all very hospitable, and it may be imagined how it sounded to our ears, for a matronly-looking woman, with a child held by the hand, to address us with, "What will you have to drink, Jack?" while everybody about seemed to regard it as a matter of propriety.

At night, as there were not beds sufficient for our accommodation, we took a shake down in the diningroom, using kangaroo-skins as blankets. We had scarcely got settled, before we were rolling, pitching, and tossing, by way of a forced accompaniment to the flea-bites that were being inflicted upon us: the numbers of these pests being myriads. Although they are little heeded by those who are acclimated here and inured to their tortures, yet to us thinnerskinned gentry these fleas now proved objects of real terror. For hours, sleep was out of the question. All of us had been accustomed to considerable bloodletting aboard from the bed-bugs that always infest old ships in warm weather; but we were by no means prepared for a wholesale depletion by these vampires. At length, towards morning, we managed to gain some intermission from their attacks, and the sun had made a great portion of his daily journey ere we broke our slumbers.

After breakfast was over, we took a tramp, and found that we were not deceived in our estimate of the country. Instead of the sandy surface we had been accustomed to see in the southern sections of the colony, there was here an excellent soil, and the appearance of the crops promised an abundant harvest; while the live stock we saw were in a good condition.

The trees here embrace all the varieties of the sheoak, bankshire, mahogany, peppermint, blackberry and raspberry jam, and some little way in the interior the precious sandal-wood is found.

The houses are of stone, and neatly fashioned: mahogany being applied to all the various purposes of the architect—its great plentifulness and durability rendering it preferable to any other wood they possess.

The following day, the wind still being unfavorable and precluding our departure, the officers in charge of the expedition began to feel alarmed as to the insufficiency of their funds — the whole amount of money brought being ten pounds, or fifty dollars; this amount would not go very far towards the support of thirteen men, for any length of time, in a place where all the necessaries of life were held at an exorbitant price. Now that their suspicions had worn off as to our true character, I do not think that they would have allowed us to want; still, we did not feel inclined to depend on their charity, so we asked them if there was any work that we could perform. The only branches of business open were wood-chopping and supplying the community with fresh fish; they possessing no boats, and the snapper banks being some distance from the settlement, it is only by chance that they are enabled to indulge their appetites for them. We, on this information, held a consultation, and one party, including the two officers, shouldered axes and went into the woods, where they gave the colonials a specimen of Yankee wood-chopping; the rest of us took the boats, and, having been supplied with tackle, made their hearts glad by a display of fish superior to any they had seen for a long time.

This was a pretty specimen of occupation for gentlemen's sons to engage in; but it only verifies our national peculiarities: and the originator of the remark that a Yankee, with or without his jack-knife, could make a living anywhere, was not far from the truth.

The natives here, as elsewhere, are the same miserable, debased race; but are ruled by an iron hand—the early experience of the colonists forcing them to adopt severe measures to secure them against the depredations of these nomadic tribes. I was informed that little account was taken of the death of one of them, by a white man's agency, if detected in any little peccadillo; but a few years since the whites were still more severe, shooting the natives down like dogs whenever they approached their habitations.

At nine o'clock on the morning of the 19th we bade farewell to Champion Bay, under strict surveillance of the authorities — they being fearful that we would convey away some of the prisoners. We were favored with a fair wind, and at 4 o'clock the same afternoon boarded the ship, perfectly satisfied with our jaunt. We found that during our absence changes had taken place—a Portuguese boy, whom we shipped at Flores, having exchanged, and gone aboard the Europa as steward; her former steward, a native of New York city, having received his discharge on account of inability, from sickness, to perform his duty. He is suffering from spasmodic stricture of the urethra, and goes with us to Mauritius in order to procure efficient medical aid. He lives in the forecastle, and, as well as his health permits, agrees to perform duty as a foremast hand; on arriving at Mauritius, it is optional with him either to remain ashore or go with us to the United States.

During the whole time that we lay at anchor here, the most intimate relations existed between all grades of the two ships' companies; every day and every night we held re-unions, in which, by merriment, we strove to dispel the recollection of being so far separated from home. A boat seldom left either ship on an excursion for pleasure, without calling on the other party to see if any wished to go; and if either ship was to be kedged ahead, or her anchorage shifted, the other crew were ever ready to volunteer their assistance.

One favorite trip was to go with the boat to within a short distance of the heavy surf that broke on the reef at low water, where live shells were to be collected. These were then buried in sand, or immersed in fresh water, until the death of the animal rendered dislodging him from his shell an easy task. In this manner we cleaned them, without impairing the enamel, which so greatly enhances their beauty.

One of our last moves previous to sailing, was to stow some two hundred barrels of salt water in our after-hold, the ship being so light as to render more weight in her hold necessary to make her seaworthy; we having put into her nothing like her carrying capacity of oil, and having eaten the principal part of the provisions, there remained but little in her to act as ballast.

Having now been from home almost our allotted period, we have exhausted almost all the original supplies. Our meat is reduced to some forty barrels, flour to ten or twelve, sugar none, molasses none, (the latter we procured a supply of from the Europa,) and our tea is so near its ultimatum that it is reserved for special occasions, and coffee takes its place as a beverage for supper. Our boats are nearly all worthless, and now only comprise the four on the cranes—two having been disposed of to Captain Phinney, of the Europa; who likewise got all of the spare oars. We have but one respectable set of topsails and courses that can be depended upon in heavy weather, and are ill provided for a much longer stay from home. Should we take another cruise or two, the expenses of refitting would be great; and, should we then do nothing, instead of a source of profit to the owners, we would prove a burden, independent of the loss of time to ourselves. At the same time we feel loath to return with so sorry a cargo; and there are a number amongst us who are anxious and willing to risk the prospect of another six months' or a year's work, so as to have something due them on their return; forgetting that, although they were to land penniless, the six or twelve months thus spent at sea, if steadily devoted to some occupation ashore, would return a much larger sum.

At 11 o'clock on the morning of the 20th, we weighed our anchors with the intention of going out; but no sooner were they tripped, than the current set us down upon the Europa, which lay a cable's length astern. All hands jumped on the taffrail and quarters, and shoving with might and main, prevented a collision. We then kedged her ahead, and, finding it impossible for us to leave until the Europa sailed, we lowered our boats and towed her into the channel. Then kedging ahead to clear the shoal, after narrowly escaping planting her stern on it, off she went in gallant style.

The Europa went out rigged as a barque. Her mizzenmast being defective, carrying sail on it would be rather hazardous; so her crossjack, mizzen topsail, and topgallant yards, were sent down, and the leg-of-mutton-shaped gaff-topsail substituted in the stead of the canvas pertaining to them.

These whaleships often undergo striking changes between the date of their leaving home and the period of their return: the captain possessing a discretionary power to pull down and build up any of his ship's arrangements. But, woe betide him! if he does anything that results disastrously, unless he makes a good voyage (which last is the New-Bedford apology for a multitude of sins). Some old-fashioned skippers are content with leaving things as they find them; whilst those of the more modern school want their quarter-deck made clear, so that when in port a fore-and-after can be indulged in by the select assemblages who then ordinarily rendezvous aboard whalers.

By the way, I recently heard a story about a party of such visitants, who boarded the ship Twilight in King George's Sound. Amongst them were the daughters of one of the most aristocratic families in the town. The steward of the vessel, supposing of course that they were ladies, had gone to considerable pains in preparing a collation, which the guests seemed much to enjoy. After concluding their repast, they stuffed their pockets with the cakes they were unable to eat; indeed, one went so far as to make her bosom a storehouse for provender. They then adjourned to the quarter-deck for a dance; and, as they displayed much activity during its progress, the hidden dainties were dropped: an eclaircissement which much surprised the neophytes of the ship, who were unaccustomed to such practices. The possessors were by no means disconcerted; but, re-collecting their prizes, continued the dance.

This relation of New Holland manners may by some be deemed overwrought and extravagant; but, as I have the story from most reliable authority, I can vouch for its correctness. I have seen the participants, and although, as I before said, they belonged to the first circles and affected to be aristocratic, were they arrayed in jacket and trowsers, they would make first-rate man-of-war's men.

And now that the Abrolhas' are dropping astern, we will contrast the present state of our feelings with what they were when we entered this channel, five weeks since. Then we were pregnant with hope: no doubt existing in our minds as to the preconceived certainty of taking several hundred barrels of oil — the only damper to our ardent expectation being the forethought of our toil in towing. The possibility of there being no whales never struck us; for we had from various testimonies of their presence put this point so far beyond all question, that if any one had started the least misgivings he would have been treated with derision. At that time, too, we firmly expected to leave directly for home on quitting the islands; having only to make a short stoppage at the Island of St. Helena for water. But now we had before us the unpleasant prospect of another cruise; and this still more darkened with the thought of our putting into ports, where the little we had due to us would most likely be foolishly spent. Instead of the hundreds of barrels of oil that we had anticipated to have stowed below, we had two hundred barrels of salt-water; and to counterbalance our other disappointments we had — just nothing at all. Yet, had we not made the attempt, none of us would have been satisfied; and I think the captain perfectly justified, although the result was so disastrous.

But there is no use in repining: for this was only one of the series of maladventures we experienced throughout our voyage. The season in the Bight and that on New Zealand (on both of which we had counted largely) returned us almost nothing. We had, however, solaced ourselves with the reflection that the Abrolhas' season was yet to come; and, although we preferred the sperm oil, still we had made up our minds to be satisfied with a cargo of that of the humpback, which we were assured we could get without trouble, except hard work. And now, when this too had failed, our sheet-anchor was gone: for, if there were any who still had an idea of making a good voyage, they were hoping against hope. For us, certainly, the day had gone by; unless, indeed, when we returned, the market for oil should by some strange revulsion have become so much exhausted as to cause it to bring an almost fabulous price. Then, and then only, would any of us make pin-money enough to repay us for more than three years of a hard, wearisome life. However, as I said before, there is no use in repining. We must grin and bear it, and at the same time admit ourselves convinced of the aptness of that axiom which reads "Blessed are they who expect nothing; for they are sure not to be disappointed."

And now, the general feeling that pervaded the ship's company was a wish for a speedy return home: all being convinced of the inutility of a longer absence. But whether the captain would act in accordance with it remained to be seen. His mind fluctuated, with the tide of time, between these two points: to go, or not to go. This was the question which he appeared to be continually debating in his own mind. One moment, "going home" was in the ascendant; the next, all his sympathies were enlisted in favor of staying out for another cruise: points which were perhaps ultimately decided to our disadvantage.

CHAPTER XII..

AFTER leaving the Abrolhas', we had a strong westerly breeze, which required us to carry sail pretty stiffly, to avoid the shore; in the course of which process we sighted the Wollaby group and Wizzard's Peak on the main.

Our intention was to cruise here for four or six weeks; but having, after the lapse of eight or nine days, seen sperm whales which were going eyes out to the westward, (we lowered for them, but did not get within miles of them,) on the morning of September 1st, we spoke the Europa, sold to her captain another boat, and, with strong southeast trades, took up our line of departure for the westward. Our ship's bottom, from long exposure, was very foul, and we tried to make amends for her dullness by packing her spars full of canvass: main royal, topmast, lower and topgallant studding sails, all assisting us on our westerly course; and, although we were not bound directly home, we were all well aware that space now crossed brought us thitherward, and would not need to be retraced by us. Hence we entered into the spirit of the passage with more alacrity than usual. There was, besides, this other consideration, that we were bound to a port within the precincts of civilization; which is always a matter of gratification to sailors, after either a short or long cruise.

At the last farewell visit from the Europa's crew, we were commissioned to deliver many a message, both verbal and written, to near and dear friends of theirs in the States; and they, poor fellows, doomed as they are, for a year or eighteen months more, cruising off New Holland's coast, could not avoid announcing their wishes to be aboard with us. They, however, bade us "God speed;" and we bade adieu to New Holland and them both at the same time, hoping to meet the latter again in the land of Washington, amid pleasanter scenes and under happier auspices than can be found within the confines of an Indian Ocean whaler's timbers.

After bidding adieu to the Europa, we occupied ourselves in sending aloft studding sails on the fore and main, from the topgallant yards to the deck; the main royal was bent, a mizzen staysail manufactured and bent, and under a cloud of canvass, impelled by the gentle trade-wind, we kept her west-north-west, fully anticipating making Mauritius within a fortnight; but, like most of our bright anticipations, this was doomed to be dashed—the trade-winds, most unusually at this season of the year, persisting in being light, so that it was not until the 21st that we saw the Isle of France. Previous to this, on the 19th, we sighted and passed close by the Island of Rodrique. This small island is seldom visited by whalers for supplies, as there is no accredited American agent resident on it. It however is made famous amongst the whaling fleet, from the fact of a captain of a New Bedford vessel having selected a lady of the island, of French parentage, as his lady love, marrying, and taking her with him to the United States, to the dismay of the fair sex in his native neighborhood, who had set their caps for him. This fact is so well known and widely spread, that I never, whilst in the Indian Ocean, heard the name of the island mentioned, without being compelled, from politeness, to listen to a repetition of the love passage.

The following day, at five o'clock in the afternoon, we sighted a school of sperm whales, consisting of cows and calves. After several hours chasing, we were obliged to relinquish the pursuit as futile.

On the afternoon of the 23d we stood close in to the land composing the Isle of France; it is rugged and mountainous, covered by immense fields of nature's own green, which we judged to be the different plantations of coffee and sugar-cane, for which the island is celebrated. At night we beat to windward, having to direct us the beacons of two light-houses, which designate the entrance to the harbor. Next morning we stood into the roadstead, which is easy of access, but only presents a secure anchorage at certain seasons of the year, being entirely unprotected from the winds. At $10\frac{1}{2}$ A. M. on the 23d we let go our anchor, amid some twenty vessels, most of which fly either the French or English flag—these two nations carrying on the principal trade to and from the port. These vessels were of the most ancient models, not a clipper to be seen amongst them; all betrayed too plainly that Yankee ingenuity had nothing to do with their construction, but that their models, rig, and lumbering appearance were all owing to some clumsy English shipwright, or French bungler in the same line.

The town, or rather that part of it which can be

seen from the roadstead, presents anything but a creditable appearance; only the outskirts can be seen, built on the base of the far-famed and world-renowned Peter Boite mountain, which rears its cone-shaped summit aloft in the regions of upper air. Midway up the ascent is a signal station, which informs those initiated into the mysteries of the system of signals, of the appearance in the offing of inward bound vessels; and when these are near enough, by the arrangement of Captain Marryatt's signals, consisting of four small flags, or rather three flags and a whip, they ascertain the name of the vessel, whence from, her cargo, and to whom consigned.

The entrance to the harbor, which, by the way, appears from the roadstead tolerably full of shipping, is guarded by two elevated fortifications and a mole; so that, from the number of fortifications, I should judge that the harbor was pretty secure in case of assault.

It is very easy to remark the difference between the English and American method of transacting harbor business. If we had anchored near an American city, within the jurisdiction of the quarantine physician, our anchor would have scarcely left the cat-head, ere he would have boarded us and been satisfied as to our general healthiness; but here, from half-past 10 until 3 o'clock, we were left in a blessed state of uncertainty as to whether we should communicate with the shore or remain stationary; when the dilatory physician boarded us, and, after marshalling the crew aft and satisfying himself as to our general sanitary condition, gave us a red flag to fly at our fore royal truck, which was our certificate of health, and guaranteed to us permission to transact business with the city. Those vessels that are condemned by the port physician as unfit to enter into communication with the inhabitants of the island, are removed to the quarantine ground, about a mile below our anchorage, where, at present, some dozen vessels lie, guarded by the police boat, that prevents any interchange of goods that may lead to the introduction of infection into the port.

The port officer, who accompanied the physician, left with us a small book containing the harbor laws and regulations, for the government of vessels of all nations which anchor within its precincts. These laws are printed both in French and English, and purport to emanate from Sir John Higginson, lieutenant-governor; they are comprised mostly of stringent quarantine restrictions, which led me to suppose that at some earlier period they had suffered severely by the importation of dreadful contagious diseases, which I can easily imagine would find abundant food amid the miscellaneous population, assisted as it naturally would be by the extreme heat of the climate.

Beside these, there are a series of signals for the preservation of vessels in the roadstead during the months which are most liable to typhoons or hurricanes. This period extends from the 1st of December to the 1st of April; at the first signal the captains of all vessels lying in the roadstead are compelled by law to resort to their respective ships; other signals are for the increase of ground-tackle, shifting of anchorage, and, finally, getting under weigh, when a longer stay in the roadstead would prove dangerous.

At 8 o'clock in the evening we heard the report of the evening gun which enjoins all keepers of public houses, and other places of business, to close their doors; a heavy penalty being imposed upon any person transacting business of whatever kind after gun fire. At 5 o'clock A. M. the morning gun is fired, when all are at liberty to open their doors, and resume their respective avocations.

On the 25th we thoroughly washed our ship, sending ashore several times during the day. When the first boat came off with provisions, comprising meat and vegetables, a boy, who constituted one of the crew, was exploding with suppressed laughter, which occasionally would escape him notwithstanding his utmost efforts. On being questioned as to the cause of his mirth, he proceeded in a very naive and humorous vein to describe his trip to the market for meat. After selecting what was wanted for the ship's consumption, a Lascar backed it, which was all very well; but no sooner had he started, than another of the same race jumped up from his squatting posture, and, by a series of thumps and rib ticklings, forced the one who acted as pack-horse into quite a nimble pace for an indolent Asiatic. The thumps and rib ticklings, which seemed a grave matter of business between the contracting parties, excited the fancy of our Yankee boy, who had never seen or heard of such a man-persuading operation; hence his violent merriment.

The meat which we procured is known by two sobriquets, being called indifferently, "buffalo" and "cape beef." The animals are procured either from the Cape Colony, or the Island of Madagascar. I saw a number of them yoked together, performing the heavy draughting to and from the plantations and warehouses. With the exception of the hump, I could perceive no difference in form between them and our own cattle. This hump is situated on the spine directly over the fore shoulders; in shape it resembles a mound, being conical as it approaches its summit, and in a full grown animal attains a height of from eight to twelve inches. The flesh of the hump is said to be esteemed a great dainty, and I have no doubt of it from the fact that whilst lying here not a particle of that portion of the animal came aboard our ship, it commanding a higher price than the other portions, and, therefore, was too expensive provender for sailors.

I have heard this meat reviled over and over again, as being tough and anything but nutritious; but I disagree with its detractors, as I found it sweet, tender and palatable, although it is very far from being fat.

Besides fresh meat we were enabled to obtain sweet potatoes — the murphies not being raised here — and so we were fain to put up with their yellow prot500
types; they were much the same esculent as we formerly procured in the Island of Lombock. Carrots, and the various garden vegetables, too, were procurable, and the most original turnips that it ever fell to my lot to behold. In form they resembled a pine-apple, and were of a deep purple color. Attracted by their savory look, I essayed to peel one with my pocket knife, but found such a proceeding

not to be accomplished with ordinary tools; with the assistance of a sharp hatchet, I managed to remove the jacket, and was rewarded for my pains by a mouthful of the hardest chewing commodity that ever was put between my masticators; it reminded me of the occasion, when a boy, I attempted to crack a hickory nut between my teeth.

On Monday morning we arose with the intention of doing a great deal of work — thinking to get off all our water in the course of the day. In pursuance of this resolution two boats were manned, and we went ashore with a raft of casks in tow, passing up the inner harbor. (But as we were to go ashore in a few hours on liberty, and would then have more leisure for inspection, we omit further description until then.) There were several hundred ships lying here, independent of the coasting-craft, and therefore on arriving at the watering-place, which consisted of an aqueduct with a single nozzle, we found it surrounded by seamen of every nation, hose in hand, patiently waiting their turns, while being scorched by the burning rays of a tropical sun. Finding that in all probability the greater part of the day would be consumed ere we should have an opportunity to fill our casks, the starboard-watch returned to the ship, in order to make preparations to go ashore on liberty; which being soon completed, a boat was manned, and away we went for a day's enjoyment after eight months of sea-life.

On our way in we passed a series of parti-colored buoys, placed so as clearly to define the entrance to the harbor. About two miles from the landing there is a curious contrivance of wicker-work, with a bell in it, familiarly known as the Bell Buoy; and a little further in, the Powder Boat, into which all vessels entering the harbor are compelled to deposit their powder. The entrance to the harbor is moderately wide, but still no vessels enter without the aid of the steam tow-boat, which they may however dispense with on leaving. Every vessel in the harbor is compelled to anchor with two stream and two bower anchors.

And now we were amongst the shipping: for the most part, great, lumbering, unsightly sugar-boxes. There, the aristocratic title, the Earl of Derby, proclaimed the Briton; the Napoleon was undoubtedly Monsieur's craft; the Esperanza, the Don's; and Peter of Hamburg, Mynheer's. But amid them all rose the lofty tapering spars of the brigantine Penney, of New York; and, on a nearer approach, we could examine the beautiful lines of her symmetrical hull, giving evidence of the handicraft of a Baltimore shipbuilder — and such was her class: a Baltimore clipper of the handsomest model. To-day she flew our glorious ensign (the stars and stripes) for the last time; having been sold to the British government, to be used as a revenue-cruiser. Her purchasers, a few days before her delivery to them, having assiduously substituted, for the Eagle on her stern, the British Lion, desired to fly that ensign at her mizzen peak; but the crew in charge of her (two full-blooded Americans) would not allow them to do so whilst they remained on board, and persisted in flying the star-spangled banner until the last day, when they left the vessel just before it was hauled down.

Near the brigantine lay a three-masted schooner,

also a creditable specimen of American naval architecture, and which was likewise sold during our stay in the port. Several other Americans came in: one, the Spitfire, of Boston, last from Calcutta—in distress, leaking badly — a noble clipper-ship, of two thousand tons; and the barque Agnes, of and from New York, whence she had been seventy-six days on her passage — also a handsome clipper. Besides these, several clippers came in under the French flag, which, on inquiry, we were informed had also been built in the United States of America. It was a matter of congratulation to us, so far from home, to know and feel our national superiority in the construction of that noblest of structures, viz., a clipper-ship, and at the same time to feel the proud consciousness that all the world admitted it.

Just above the harbor there is a dry dock, on which quite a number of vessels were hauled up for repairs.

Our boat now glided up to the steps of the landing, which we mounted, and once more trod upon terra firma. From the different languages that fell on our ears we were at a loss to tell what countrymen we were among. First, from the number of turbans and white robes, with the faultlessly regular oriental features, we were induced to think that we had landed amid an Arabian population; then, the vast number of gaudy caps, surmounting shaven crowns, caused us to change our opinion, and imagine the greater portion of the mass before us derived from farther down the Malabar coast; but, again, we saw the barbaric ornaments, dusky features, and scanty clothing of the Madagascar native, followed by the various Hindoo tribes, representatives of the other East India colonies belonging to Great Britain; and next the Chinese, the Malay, the Creole (a production of the amalgamation of some one of these races with the European); then, lastly, there were the French and English, intermingled with people from every civilized country of the globe: and hence it may well be imagined, from these incongruous features of the populace, that the commingling of all their different languages must produce a most Babel-like confusion. Then the donkeys, too, which at all times of day are about the docks in great numbers, added their harmonious voices to the confused din. At the moment of landing, I was struck with the sparsity of the white population. It was only at rare intervals, as I penetrated into the city, that an European face could be seen; and I have walked for hours in utter ignorance of my whereabouts; for, although I frequently inquired of whomsoever I met, I was unable to find one who could speak English enough to direct me.

After a short walk through the macadamized streets, feeling that I was utterly out of my element, (all sailors, who have been a long cruise at sea, are poor walkers,) and inquiring for some time as to the direction of Paul and Virginia's grave, (the hero and heroine of the beautiful French novel, which designates this island as Cypress,) we succeeded in finding an English chaise-driver, who soon had us stowed away in his vehicle, and bowling along over a good road into the country. Our ride extended for seven miles, through a populous and fertile country: the inhabitants being of the same class as in the city.

On arriving at our destination, we were sadly disappointed; as we had formed the idea, that we should see a stately mausoleum erected over the remains of two such renowned characters. A dilapidated sandstone monument, enclosed by an iron railing, was, however, the only memorial by which to distinguish their last resting-place. On this monument there had once been a tablet, which either the ruthless hand of time, or the eagerness and avidity of curiosity-hunters, had rendered illegible. The latter class of persons, we were assured, had carried the greater part of it away piecemeal, notwithstanding the notice, printed in French and English, which forbids trespass.

Inquiring from our chaperon for the other "lions" of the port, we were shown the Peter Boite Mountain, and were assured that a view from its lofty summit was well worth the trouble of ascending; but, unaccustomed as we were to the seething heat of the sun ashore, we were not at all anxious to attempt such a task.

Close by the tomb there are beautiful botanical gardens, a visit to which disclosed to us the beauties of tropical vegetation. Here the pine-apple, bananas, clove, nutmeg, allspice, coffee, and other plants, bloomed in luxurious profusion. There were, too, many of the products of the temperate climes: presenting to an American's eyes the aspect of a great hot-house. The walks and drives through these splendidly arranged grounds are of the most beautiful description.

Having satiated our appetites for seeing and tasting, we retraced our way to the city; and I sat down in the coziest corner I could find, to make some observations on the general aspect of the city, and character of the inhabitants.

The part of the city adjoining the wharves is laid out with little attention to regularity — the streets describing most tortuous courses. At the outskirts the avenues are at right angles, and that part of the city presents a better appearance. All the streets are macadamized; but few of them are named, or rather they have no names at the corners to direct the stranger. I remember seeing but a single signboard, and that was in French, having on it Rue de Rivoli. On the other avenues the signboards only displayed the number and the first and last letters of the name.

The tenements and business-places are generally two stories in height, and built of stone, bricks, or wood. On the wharves are iron-framed warehouses, built in the most substantial manner, so as to withstand the violence of the typhoon. They are not enclosed, but resemble our market-sheds. The market-house, situated in the centre of the town, is built in the same manner, and divided into four departments, one of which is the meat-market, where I saw nothing but beef and fish exposed for sale; the latter not of the description admitted to our tables, as on the shambles of one victualler I saw two monstrous sharks, from twelve to sixteen feet in length, which he was cutting up, and selling to the dusky portion of the inhabitants. Another department is devoted to the coffee-venders, where any person can get a cup of excellent hot coffee for a penny; and to judge from the number of their customers, these petty merchants are driving a lucrative business. The third department is occupied by the sellers of vegetables, birds, &c. The fourth, known as the bazaar, is apportioned into stalls, each under the supervision of a brown clerk, who uses his utmost endeavors to attract customers. These stalls are furnished with fancy articles, perfumery, cutlery, hosiery, cambrics, and a variety of Eastern articles quite unknown on our shores. Each of the merchants is adorned by a streak of India ink, running from the center of the scalp-lock to the bridge of the nose, which is said to be a mark of distinguished caste — the wearers of it being known as Parsees. They display considerable acumen in conducting business, and offer inducements to purchasers scarcely inferior to those presented by salesmen in our clothing establishments on Market street. One miserable practice prevails, which is general amongst all classes of merchants throughout the city; that is, the abominable custom of asking three prices for an article, with the expectation of being beat down to a reasonable one: doctors, lawyers, merchants (wholesale and retail), druggists, and other dealers, all persisting in it. I had occasion to go to a first-class drug-store to purchase some articles for the ship's medicine-chest. Here I confidently expected to see a rational method of doing business; but, to my utter surprise, I was asked twenty-one dollars for a package that I could purchase at home for five. After considerable chaffering, I succeeded in obtaining it for twelve dollars. Under this phase of bargaining, it was a matter of time to make the most trifling purchase; and, whenever at a loss for occupation, it was customary with us to resort to the bazaar, and inquire for an article which they, from their inadequate knowledge of English, could not comprehend, and then watch their anxiety in displaying every article they had for sale, in hopes of hitting upon the right one. No sooner had you been given up in despair by the occupant of one stall than you were seized on by his neighbor; and if, attracted by the quaintness of any particular article, you should make a purchase, however small, your former attendant would show his chagrin in a garrulous and amusing manner.

One day whilst thus perambulating in Yankee fashion, with our hands deep in our pockets, as a protection from the wonderful sleight-of-hand possessed by this people, one of these merchants, attracted by a whalebone stick our steward carried, offered a pound sterling for it. The steward agreed to take it, but then the native would not purchase, without a bill and receipt. Being penman and amanuensis for all hands, I was desired to make out the necessary document. After writing it, I was requested by the steward to sign his name; but it was no go. The native, albeit he could not read a single word of English, knew that this was not the proper mode of doing business, and obliged the steward to sign his name himself; when, after calling an English policeman, and submitting it to his inspection, he was satisfied of its validity, and paid down the dust.

The Governor's House has no pretensions to beauty. It looks like an old-fashioned farmer's homestead, and no one would think it had a claim to aristocracy, were it not for the presence of the red-coated sentry, who continually paces in front of it. The only building which I saw that presented any real pretension to beauty was a mosque, built in the Egyptian style, with mimic towers. Strangers were not admitted within it on the days when I was ashore; so I had to be satisfied with a glance, that revealed to me the handsome decorations of a very small part of it, and a massive chandelier, pendant from the dome which formed the roof.

The Hospital is a large, commodious, well-ventilated building, surrounded by verandas, healthily situated, and close by the water's side. It comprises three separate departments. One building is devoted to the military, and is known as the Military Hospital. A second building is known as the Civil Hospital, where the citizens are admitted at a charge of a shilling, and seamen of other nations at two shillings, per diem. The ground-floor of this building is set apart for the use of the black Asiatic population — French, English, and American negroes being admitted to the same apartment as the whites. At the time we were there the dysentery was so prevalent amongst the Asiatics, that it was found necessary to extend their apartments, and for this purpose a part of the upper portion of the building was devoted to their use.

Having sent two of our men to this hospital for treatment for stricture of the urethra, I visited it, and found it clean, orderly, and well conducted. The resident and visiting physicians are all Englishmen, and, from their mode of operation, I should judge them to be scientific and skilful surgeons. The Malabars are attended to by creole physicians, who have received thorough medical educations; two-thirds of the patients were under treatment for dysentery, which, from the symptoms and treatment, I am certain is nothing more nor less than Asiatic cholera; the remaining varieties are mostly venereal affections, which, in this hot climate, assume their most violent and disgusting forms.

There are a number of Americans here; some resident ashore, and others from the American vessels in the harbor; those from the vessels being discharged sick on the consul's hands, who provides for them at the hospital until recovered; he then finds them ships and sends them to the United States.

Neither of the men who were sent from our ship to the hospital recovered so as to be able to go out with us. One of them, a New Yorker, the former steward of the Europa, anticipates remaining on the island some time; the other, John Cunningham, of New Bedford, one of our original crew, is left in charge of the consul, to be sent home as soon as the state of his health will permit. Our captain was very desirous to take this young man home with him for the sake of his widowed mother; but as the invalid objected to going before he was perfectly recovered, and the doctor's authority was paramount to the captain's, we were forced to leave him in a foreign land, in a foreign hospital, amongst strangers, to look out for himself, with the assistance of the consul: a fearful responsibility for a boy of eighteen, unacquainted with the world.

There is also another institution for the reception and relief of destitute seamen, known as the Sailor's Home: its accommodations are said to be excellent.

At this house were part of the crew of the whaleship Nauticon, of Nantucket, which ship was lost a few months previous at, or near, the Seychelle Islands. All seamen's boarding-houses in Port Louis are bound by law to afford a seaman two weeks' board, at the expiration of which time they can expel him from the house, if they feel so inclined; but it generally happens that they ship before the fortnight expires, and pay their board with part of the advance money they receive from their new employers. The usual charge for board is a guinea a week.

Connected with the Home is a floating bethel, moored close by the landing stair.

Another feature of the city is the park. Some of our boys from the rural districts having visited it, and found several fountains on its grounds, gave so animated a description of its beauties as made me eager to visit it. I went, saw, and was neither overwhelmed by astonishment nor pleasure; the walks were well enough, so were the fountains, but the trees appeared uncared for; and the grass, what little there was, was parched by the heat of the sun to a straw color. This park was about two hundred feet in width, and several hundred yards in length. The peculiar attraction of this place is that it is the resort of the children of the European residents, and from their presence one argues the existence of white women in the neighborhood; but where they seclude themselves I cannot perceive, for if the very small number of white ladies whom I saw in Mauritius were the maternal relatives of all the children I saw in the park, verily the climate of Port Louis must conduce greatly to the fecundity of our race.

Occasionally, in the park, may be seen a Miss who has discarded pantalettes, and, when seen, her rosy cheeks and white transparent skin contrast so favorably with the universal yellow and brown hues of the East Indian dames, that one could almost and without any great expansion of the imagination, think her an angel from the ethereal regions sent to illuminate the dusky scene.

A few miles from the landing is a cemetery, which I visited. The road to it embraces a beautiful walk or drive through a long shaded avenue formed by rows of cypress trees; the cemetery is laid out in the form of a square, and is well filled with monuments, the styles and workmanship of which would do no discredit to Laurel Hill or Greenwood. Most of them bore inscriptions in French, several were devoted to the last remains of English naval commanders who had died whilst on this station. Over the remains of one of these, a comparatively young man, was erected the base of a column, a few feet above which the column was fractured, signifying that the deceased was cut down by the fell destroyer in the spring tide of life, and ere he had arrived at the goal to which his talents would have conducted him.

One beautiful tribute to the memory of the departed prevails—on each tomb is a vase containing flowers, which, from their fragrance and freshness, were apparently renewed by no niggard hand. This beautiful custom reminded me of the oft-repeated wish of the old man in the best of Dickens' Christmas Stories, "Lord, keep my memory green." On my way back from the cemetery, I came in contact with a crowd of Malabars, whom an old woman was haranguing from a rostrum consisting of a large stone, in the most approved manner of stump speaking. She was in a state of semi-intoxication, yet her auditory yielded her implicit attention. Not understanding a single word that she uttered, and being unable to obtain an explanation of the scene, I was on the point of withdrawing, when her change of manner, from a state of ecstacy to that of frantic despair, led me to approach the house to which she was continually pointing during her oratorical effort. In the house I saw a rude pine coffin, around which the relatives and friends were collected, all half-drunk and pugilistically inclined, arguing some point with much vehemence. Disgusted with the affair I withdrew, thinking I had witnessed as serio-comic a scene as the wake of Teddy the Tiler.

In my walk up to the residence of the American consul, I saw the barracks of the soldiery, and heard the performance of their excellent brass band. The consul's residence is about a mile and a half from the landing. It, with the other buildings in its neighborhood, are built in cottage style, and present the best appearance of any in the port. The consul is a New Yorker named Fairfield.

The few white inhabitants engaged in business are mostly in the wholesale branches of trade; the other positions which the whites fill are the police bodies, and the plying of boats to and from the wharves and shipping. This police body is the richest farce, in regard to the preservation of law and order, that ever was endorsed by the city fathers of any municipality under the sun. The force consists of two bodies — the Government and municipal police — the former body, or at least that part of it on duty in Port Louis, contains three hundred men, two-thirds of them being whites; this proportion is made up entirely of seamen, French, English, American, and German — the Government, eager to have a white police force, accepts all who offer to enlist for a term of from one to three years, providing they possess a certified discharge from the vessels in which they have last served.

It may be better imagined than described how a body of men, composed of such reckless material, would conduct themselves; they create more disturbance by far than those under their surveillance; and it is not unusual for them, at the close of the month, to be mulcted in the greater part of their wages—retained by the authorities as fines for disorderly conduct.

They receive four pounds sterling per month, and live in barracks resembling those of the soldiery; those who are married are allowed to live where they please. Their uniform is duck trowsers, a jacket of blue cloth reaching to the hips, and closing tightly with brass buttons, each displaying the crown, and a blue cap, the top of which is of white glazed oil skin — this cap is also surmounted with a crown; in the hand, day and night, is carried a baton, beautifully ornamented with Chinese characters.

We were much surprised to find in the police force a number of Americans who had deserted from whalers, and whom we had seen before in the eastern ports of the Indian Ocean; amongst these were several of the Elisha Dunbar's crew. One of them, a Bostonian, had been promoted to be sergeant, and was living with a great, greasy, disgusting-looking squaw, as black as the ace of spades, thereby carrying out the doctrine of amalgamation to its fullest extent.

None of the members of either of these bodies are allowed to go beyond the precincts of the city without a pass — the authorities being extremely fearful of desertion; and with reason, too, as, although these men are induced to enter by the prospect of easy times, (and they are easy, indeed, duty only being required of them for four hours out of the twenty-four, after which time they are at liberty to dress and act as citizens, only they are not permitted to engage in any other business,) yet their very inactivity disgusts them with their billets. Men, like sailors, who have been accustomed to a stirring, active life, ever on the alert to anticipate the storm king's movements, cannot at once divest themselves of their sea-going habits; hence their uneasiness and determination to desert. When we left Mauritius, two of them, who had been part of the force for several months, were snugly stowed away aboard our ship, preferring life in a whaler's forecastle, to ease and comfort ashore.

The boatmen comprise two distinct classes: the white and the native. The whites are generally seamen, and in this avocation I saw manual labor performed by them only. The principal and most business-like of these aquatic carriers was a man who had fled the city of New Bedford for no less a crime than manslaughter, and thereby escaped punishment by the laws of his country; but being now doomed to perpetual exile from home and kindred, he could feelingly say, "Verily, the way of the transgressor is hard!"

And now that we have pretty thoroughly analyzed the city and its suburbs, it is quite time that we should speak of the tawny inhabitants of Port Louis. Having mentioned the whites, we will first glance at those who most nearly resemble them in color and form: the Arabs — a fine-looking, large and symmetrically built race of men, who wear the turban, a white robe, and sandals, of the same form as did their ancestors in time immemorial. They are a very intelligent-looking people, with perfectly regular features, grave in deportment, respected, and reputed wealthy. Most of them are merchants.

The next class we will notice is, the Chinese. These, without being in great numbers, wield considerable influence. Their strict attention to business, and speedy method of amassing money, by sobriety and regularity in living, soon render them independent through their own exertions. They are mostly engaged in the grocery and dry-goods businesses. They adhere to their native costume, sporting their pigtails, wide trowsers, conical hats, and satin slippers, alongside the turban and sandals of the Arab.

Next comes the Malay, with his dusky features. They are few in number, and partake in some degree of the peculiarities of both the former nations. Like the Arabs, they are strict Mahometans, turning their faces towards Mecca whilst at their devotions. These people are employed both in humble avocations and in the higher walks of life.

Next, we notice the people known as Malabars. Under this patronymic, not only the natives of the Malabar coast, but those from the shores of the Bay of Bengal, are known; and consequently, coming from so extended a line of country, there is a vast difference in their appearance: those from one part of the country being small in person, with scarcely any muscular strength; whilst those from the Ghaut mountains are a tall, muscular race, capable, for Asiatics, of great bodily exertion. All are subdued, and appeared to me as the most abject of any servile people. They are, emphatically, "hewers of wood and drawers of water." Few of them are employed in trade, except as segar makers and sellers. All the manual labor peculiar to shipping is performed by them — caulking, loading, and discharging; and the way they work is a source of pain to an enterprising spirit. For instance, four or six of them will arrange themselves around a bag of guano, or other package of merchandise, and at a signal from their overseer (who wields a bamboo, with which he very often administers hearty thwacks on the heads of his employees; and, as they are closely shaven, their crowns possess no protection from the blows), commence a monotonous melody, which they continue for several minutes, before touching the bag; then, as many seizing it as can get hold, they swing it on the cart or scales arranged for its reception: during which operation they consume more time in handling one bag than one-third their number of our men would do in disposing of a dozen bags on the wharves at home.

Besides this, they are the barbers, coopers, and stone-cutters of the port. I saw boys, of ten years and upwards, and possessing the most effeminate bodies, with mallet and chisel, working away at the last-named business like good fellows.

In coopering they pursue a novel mode of operation: one getting on top of the cask and holding the driver on the hoops, whilst the other uses the hammer. This is done, of course, after the head has been adjusted; previously to which the helper stands in the center, and arranges the staves.

Barberizing, from the universal practice of shaving the head, seems to be a thriving trade. The person undergoing the operation squats cross-legged, whilst the barber works around him, removing his hair in a very short time. I think this a most excellent custom in this hot climate, so conducive to the fostering and increase of vermin.

From this class servants are selected, who perform all the various functions of waiters, footmen, runners, &c. There are few women and children imported, in comparison with the number of adult males: possibly, owing to the greater usefulness of the latter. Their costume varies—some wearing the turban; but generally a plush cap is worn, ornamented with gilded or silvered braid, arranged in fanciful forms. All wear the breech-cloth—the upper and lower portions of the body remaining bare. They live any and every where — the ground-floors of the dwellings throughout the city being crowded with them; and ten or a dozen will occupy one apartment, with scarcely moving or breathing room—sleeping on the bosom of mother earth, and covered only with their breech-cloth, which is of the lightest texture. They receive very trifling wages; but as they live principally upon rice and curry, which cost scarcely anything, they are able in the course of their apprenticeship to save what is, to them, a considerable sum of money.

These people are anything but temperate as regards the consumption of ardent spirits; but I never saw one of them display the slightest approach to intoxication. Their favorite beverage is the fiery arrack, (distilled from rice,) which they buy for a trifle, and consume in large quantities.

And now we come to the most influential, wealthy, and thrifty people in the port. I refer to the Creoles, the issue of a union of some one of the white races with the East Indian. They are mostly French, and nine-tenths of the mercantile business is conducted by them. Their distinguishing traits are — industry, neatness, and exact business qualifications. They are also enterprising, and possess all the politeness and suavity of Monsieur himself. It is not at all unusual, on going into their business-places, to be waited upon by a bevy of saffron-colored clerks, whilst at one side sits the maternal relative, dressed in the handsomest manner, but with a skin as black as ebony. The Creoles treat these relatives, notwithstanding the difference of color, with a degree of filial affection pleasing to witness.

These Creoles, on account of their wealth, and character as substantial men and good citizens, are much respected, even more so than the white residents, and are freely admitted to all the privileges and immunities possessed by the latter.

In speaking of the Malabars, I omitted to describe a funeral procession in which they were the participants. The corpse was borne in a coffin, on a hurdle, supported on the shoulders of six men. Preceding the coffin was a musician with a horn in the shape of the letter S, from which the operator produced more noise than music; next came two drummers with their instruments, and then two tambourine players—all uniting in making as much din as possible. Those in the procession not engaged in discoursing the melody, were dancing and shouting. This manner of testifying grief seemed rather odd, and diametrically opposite to all my preconceived notions of these people, as I had judged them to be incapable of any joyous demonstration; but it seems they can act a farce, although they choose a rather sombre occasion to indulge it. I have not, however, done with the funeral, not having as yet mentioned its most peculiar feature. Over the coffin was erected a bower of twigs and green plants, intended to represent, as nearly as possible, a temple. I followed the procession to the cemetery, which is an unenclosed piece of ground, situated just outside the European cemetery, and unmarked by a single headstone. Just previous to arriving at the cemetery, the policemen, who accompany all such funerals, obliged them to desist from their merry-making. At the grave, which was not more than four feet in depth, the bower was opened, and a young chicken taken from it, which a near relative placed in his bosom very carefully. This form, I suppose, has something to do with the doctrine of the transmigration of souls — these foolish people imagining that the spirit of the deceased is obliged, after death, to take refuge in the body of some animal; and the chicken is carried thus, so that the spirit of the defunct may easily find a tenement. All this seems to us supremely ridiculous; but, on the other hand, these people are just as much amused at our forms of worship as we are at the unreasonableness of theirs — education and the early instillation of traditionary or other precepts, making a believer of any race in the doctrine of their forefathers.

And now the question arises, how these Malabar and Madagascar natives came here in such numbers. Fortunately, it is very easily solved. Their presence is the natural fruit of the French and English apprentice system — a mode of procedure as much blacker and more disgraceful to the nation engaged in it, than the slavery of our Southern States, inherited from these same nations, as the pirate's bloody pursuit is to that of the legitimate merchantman. I will merely state the manner in which these people are *purchased*. An English, or French vessel, runs into some out of the way port in Madagascar, lets go her anchor, invites the king aboard, makes him presents of articles trifling in value to us, but in the eyes of the savage of intrinsic worth. After flattering his vanity and cupidity they broach their object in visiting the coast. The king, nothing loath, invites the supercargo ashore, and shows him the flesh and blood he has for sale. The merchant in human slavery carries ashore old condemned muskets, kegs of powder, jack-knives, hoop iron, trinkets, beads, and calico (these being the articles most sought after by them). He then selects the most fitting objects for his purposes, and, after considerable chaffering on both sides, the purchases are taken aboard ship to be conveyed to a foreign country, ostensibly for a term of years, but really for as long as their owners choose to detain them. At the same time the purchasers do not know whether they are prisoners of war or the king's own flesh and blood; neither do they care, their object being to gain money by making merchandize of a free people. The governor of Mauritius receiving so much per head, as a perquisite, for each one that is imported into the colony, holds out every inducement for their introduction into the island; and I should judge, from the crowded state of the ships that arrived with them as cargoes, that the trade was most thriving. In fact, at the time we lay here, this was the only freight procurable, shipmasters complaining that they could not find employment for their vessels; some of them having laid here for months without being able to engage a freight. I should think that at least two thousand of these pseudo apprentices arrived whilst we were here; they embraced for the most part the natives of the Malabar coast, and of the Island of Madagascar. I omitted, in my description of the latter, to remark upon their fondness for ornament; scarce one of them can be seen, male or female, young or old, whose arms or ankles are not covered with silver wristlets and anklets; those whose finances will not admit of their wearing the precious metals for ornamental purposes, use those made of clay, neatly ornamented and gilded. Many of the women wear jewels, which, by some contraction of the skin of the forehead are so arranged as to always remain there. They are worn in its center, directly over the bridge of the noise; they are diamond- or lozenge-shaped, and, for the most part, of an emerald green.

One day, whilst strolling up an avenue contiguous to the wharf, I was attracted by a crowd assembled around a walled enclosure; taking the privilege of my nation (curiosity), I elbowed my way through the mixed assemblage, and saw ("tell it not in Askalon, publish it not in Gath,") two English auctioneers, in a country under England's control, and governed by England's laws, mounted on their rostrums, selling what they call in the British Isles, their fellow-men, co-equal in all respects to themselves. To say that I was surprised would convey but a faint idea of my feelings—I was really astounded. After recovering somewhat from my astonishment, I was so thoroughly convinced of the ridiculousness of England's so often vaunted philanthropy, that, had I been in a proper place, I could have indulged in a hearty burst of laughter. As it was, I could not, without an effort, control my risibilities. This feeling soon gave way to that of indignation at the recreant sons and daughters of our own soil, who disgrace our country, after having been nursed and rocked in the cradle of liberty—as soon as they are out of their swaddling clothes, turning upon and stinging their nurse, and for the sake of political or monetary personal aggrandizement, publishing wishy-washy novels containing such perverted descriptions of our Southern slavery system, as to induce foreigners to think our boast of liberty and a free government is but a farce. Such persons do not merit being dignified by the notice of honest men, which they court; and, whether it be in the form of a favorable mention or a criticism, is all one to them, so long as it gives them publicity. As they cater for the morbid literary appetites of the sycophantic courtiers of the Old World, who are only too eager to pick holes in our beautiful and, to them, unattainable system of government, a notice, to these horror fabricators, answers all the purposes of an advertisement; so I shall bid them farewell, only exhorting Americans to cry shame on such scorpions.

To return to the slave-mart. As I before said, there were two rostrums erected, on each of which an auctioneer was busily employed crying the merits of the merchandise, and eagerly soliciting a bid; both were crying the same article — the second repeating, word for word, all that his superior said in regard to the price and quality of the article put up.

The slaves were gathered and arranged in groups close by the rostrums. Neither sex had any other covering than the breech-cloth, so as to display the mucular system to the utmost advantage. The purchasers, who for the most part are French planters, walk in amongst them, examine their muscles, teeth, and joints, make them leap to show their activity, and in every way that their experience suggests satisfy themselves with respect to the availability of the slave. Their almost nude condition displays to advantage their erect and symmetrical forms, and in the women particularly, those points for which the females of the East are so justly celebrated.

The only saving clause in the whole transaction was, that, in case any of the slaves had a family, the purchaser was compelled to buy them all together, or not at all.

Instead of having the gloomy faces and downcast mien that one would naturally expect to see in rational beings under such somber auspices, these people, with the thoughtlessness, or recklessness, of their race, were laughing and joking apparently with heartfelt glee. The younger portion engaged meanwhile in little love-passages; and I was struck by the coquettish archness with which the young women naively avoided the too pressing advances of their admirers, by gracefully shaking their beautifully-formed heads, adorned with the glossiest of ebon hair, and at the same time accompanying it with the most roguish expression from their deep black eyes, while merrily laughing and displaying their pearly teeth. At such times, and on such occasions, the beholder, albeit he may belong to a superior race, is apt to forget his prejudices, and think that the poor slave before him is susceptible of truly loving, and of being loved, as well as the fair representatives of his own race.

After purchasing as many as he wants, the planter arranges his slaves in Indian file, proceeds to the warehouses where he purchases his supplies, and each member of the file poises some article or other on his or her head; and thus they march to the plantation, where they are to remain until the expiration of their servitude — never coming to the town, unless accompanying their owner.

These people are very expert in carrying burdens

on their heads, and in this way we may account for their erect carriage. At any minute in the day women and children may be seen carrying earthen jars containing molasses or oil, threading the crowded thoroughfares, and bringing their loads safe to their destination — a feat not to be accomplished by those unaccustomed to the practice.

On the principle that sparing the rod spoils the child, (for these people are viewed only as children,) their owners are not at all reserved in the use of this instrument of chastisement; and along with the gangs at labor may the overseer be seen applying it without remorse. As the blow generally falls on the skull, I can see little reason for a preference of this to the method of punishment by lashes on the back in vogue in our Southern States. This, however, is not their only way of punishment. I saw several instances of gross personal abuse. In one case I saw the slave thrown down, and dragged by the waistband over the sharp points of the macadamized street, with nothing to protect his buttocks from laceration except several thicknesses of calico. The poor fellow, apparently aware of its uselessness, made no complaint. This occurred, not in an obscure place — not in the purlieus of the town, but in a public street, where people were constantly passing, and who, if any feeling at all were expressed by them, only laughed at the ludicrousness of the scene. A police-officer stood looking on apathetically, as though the whole affair were a matter of course.

Impelled with a desire to know what Englishmen thought of the apprentice-system, I put the question to every intelligent one that I could get at. In nine cases out of ten my auditor would waive the question by starting some other subject of conversation; but by the employment of a little finesse I generally managed to corner him, when, upon argument and hearing explanations of our system, he would confess that there was but a shade of difference between the two. One candid specimen of the John Bull character, whom I accidentally formed an acquaintance with, (and one, too, who had made the tour of our Southern States from Delaware to Texas — a man of strong mind and superior intelligence, and from the knowledge he possessed of the subject, also a man of observation,) stated that our slaves were better housed than the apprentices under the control of magnanimous and philanthropic Britain! Verily, England should look at home; and, if she can, apologize, and legislate for her factory-system, which heretofore has been the set-off advanced by Americans to her abuse of our slavery-system. Here is the same system, with such a close affinity to ours, that she cannot apologize for or mitigate it, without rendering us justice, and thereby exposing her previous hypocrisy and selfishness.

Strange — strange, very strange — it is, that the philanthropists of the United Kingdom have never taken cognizance of these facts. What a splendid theater Mauritius presents for the Address drawn up by the Ladies of Great Britain and sent to the Ladies of the United States, (which, however, to the honor of our countrywomen be it said, was contemptuously rejected,) and signed by I do not remember how many thousands of the mothers, daughters, and wives of Merry England and her dependencies; which ladies, in a body, had the most disinterested wish for the amelioration of the condition of the black races held in thraldom by their white cotempories, (or, to use the words of Lucy Stone, they had "a fellow-feeling in their bosoms for the oppressed of all nations," though whether the "fellow" ever found these martyrs I do not know). Here, I repeat, is an excellent field for their Address; though, as to whether it will meet with the same contumelious reception as it did in the "land of the free," or meet with a reception adequate to its fitness for the city of Port Louis, a trial only can determine. Perhaps the editor of the Thunderer could bring the feasibility of such a proceeding to the notice of those fair reformers through the columns of his widely-circulated journal.

In writing the above description of the apprentice-system, I have not only embodied my own, but the collective convictions of the whole crew of the vessel; and, as two-thirds of them were from Massachusetts, their opinions, if not my own, are worthy of belief: beside, there was no Southerner aboard, to convert us to Southern opinions—not one of us having been reared to the southward of Mason and Dixon's line; so that no personal interest or feeling sways our description of this evil. Hence I think that our observations are entitled to the regard of those who laud the freedom, philanthropy, and disinterestedness of the government of the British Islands at the expense of our own; and if I can enable but one of them to see and confess the error of his or her ways, I shall consider my labor well repaid. And here I now leave this subject.

I cannot imagine why whalers visit this port in

preference to others where they could be much better supplied. To be sure the American consul is resident, and through him they can draw money to the extent of their necessities; but, on the other hand, provisions are excessively dear, and so are all other supplies needful for shipping. Two articles are cheap — liquors and segars; the latter being made from tobacco grown on the island. Instead of being filled, as with us, and enclosed in a wrapper, the natives make them entirely of wrappers. They are very mild, and can be purchased for a song; everybody smokes them and the consumption must be immense. The plug tobacco is of American manufacture, and, from the duty imposed upon it by the government, commands a high price.

Notwithstanding the cheapness of liquors, there is but very little intoxication to be seen amongst the community, although all seem to indulge, more or less, in its use. The favorite drinks are the lighter wines, such as the claret and Vermouth; these are pleasant, but are detrimental to a healthy condition of the bowels, and, therefore, excessive indulgence in them in this climate is purchased at a dear rate.

There is no scarcity of money, most of the exchanges being made in the metallic currency of Great Britain, and as our Scrimschawing, or to use a less outlandish term, our different manufactures from the bone and ivory procured from the whale, were to these people great curiosities, they commanded good prices. It was not unusual to get from twenty to thirty shillings for a bone cane; and jagged knives, used by the pastry cook for filagreeing the edges of his pies and tarts, were eagerly bought up at a pound the pair. Consequently, all our boys who possessed numbers of these articles were well supplied with the rhino. The reason these articles are so eagerly sought for in this port, is that no whalers are fitted out or belong here; neither is there any market for the sale of whale oil — the inhabitants universally burning the oil expressed from the cocoa-nut; and as the cocoa tree is indigenous to the island, and grows in great profusion, it is readily obtainable at a low rate. The captain of the Nauticon, who lost his ship among the Seychelle Islands, is here, and has been importuned over and over again by the merchants of the port, to return to the United States, build and fit a vessel with all necessary accouterments, and bring her here to sail as a colonial whaler belonging to Port Louis. The future must decide as to whether he coincides with them so far as to act out their wishes; but it is easily seen that such a proceeding must necessarily be remunerative, as no sooner has a whaler left the port than she is on the very best sperm whaling-ground in the Indian Ocean, and the prevalence of the trade-winds and general good weather for nine months of the year, render it an eligible cruising ground.

There is an excessive jealousy existing between the French and English residents — the French considering themselves as the rightful owners of the soil, lords to the manor born; whilst the English plume themselves upon the conquest of the island, and consider possession nine points of the law. Little intercourse, apart from their business relations, exists between the two nations, and the same feeling prevails, not only among the residents, but among the sailors of ships belonging to the two countries. Sunday night, generally, is the occasion of broils between them, and these, the police informed me, were the most serious disturbances they had to contend with.

The German sailors were the merriest of any nation whom I saw on liberty — gathering in little knots, and singing the songs of their fatherland with the utmost good-fellowship, and not without melody. They were very exclusive in their associations, and mixed with none but their own circle of shipmates.

The markets of Mauritius were filled with fruit of the various kinds to be found in tropical climates — the pine-apple, cocoa-nut, banana, oranges, lemons, and limes, all being found here in abundance. The favorite condiment of the blacks is the sugar-cane, which they suck in pieces as long as themselves; and two youngsters may be seen, each supporting and sucking away at either end of a piece of green sugar-cane a fathom in length.

This city differs very much from Hobartown in two of its striking features. In the latter city, at every corner is to be seen a mendicant; in Port Louis I did not see a single person soliciting charity. The other feature that I refer to is the absence of all itinerant hawkers, except the cake venders, who are the only class of petty tradesmen who make a depot of the streets for the sale of their goods; whilst in the capital of Van Diemen's Land, as I have remarked elsewhere in my notice on it, at every step one is beset by these pertinacious leeches, anxious to make a sale.

But in another point there is a perfect resemblance

between both cities — that is the presence of a regiment of British infantry; a provision that Great Britain never neglects in any of her colonies, governing her subjects by appealing to their fears of the bayonet, wielded by a hireling and remorseless soldiery. This regiment is about leaving its station here for the seat of war in India. I conversed freely with several of its members, and although they displayed no symptoms of fear at the prospect of being engaged with an enemy, still there was a total lack of enthusiasm or patriotism. From the atrocities so glaringly held before the public by the English journals, as committed by the Sikhs on British residents in India, I had expected to find an eagerness on the part of the gentlemen with the red coats, to avenge their countrymen and countrywomen so barbarously maltreated; but so wags the world, one half caring not or feeling not for the miseries or misfortunes of the other half.

Now I shall change the subject from a consideration of the biped portion of the population to an analysis of the condition and quality of the quadrupeds. On account of the trouble and expense attending the procreation of the horse, he is here quite a dignified animal, and is only used by the aristocratic portion of the population for the lightest draughting. His high price, too, ensures his careful treatment; and all who can afford to keep a carriage, whose business requires its use all day, change the animal and put a fresh one in the traces at noon. The reason why the horse commands so high a price here is, that the Government interdicts the introduction of mares into the island; whether the climate is prejudicial to the breed of the animal, or Great Britain, in her forethought, vetoes their importation, for the purpose of securing a market for the surplus stock of her Australian colonies, is a point which, in the absence of any authority, I am unable to decide.

The vehicles are of English construction, and are moderately light; the rattan body, which is so conducive to ventilation and comfort in warm weather, being in general use. Their harness, too, is of European manufacture — made light, to conform with the oppressiveness of the climate.

And now that we have pretty thoroughly reviewed the town and its purlieus, we will return to our proper element, and give an account of what transpired in the harbor during our stay. First we will notice the whaling barque, Belle of Warren, which came in to post letters; of the boat's crew who went ashore for this purpose, one did not return, having taken leg bail for security. I saw him ashore several times afterward, and he was wandering about without a discharge and without a home, looking destitute and woebegone. The Belle remained but a few days; meantime the whaleship Martha made her appearance, for the purpose of landing her third mate, who goes to the hospital to be treated for a pulmonary affection. The Martha reports that the portion of the whaling fleet which went to the northward humpbacking, were as unsuccessful as ourselves; seeing nothing, and, consequently, doing nothing. This goes to strengthen our theory of the absence of whale feed on the coast during the preceding season. The Martha made as short a stay as the Belle — both vessels having, like us, seen sperm whales near the

Island of Rodrique, and both intending to return there. Hence their haste to leave port.

The next whaler that made her appearance was the barque Columbus, of New Bedford: she, like the Martha, had accomplished nothing humpbacking, but on her passage from New Holland to this port, had captured three hundred and fifty barrels of sperm oil, in the vicinity of the Island of Rodrique. Like us, the Columbus came in for provisions, and to give her crew liberty. Her crew comprised, for the most part, men who had been shipped in Hobartown; and they had scarcely set foot ashore when they were squabbling.

Soon after the Columbus's arrival, the barque Mechanic, of Newport, came in. She was seventeen days from Angiers, and, although there was no sickness on board, was compelled, by a law of the port, to go into quarantine until the expiration of twenty-one days from the time of her leaving Angiers, that being the time set by the law. After performing the quarantine she was hauled into the inner harbor to undergo repairs.

And now, for the time being, we have done with American whalers, and come to one sailing under the flag of England—the brig Elizabeth and Jane, of Hobartown. She was fitted out as a tender for some larger vessel, and sent to Desolation for the capture of whales, sea-elephants, and seals, indiscriminately; she had a Yankee mate, and was intended by the Hobartown merchants to be the pioneer of a fleet to compete with the Yankees in the procuring of oil, which trade has, for many years, been a prolific source of wealth to those engaged in it; the bleak shores of Kerguleus land being a favorite resort for those creatures so eagerly sought for by the whaleman. Scarcely had the brig arrived at the scene of her anticipated operations before she commenced leaking so badly, that the crew were kept continually pumping, day and night; necessitating her being carried into port, and either being thoroughly repaired or condemned as unseaworthy. On bringing her into Mauritius, the captain preferred a complaint to the authorities against his men, charging them with mutiny and threatening his life. Before the authorities had time to act upon his information, about one half of the crew took one of the boats, went ashore, and got drunk. A fight followed as a matter of course, and in this condition they were easily captured by the police. Those who were left aboard were brought ashore in irons; but they did not seem to mind the manacles, all of them being convicts, who, no doubt, had been accustomed to such bracelets before. After landing, they were conveyed to the jail, where their companions were already lodged. The following morning they were brought before the magistrate, who, after hearing both sides of the case, dismissed the charge as unfounded and frivolous, at the same time adding some wholesome advice to the master of the vessel for the future government of those under his command. A few days after the brig was condemned as unseaworthy.

We will now return to our own vessel and crew. As I stated in the former part of my journal, we shipped Irishmen in Hobartown, and Englishmen in Vasse. During the time they have been aboard we have been thoroughly convinced of their utter uselessness—their indolence preventing their acquiring sufficient insight into a seaman's duties to render them a useful part of the ship's company; and our captain was anxious to get rid of them. On the first liberty-day, two, whom we shipped at Vasse, overstaid their liberty, and were informed by the captain that he would not receive them aboard again. On the same day, one, whom we shipped in Hobartown, was discharged for inability to do duty. W. B. Wood, whom we brought from New Bedford, was also discharged sick. Joseph A. Lewis and John Cunningham, discharged sick, and sent to the hospital. Wood and Cunningham were both of our original crew; the remaining one, whom we shipped at Vasse, deserted. A seaman, shipped in Hobartown, was discharged with the consent of the contracting parties; one, shipped in Vasse, in January, 1857, and who, during the time he has been aboard, has been acting as fourth mate, was discharged with his own consent; and one, whom we got in Hobartown, is in jail—so that we are ten less in number than when we dropped anchor on the day of our entering the harbor. In their places we have shipped five men, all of whom are Americans, and have been whaling before. I said that we had shipped five, but two of the five came aboard without any agreement with the captain. These two were policemen, who had become disgusted with wearing her majesty's button, and on their hinting their wish to get afloat again. our boys readily offered to assist them. Besides these, we shipped a lad of fifteen as steerage-boy.

Although we had thus replaced the ten with but five men, we found, as soon as we got into blue water, that we had a much more effective crew than we had had at any time during the preceding sixteen months. The ten discharged and deserted comprised all the useless material in the ship — the foreign portion of them, in fact, being worse than useless; for, together with their incapacity, they had a propensity to growl, and made both themselves and those with whom they were associated uncomfortable. Their thievishness, too, had still adhered to them, notwithstanding their penal servitude. One of them, we discovered after leaving port, had on his dismissal carried away with him a considerable portion of the cooper's tools. This was Leonard, professedly a cooper by trade.

CHAPTER XIII.

AT two o'clock in the afternoon of October 11th we weighed our anchor, and, with a fair wind, stood out to sea. Twenty-four hours afterwards we sighted a school of sperm whales, consisting of cows and calves. After some little manœuvering, we lowered away all four boats; but the whales going to windward, the captain and mate, after an hour's chase, deemed farther pursuit useless, and returned aboard. The other boats, however, continued the chase; and at about 5 P. M. the third mate's boatsteerer fastened, killing the whale with his irons. Whilst hauling up to him, the line became entangled in the jaws of another whale, and was severed. The third mate then lanced and killed three more; but night coming on, and the weather becoming rugged, he was unable to save any of them, and obliged to return to the ship empty-handed. The mate, in the interim, had fastened to a cow, and killed her and her calf, both of which were saved; but it was midnight before we had them secured alongside. These two were the most diminutive whales it has been our fortune to capture. The cow, which was the first female of the species we have had alongside, was about thirty-five feet in length, and of much inferior bulk to the male. Her skin was smoother, glossier, and of a deeper color; and, taken altogether, she was a much handsomer fish than the bull sperm-whale. The calf was about fifteen feet long — lacking none of the peculiarities of the older fish, except the teeth, which as yet were not cut; but on getting the jaw on deck we penetrated the gum, and found perfectly-shaped teeth, about an inch and a half in length. The following day we cut them in, and tried them out. They yielded, altogether, a trifle over twenty barrels of oil.

After taking these whales, we ran several degrees to the eastward, and spent a week in cruising, during which we saw whales three times — in each case going to windward eyes out, without giving us the shadow of a chance to lower for them. We retraced our course, and on the 23d passed Mauritius. The following day we coasted along the Isle Reunion, or Bourbon — an island under the dominion of France, and so beautifully fertile as to be called the Garden of the Indian Ocean. From hence the Mauritians obtain most of their agricultural supplies, and quite a fleet of coasting vessels is employed in the carrying trade between the two islands. Some idea may be formed of the amount of this trade when I quote the remark of one of the citizens of Port Louis, that, "were it not for the productions of Bourbon, all the inhabitants of Port Louis would starve to death." All the tillage and other laborious work on this island is performed by the natives of Madagascar, introduced here by the French, under the same apprentice-system as that practised by Great Britain.

The island, like Mauritius, is composed principally of very high land, some points being elevated many thousand feet above the level of the sea. A volcano, for the name of which I am at a loss, towers far above all. It being a moonlight night when we passed, we saw but little of its eruption, which is continual — lighting up the surface of the ocean for miles. This island has since been made the French Naval Depot for the Indian Ocean.

There is no good harbor on this island, which, together with the fact of there being no resident American consul, is the reason for the rarity of whaleships visiting it.

The three islands, Bourbon, Mauritius, and Rodrique, were first taken possession of by the French, and for many years were known as the French East India Islands. During the wars between France and Great Britain, Mauritius was the naval depot for the former power, from which her cruisers were fitted out for the annoyance of the East India commerce of the enemy; but during the time of Napoleon, (when England's operations were restricted to the ocean,) as an offset to the conqueror's successes on land, the wooden walls of Old England were busily employed in making captures of the various colonial possessions of France, both in the East and West Indies. Many of these, subsequent to the negotiations for peace, were restored. But Mauritius was too important a place to let slip, after being once occupied; wherefore a British regiment became part of its population, and the meteor-flag of England waved over its battlements. This group is often called the Mascarenha Isles.

On Sunday (October the 31st) we spoke the ship Brewster, of Mattapoissett. A few days before, she had a man killed by a sperm whale: the officer in command of the boat having been foolhardy enough to run on the fish whilst in his flurry, his amidship oar's man was instantly swept from time into eternity by a stroke of its flukes; but, fortunately, no others of the crew were injured.

October the 25th we sighted the southern part of the Island of Madagascar, which was to be our cruising-ground for the next two months. It is anything but a comfortable latitude to make a prolonged stay in; for, on an average, once every twenty-four hours, violent rain-storms of from one to four hours' duration thoroughly drench the crew and vessel. These squalls are attended with any quantity of thunder and lightning, which adds very much to the disagreeableness of their visitations.

This ground is the point to which we endeavored to beat up three years ago, with the intention of whaling, before visiting New Holland. It bears a good reputation as to the presence of whales; but the fish are noted for their fighting on being struck, so that it is no easy matter to make a capture, after once striking. Whether we should have been any the more successful had we visited and cruised on this ground in the earlier portion of our voyage, deponent, from his ignorance, saith not.

I omitted to mention that on account of the extension of the term of our voyage, meat had been purchased in Mauritius; also, ten barrels and a half of colonial beef (of a very inferior quality) packed in Melbourne, and thirteen barrels of American pork purchased from the ship Robert Patton, of Boston: which, together with what we already had aboard, was deemed amply sufficient for our consumption on the short cruise off Madagascar, and during our passage home.

The time of our leaving for home was now set to be New Year's Day, 1859. This period, so long and devoutly prayed for, we were assured would not under any circumstances be again postponed, and we hoped that it would not; for we had been out very long, and all were thoroughly convinced that longer cruising for whales would be entirely useless. To be plain; all wanted to get home. The whole ship's company, too, felt and expressed the opinion, that the voyage was unlucky, and they wished to begin a new one, under better auspices. Our continual ill fortune in not seeing whales, and having our boats stoven, had so deeply engendered this feeling that a general lukewarmness prevailed, which could only be dissipated by a notice from the masthead that sperm whales were about, when indeed all would again become as eager as we were at the commencement of the voyage.

There were now, of the thirty who sailed from home in the vessel, but twenty-one remaining; yet even this is a much larger proportion of the original crew than is usually carried home from a voyage of such length as ours. The cabin had lost one of its members; the steerage was intact — the same boat-steerers remaining as when we first set sail; and of the foremast hands ten, besides the cook, remained: making twenty one in all. We had now been so long together, that the withdrawal of one of our number would produce a feeling like that caused by the separation from a member of one's own family;

and it was not without much regret that we thought on having parted with the two of our original crew in Port Louis.

We continued off the Island of Madagascar up to November 27th, without aught to mar, or rather improve, the general and almost uninterrupted bad weather — thunder and lightning storms following each other with scarce any intermission. During this time we occasionally saw a whale-ship, and, if the weather permitted, failed not to while away a part of this dreary period in gammoning. One day, whilst so engaged, we learned that the chief mate of the ship Martha, of Fairhaven, had lost his life in much the same manner as did the seaman belonging to the Brewster. The mate was not seen to leave the boat, neither was any other of the boat's crew injured; but it appears that the boat had been rashly carried into a perilous and unwarrantable situation by the mate, and, in the bustle attendant to extricating the boat under such circumstances, it is supposed that whilst the others were busy in trimming boat and attending to the line, the whale, by a sweep of the flukes, struck the officer so suddenly and so severely as to put it out of his power to give an alarm, whereby to attract their attention. Undoubtedly his death was instantaneous; but little exertion on the part of the whale would be required to supply a sufficiency of force to crush vitality from the frame of the strongest or proudest of the human race.

This accident is attributed to carelessness, and, from my own observation, I should say that at least two-thirds of the fatal accidents that occur to whalemen, in pursuit of their prey, result from gross carelessness or recklessness on the part of the boat-header. Some years ago it was unusual to hear of a fatal accident to those engaged in the pursuit of the whale. At that time the fish were plenty, and boatheaders, as a class, were cool, sagacious, and experienced men, who had been accustomed to and occupied in the whaling business for years. These men would not risk their boat and crew to almost certain destruction to strike a whale, or to be the first boat fast, or to get a fatal lance before another boat arrived; but, working carefully and securely, they bided the time until a fit opportunity presented itself, and then, guided by their long experience, applied the lance expeditiously and fatally. This race of whalemen has, however, been supplanted by another of younger men, who were brought into the field by the prolific grounds of the Arctic Ocean and Ochotsk Sea, inhabited as they were by myriads of bowhead whales that had never been chased or interfered with by whalemen; consequently, they had not learned from the past to use all the expedients furnished them by nature to avoid and combat against the wiles and stratagems of men. Hence, little else was necessary to capture the bowhead but to have a boat and crew, pull alongside the fish, dart the irons into him, and, ere the bewildered creature had recovered from his astonishment, drive in the lance and kill him; but now that the bowhead has grown more wary, and to take him is a work of difficulty and danger, ships do not make such remunerative voyages in their pursuit as formerly; therefore their owners, instead of directing their vessels only to the Arctic and Ochotsk, began again to turn their attention to the, for a few years, comparatively neglected grounds of the Indian Ocean; but they do not venture without many misgivings as to the probable success of their vessels. A few ships are fitted out, they sail, and in the course of a few years return with excellent cargoes — the whales, having enjoyed somewhat of a respite, again resorted to their former haunts. All is now hurry and bustle in New Bedford and the other whaling ports. These voyages act as an incentive to further operations—mechanics are incited, by liberal offers, to extreme exertion; and in a short time the vessels are ready for sea. The north-west whalemen have also heard of these voyages; they apply for berths, and the owner, or agent, in making inquiry as to their qualifications, learns that he or they got so many whales during the last voyage. In the absence of information, the shipper, supposing that if the applicant can strike and kill one description of whale, he will have no trouble in capturing the others, engages him at a good price, which he commands on the strength of his reputation. The ship sails; but when the north-wester gets into the Indian Ocean, he finds many ships, but few whales, and those few requiring different manipulation on his part, if he wishes to capture them, than those with which he is better acquainted. He strives to become familiar with their habits, but, unfortunately, the whales being chased daily, and almost hourly, by some one or another of the various vessels that occupy every nook and corner of the ocean where there is any likelihood of seeing fish, afford him but few opportunities of adding to his stock of experience; so that it is not until near the

CAUSES OF ILL-SUCCESS. 343

close of the voyage that he becomes *au fait* in the discharge of his duties. By this time the golden opportunity has passed, and, but a few months remaining, he strives to make up by rashness what he lacks in skill, exposing himself and crew in situations against which his better judgment, in cooler moments, would revolt; but this is a losing game, as his crew, who, with equal opportunities and equal intelligence, well know when a whale is approached in the proper manner, and, following the precept that self-preservation is the first law of nature, hesitate to pull anywhere and everywhere, without satisfying themselves that they are right, which they would not if they had full confidence in their officer. Hence, the want of a perfect understanding between the boatheader and crew is another prolific source of accidents. To sum up, every day increases the difficulties and dangers presented to those whose calling is the pursuit of the whale: the fish are either becoming much less numerous, or else they are retreating to the frozen North or South, where the climate forbids man's encroaching. They are also becoming more wary, and it is only by the most careful management that a boat can approach so as to strike them; they taking the alarm at the least variation in the motions of the waves, and the slightest noise being sufficient to alarm them. Formerly, if we are to believe tradition, such was not the case; and certainly the following anecdote, which, I engage, will be told for many years to come by men who will attest to its perfect reliability, will, to some minds — though I must confess they will be of small caliber if they give credence to it — go to substantiate such a premise, to wit:

It formerly was the practice to provide each boat from a whale-ship with a number of bricks. On lowering for, and approaching within a respectable distance of the whale, the boatsteerer was directed to heave one of these bricks at him. If he took no notice of the insult, he was pronounced perfectly safe and tractable, the boat was then laid on and the irons darted; but if, on the contrary, he used his flukes or fins, and made the white water fly, the boat was pointed for the ship; the fishermen being perfectly satisfied with the display of his belligerent powers without a nearer approach, and very well contented to await a more safe and favorable opportunity of increasing their store of oil.

On the 27th of November we gammoned the ship Plover, of New Bedford; her mate and his boat's crew being on board our ship, and our captain and a boat's crew aboard of her. At 3 o'clock in the afternoon, our masthead's man sung out for sperm whales. After a short observation our mate lowered away, and in less than ten minutes fastened. Immediately the Plover's mate and our second mate dropped their boats, and several boats from the Plover pulled for the scene of operations. After some little difficulty, a second boat fastened. Our mate, going on to lance the whale, had his boat crushed to pieces, the whale having turned towards him suddenly and grasped the boat in his jaw, making it a wreck in a moment; the crew were pitched head over heels into the water, whilst the boat, being so much damaged, as to be useless, floated away without being taken notice of. The crew were soon picked up, and in other boats were trying to revenge their sense of injury on the whale. The third mate of the Plover now essayed to lance the whale, but with no better success, his boat being stove in the same manner. Our second mate next tried and succeeded; the other boats, having encircled the whale, diverted his attention, and we turned him up. The whales on the Madagascar ground are notorious for their belligerent propensities, and I have been assured by old habitues of the vicinity, that if a boatheader escapes once in three times from having his boat stove, more or less, he is either an admirable manager, or a wonderfully lucky fellow.

The Plover is but five months from home, and her crew had previously done no whaling — she having taken no oil; therefore it was amusing to watch the woebegone and rueful countenances with which the boats' crews obeyed the order of their officers to pull up to the whale, whilst, on the contrary, when ordered to pull in the opposite direction, their faces would brighten up with an expression of heartfelt relief; and then to look at our own fellows, inured to all the vicissitudes of this adventurous pursuit, taking everything as coolly as if engaged in the most ordinary occupation; making sport of hardships and a jest of danger; eager as the most insatiate sportsman to be in at the death; assisting their boatheader to the utmost, anticipating his orders, and acting out all his requirements; so that boat, officer, and crew, seemed to be a nicely constructed machine, working by a secret spring actuating the muscles of each of its occupants with the self-same power. Even when their boat was stoven they had a jest to crack at the greenhorns. Poor fellows, they were much more entitled to our commiseration than derision; we have been through the mill, and have seen and suffered, whilst they, unless circumstances should very much favor them, are doomed to a three years' stay in the Indian Ocean, where, if "forthcoming events cast their shadows before," they are fated to discover that their one stoven boat is but a foretaste of what they will experience in that line before their time is up.

Before we saw the whale we observed a ship some five miles to windward, with her boats down, and another about the same distance to windward of her, manœuvering as if for whales. We subsequently ascertained that, between noon and the time we struck, five vessels had attempted to capture this whale. All these vessels being in a direct line with our own ship, the whale following a straight course and going to windward, they gave up the chase as useless. We only succeeded by dropping our boat when he was a short distance to leeward, and at a time when the sun's rays favored a near approach to him. He was a noble fellow, and well worthy the trouble we had with him.

After turning the whale up, we took him alongside our ship. When ships' boats in company take a whale, it is customary, either to give one party the head and the body to the other, or else to release the ship whose boat fastened first from all further trouble with the prize: her companion taking the whale alongside, cutting him in, trying him out, and then either stowing down, or rafting half the oil to her companion. In case she stows it down, one-half of the barrels are branded with the other vessel's name, and credited to her account. In the present case, Captain Perkins of the Plover wishing to make through us a consignment to the owners, we took the whale, and a boat's crew of his assisted us to cut in. After trying out, one-half the oil, amounting to forty-six barrels, was stowed between decks in casks brought from his ship for the purpose and duly branded. We engaged to carry it home as freight, charging six cents per gallon for the carriage. We had also twelve hundred pounds of right whalebone on freight, from the ship Martha, of Fairhaven. This freight-business pays no one but the owners, and perhaps the captain: the proportion of it that any one else gets being so small as to make it a trifling object.

On the same day that we stowed, we gammoned the barque Iowa, of Fairhaven. She had been very successful, having filled up with humpbacked oil at the Rosemary Islands. She was but a short time from Mauritius, and brought us the sad news of the demise of John Cunningham, of New Bedford, whom we had left at the hospital in Mauritius. The cause of his death was to some degree enveloped in mystery. It appears that on the day previous to his decease he applied to the resident physician of the hospital for a discharge, stating as his reason for it the many deaths that were daily occurring in the same ward in which he was (the dysentery having assumed a fatal type just after our leaving the port). The physician told him that he was loath to discharge him as yet, for his stricture was not entirely removed; but, after some urging on Cunningham's part, the doctor directed him to apply on the following day, and he would make out his discharge. The morning following his attendants found him dead in his bed, without an external sign to show why the spirit had fled. The physicians, at a loss to account for so sudden and unexpected a termination, held a post-mortem examination upon his body, and finding all the organs free from disease, they gave in as their opinion that he had died from fright. Poor fellow!—his health aboard ship had been almost uninterruptedly good, and he bade fair to live as long as any of us. But Providence, for His own wise purposes, saw fit to call him away from life to (I trust) a better and happier sphere; and although in this world he will no more hear the storm whistling through the rigging, or the sudden boom of the tempest-tossed ocean, yet I hope that he

> "Shall find pleasant weather,
> When He who all commands
> Shall give, to call Life's crew together,
> The word to pipe all hands."

This young man was the eldest son of a widow in New Bedford. His father was for years engaged in whaling, and some eight years since, whilst master of the ship Florida, was drowned in the surf, off the Island of Rorotongu, in the Pacific Ocean; and now his poor relict is called upon to weep over the untimely end of her eldest boy, in a foreign hospital, unattended by a single friend to soothe his dying-pillow. He whom she looked upon as the stay of her declining years, like her husband, engaged in the same perilous pursuit, and died thousands of miles from home, under painfully afflicting circumstances.

He was the third who has been called away out of our bonnie crew, who in July, 1855, sailed from New Bedford full of life and hope: all at that date feeling assured of returning with a well laden ship and full crew—with stores of curiosities, gleaned from foreign ports, as keepsakes for the loved ones at home: all were sanguine, and certainly expected to make a good voyage and return by July, 1858.

But "man purposes — God disposes;" as a proof of which, let us review our relative positions now, and then. One of our men was discharged, sick, in King George's Sound; from thence he went to Melbourne, since which we have heard of his death. Our second mate was discharged at Vasse, went home as mate of the barque Pamelia, and is now, I hope, in the full enjoyment of every blessing, surrounded by an affectionate family. Three of our original number deserted, and through the example and influence of evil-minded associates, allowed themselves to be made parties to the origination of a false report, according to which our vessel had foundered on a tempestuous night, and the greater number of the crew set afloat in open boats off the inhospitable coast of New Zealand. Poor John Walters has gone to his long home! the blue waves of the South Pacific having closed over him whilst in the discharge of his duty. We learn from the Iowa's report, that another one of our original crew, whom we discharged at Port Louis, has shipped aboard the barque Agnes, of New York, bound to Batavia for a cargo, thence homeward. And, lastly, Cunningham too is gone! Whilst we, who are left, have been forty months from home, and are still battling with the ocean's elements — alas! in pocket, poor indeed, and hopefully longing for home.

We also learned from the Iowa, that the New Yorker, whom we left at Port Louis, had been discharged from the Hospital, perfectly recovered; and that he, together with an Irishman, also discharged there by us, had solicited and obtained employment in the police-force of that port.

The rest of those whom we left at Port Louis, never having done anything to entitle them to remembrance, we neither know nor care what has become of them, with the exception of our late fourth mate, who deserves mention singly on account of his utter uselessness. From the same source, we learn that he shipped, and left Mauritius in the barque Eagle, as boatsteerer. In this new position he will, no doubt, act with about as much credit to himself, and receive as unenviable a name and reputation, as he did among us.

A few days subsequent to the above date we saw and gammoned the barque Coimbra. She had sailed from Mauritius a few days after our leaving; but, owing to the sickness of her captain, was forced to return, and remain ten additional days. The captain of this vessel, quite an original, hailed from New Brunswick, and was a veritable Blue Nose — long, lank, and parsimonious. He has had during the voyage three different crews, who for some reason or other left him after a cruise or two. Early in the voyage a veto was put by the authorities of Vasse upon his entering any port on the coast of New Holland, owing to his having carried a prisoner away in his vessel. This prisoner, who was a thief, doing a good business at Freemantle, report says, paid one thousand dollars for the accommodation. The captain of the Columbus had little or no trouble with him — merely carrying him outside, and then transferring him to a merchant-ship. Being debarred from entering these ports, where the cost of recruiting ships is comparatively trifling, and having kept his crew out of port as long as a wholesome dread of the scurvy would allow, he, with an eye to economy, made the following address to his men, to wit: "Boys, I would like to go into a good port, where we could all enjoy ourselves. Such a port is Hobartown; but the limits set to my expenses by my owners will not allow of my indulging in such an outlay as lying with the ship in that harbor would occasion; but, if you by subscription pay a certain sum apiece out of your earnings, I will go there." Several of the ship's company assenting, a document was drawn up, and most of them attached their names: agreeing to contribute towards the port-expenses sums varying in amount from two to twenty dollars. One of the foremast hands demurring to this arrangement, the old fellow told him that he would get it out of him some way or other; and so he did, by persisting in tormenting him until his victim was glad to pay the two dollars, and thereby gain somewhat of an exemption from further bad treatment.

This is not a solitary case of such sharp business-operations. A certain captain once boasted aboard our barque, that by his finesse in settling with those whom he discharged in Hobartown he had made the clear sum of two thousand dollars for his owners; in other words, that by misrepresenting the quantity of oil taken, he had cheated his crew out of so much money. A most creditable boast! Of a piece with such conduct was also his mode of serving out meat. A barrel was broken out, brought on deck, and divided into so many portions as were equivalent to his idea of a day's allowance (which was about one-third of that prescribed by law). It was then tied together, and strung up on deck; whence if a remnant of it disappeared, it was charged to the steward and cook.

We saw the vessel under the last-mentioned individual's command on the first day of December. She was then bound home, and had but ten barrels of meat aboard for the consumption of the crew during the passage, which, as she had been out about four years, will consume at least ninety days. This quantity of meat would last us with the same number in the ship's company as she has, but thirty days. For such conduct this man could not plead non-success, as he had on board one of the best cargoes on the ocean — his quantity of oil being no less than two thousand barrels, of which sixteen hundred contained sperm oil.

On learning that the Coimbra was bound direct for home, several of us put letters aboard of her, and as she kept off and receded from our sight we naturally wished that we were pursuing a course in the same direction, and were agreeably astonished the next morning (December 5th) to find our captain keep off to the southward, and learned that we were bound round the Cape. In the afternoon we saw the Coimbra, overhauled and passed her; our studding-sails giving us a great advantage over her when the wind is free. The following day, in order to compete with us, she made and bent studding-sails; but this was as far as she could go, and we were still to windward of her, as we had made and bent mizzen, maintopmast, and maintopgallant staysails, which gave us a slight advantage.

On account of the length of time, and the chafing of whales alongside and under the ship, the copper was in a desperate condition. Looking at her bottom, when the sea was calm and clear, nothing could be seen but an irregular bunch of vegetable matter; looking, from her waterways to the kelson, as much like a collection of old rags, as anything else that I could compare it to, whilst in many places whole sheets of copper were gone, and in others it was rolled up in scrolls. I hooked up a piece, and, on examination, found it of an almost transparent thinness. All these inequalities in the surface of the bottom naturally tended to retard the speed; and, consequently, when whalers start for home, they strive to make amends for all deficiences by a greater spread of canvass, and venture to carry it longer than any other class of vessels afloat, relying on the number and skill of their men to prevent disaster in time of emergency.

We kept on with a light fair wind to the southward and eastward for some days, and, from the agreeableness of the weather, augured a pleasant passage around; but when opposite Cape l'Agulhas the wind hauled ahead, and we had it first light and clear, then strong and cloudy, with showers of rain and thick fog. For the benefit of those who imagine that sailors have but little to do when afloat, I will copy from my log-book the proceedings of several days (whilst in this baffling weather), *verbatim et literatum.*

December 16*th.* — This day opens with a strong breeze from the eastward, cloudy. At midnight running before it, with maintopgallant sail, fore, and foretopmast studding sails set. At 1 o'clock A. M. the breeze increasing to a gale, we took in the studdingsails and topgallantsail; at three, double-reefed the topsails; at 6 A. M. the wind hauling forward, loosed and set the mainsail; at 8, were obliged to furl it; at 9, shook a reef out of each topsail, and set jib, spanker, and mainsail; at 11, the wind hauled to the S. S. W., clewed down the topsails and close-reefed them — thus remained for the balance of the day.

December 17*th.* — At 1 A. M. shook a reef out of each topsail; at $4\frac{1}{2}$, struck by a squall that hove her down rail to, hauled up the courses, kept the ship off to haul down the jib, which was done, and furled the sail; then furled the spanker, luffed to, close-reefed the topsails and furled the mainsail amid torrents of rain; at 3 P. M. furled the foretopsail; at 6 P. M., after having shipped a sea that filled it full, took in the bowboat; at $6\frac{1}{2}$, furled the foresail; at 7, clewed down the maintopsail, shook out the reefs and reefed it over; at $7\frac{1}{2}$, loosed the foretopsail, shook out the reefs, reefed it over, sheeted it home and set it.

December 18*th.* — At $1\frac{1}{4}$ A. M., furled foretopsail;

at 4, set close-reefed foretopsail and foresail; at 7, made all sail; at 3 P. M., furled the light sails, and double-reefed the foretopsail; at 7 P. M., shook the reefs out, and set the flying-jib and maintopgallant-sail; at 10, furled the light sails and double-reefed the foretopsail, and at midnight double-reefed the maintopsail.

Here was work enough for three days, and hard work, as any one may discover, who doubts the fact, by, like me, participating in it; but handling, reefing, and steering, are by no means all the employments of the seamen when afloat. Everything being kept taut, the strain on the rigging, in heavy weather, is tremendous, so that some little thing or other always needs repair; and in fine weather the sailor is sent with his marlinespike, slush, and tar-bucket, into the rigging, where he not unusually stays a whole watch, busily employed in putting a seizing here, or seizing on a ratline there, repairing the service, or other chafing gear. These, with other duties of a like description, keep a merchantman's crew continually on the move; but where there are so many, as with us, the labors are performed without making the task irksome to any.

Wishing, in doubling the Cape, to near the land, so as to take advantage of the westerly current (which here is said to run with a speed of four knots hourly), we done all we could to hang on; but the wind forbade us arriving at this desired position; and as we drifted considerably to the southward, we were two degrees from Table Mountain on the 21st, when, with a fair wind and plenty of it, a clear sky and smooth sea, without let or hindrance, we passed into the blue waters of the Atlantic Ocean; just three years, two months, and eleven days from the time we passed from it into the Indian Ocean, with a prospect of three years whaling before us; all buoyant with hope, and not a doubt entering the thoughts of any that, by the time we were thus far on our return passage, we should be full of oil. But it is needless to say that such is far from being the case.

It cannot be supposed that we left the Indian Ocean, whose broad bosom was our home for so many months, with any regret. Indeed, there was little to endear it to the remembrance of any one who ever experienced its changeable and heavy weather, and who has been obliged to visit its miserable ports. We have had a pretty thorough acquaintance with it, having navigated its entire length, and cruised, day after day, in its waters, from latitude 8° to 42° south.

After entering the Atlantic Ocean we steered to the northward and westward, until we arrived in latitude 32° south, longitude 7° east. This locality is known as the Carroll ground, and is a favorite resort of the South Atlantic whalemen. Here, as we had good weather, but saw no whales, all hands were occupied in repairing and renewing the rigging, to get the ship in order for a return home. It is a great point of honor among seamen to return their rigging in as good, if not better order than when they received it, with a view to commendation from their owners; consequently the lower rigging was turned in anew, particular care being taken to have everything as nice as possible: blocks must be new-strapped, and neatly covered with canvas; all service that looked in the least chafed, or white, must be removed; the yards stripped and rigging-fitted; the ratlines taken off the mizzen topmast and foretopgallant rigging; the rigging fore and aft, alow and aloft, must be rattled down, and a coat of tar then applied to all the hemp material; the paint-work, inside and out, from the copper to the trucks must be renewed, and the spars scraped: then we will be ready for home. All this must be done before the 27th of January, at which time we are to leave the whaling-ground; so that we will have nothing to occupy us after that date, except to make as speedy a passage as possible to New Bedford.

On the Carroll ground we entered upon the New Year. On the 4th of January we gammoned the ship Messenger, of New Bedford. She left the Madagascar ground four days after us, and had been boxing off the Cape for twenty-one days; so that we esteemed ourselves fortunate in having escaped such miserable weather with no further detention than we experienced. Her crew were affected by a peculiar malady, which somewhat resembled moon-blindness: more or less of them had been affected with it during the whole voyage; and at the present time there were eight men in her forecastle who could not see each other after dark, but whose vision during the day was perfectly good and clear. One of them whilst aboard of our vessel complained of pain across the temples in the daytime. He was the only one of those afflicted who expressed a sense of pain or inconvenience, apart from loss of sight. I have seen individual cases before, but never in such numbers aboard a single ship. Their captain attributed it to moon-blindness; but these men positively assured me that they had not slept with their faces exposed to the moon's rays. Again, it disappeared on their near approach to land; and at one time they were completely relieved of it by the use of Irish potatoes. The men themselves attributed the malady either to the tarræ root, of which they had consumed a large quantity on the voyage, or else to their water, which, as they stated, had been for a long time brackish and unwholesome. I am inclined to think that it originated from the bilge-water; for a similar case from this cause came under my notice some years since.

Whilst amongst the Abrolhas', I was called upon by the captain of the Europa to administer to a Portuguese, whose eyes were affected by sleeping in the moon's rays. I bled him, and applied blisters to the temples. This treatment produced almost instantaneous relief. I informed the Messenger's people of this; but their captain was one of the old school, who believing that all the ailments mankind are heir to can be cured by salts, would employ no other remedy; and, whether the disease was a cold, a fever from a broken or dislocated member, or what not, his prescription was a full dose of it, whereof he constantly kept a large quantity on hand, of the denomination known as Glauber salts, used ashore for horses.

On the 16th we gammoned with the ship Mary, of New Bedford. Her captain requested me to go aboard of her, and administer to her cooper, who had for a long time been very sick. In compliance with his request I did so. In her steerage I found the wreck of an unusually symmetrically-formed man, suffering from an affection of the liver. I did what I could for him; but then, as the boat would not return to our ship for several hours, I began to fear that the time would pass tediously. My apprehension, however, was speedily banished by the attention I found myself compelled to give to the yarns of my patient, who, like all old seamen, was garrulous; and, as I was a good listener, (of which I pride myself,) he was soon rehearsing his manifold adventures from his youth upwards, embracing forty-five years of sea life. He told me, that during this time he had served in every situation aboard a whaler, from cabin-boy to master; and he mentioned some half-a-dozen well-known whaling captains who had served their novitiate in his boat. He stated, that during the South American revolutions he had been privateering, and was for many years in both the naval and merchant service. He had visited almost every country of the globe to which commerce directs her conveyances: at times (to use his own expression) flush, with plenty of money; at others, alone, without a change of clothing, amongst semi-civilized nations. He was a grandfather; and stated, that his first wife, with whom he had lived for many years, had taken umbrage at his assuming the sailor's privilege of having a wife in every port, and left him. After the legal forms had been gone through with, she consoled herself by taking another spouse.

Her husband, not to be a whit behind her, took his ship home again, sailed to the island of New Zealand, and in Mungunui married an English girl, twenty years his junior. He then engaged in the English whaling-service, wherein he accumulated considerable money, and after the lapse of a few years returned to the States, taking his wife and their two children with him. At home, he for some years rested; but the continual yearning for the sea experienced by all who have once been afloat, and not been disgusted with life thereon, induced him, in his old age, to ship as cooper of the Mary. No sooner was he afloat, however, than on exerting himself he found that his was not now a system such as that which had carried him through so many years of hardship and exposure. Fast living and imprudence had done their work, and his constitution was gone. The bracing sea-air, instead of invigorating, depressed and weakened him. Dispirited, he was at last laid up, like a worn-out hulk, without power or will to be engaged in aught but the most puerile employments. During his stay aboard the Mary (rather over two years) he had not heard from home; and, being very ingenious, he had, to occupy his mind and drive away heart-sickness, employed himself by scrimschawing, and had completed a store of unique and carefully-fabricated articles of various descriptions, from woods he procured in the different ports he had visited, or from ivory and bone.

The boat being now ready to return, I left the narrator, and went aboard our own ship. I informed the captain that he must send him into the nearest port, (St. Helena,) where he might procure rest and good medical treatment. This he thought inexpedient; but, by dint of pressing, I convinced him of the absolute necessity of such a course. After carrying my point, I had the curiosity to ask him about the cooper's antecedents; because I had not given full credence to all his story, inasmuch as old sailors are so famous for drawing a long bow. The captain gave me a rehearsal of his past life, which fully substantiated all that he had said of himself; and, after he had finished it, I left him, with the conviction that I had seen the most practical illustration possible of a career at sea, where Christianity or morality had not held the helm. Here was a man, who had made much more than a competency during life, and who had walked his own quarter-deck, after having gained his position by his own unaided personal exertion, reduced at the end of a life-time of battling with the elements to a subordinate station — sick, debilitated, and uncared-for — aged, weak, and careworn — far away from home, without the fostering attentions of a wife or children to render the couch of sickness other than a bed of thorns; and this lamentable situation brought on, not by the villany or mismanagement of others, but, according to his own confession, by his individual imprudence.

The Mary, like the Messenger, had on board some half-a-dozen persons whose eyes were affected mysteriously. She was down by the head, and had (as was also the case with the Messenger) been so trimmed on the whole voyage, which trim facilitates the collection of putrid water in the forward part of the ship's hold; hence, by taking into consideration these singular coincidents of the vessels, together with the fact that no one who lived abaft the mainmast had been so affected in either, the disease may, I think, be safely attributed to bilge-water.

After gammoning with the Mary, we ran close in to the African coast, and fell in with several Atlantic whaling-vessels. These crafts are usually small, and carry but two or three boats. By the class who go farther from home, they are facetiously denominated Plumpuddingers. The length of the voyage ranges from six to thirty months. From the specimens of these cruisers, I should say, that there is little difference in their arrangements and those of the whalemen of the Indian and Pacific oceans. One characteristic was, however, distinctive; that is, the greater proportion of foreigners before the mast. In one vessel (the Cornelia of Edgartown) there was not a single individual of American birth in her forecastle; and on board the Keoka, of Westport, there was a large proportion of dark skins from the islands of the North Pacific. Their voyages are shorter, their crews generally fare better than those of the larger ships, and, as was my impression up to the time we fell in with them, they made better ports — but this, upon inquiry, I found to be a mistaken idea; for those on board the Keoka stated that they had not been into a port where English was spoken during the whole time (some eighteen months) they were from home; and, furthermore, that they had only visited Walfisch Bay, a Portuguese settlement on the coast.

These vessels averaged about the same amount of oil, considering their time out, as other ships of their profession in the Indian Ocean. Their crews were, also, just as much discontented with whaling, and as anxious to get home, as we were. In unqualified terms they expressed their envy of us lucky fellows, as they termed us, who they supposed would in a few months be in New Bedford. Our diminutive cargo did not seem to act as a damper upon their

ANOTHER STOPPAGE AND DISAPPOINTMENT. 363

wishes. They said that they did not care, when it came to the question of getting home, whether they had anything coming to them, or not. Neither did the prospect of cold weather appal them; for one enthusiastic fellow assured me, that he was willing to be landed on a snow-bank, in a costume but little preferable to a straw-hat without trimming, for the sake of being delivered from the monotonous life he was now leading.

After leaving these vessels, we squared our yards, and rolled before the delightful southeast trades (the elysium of the seafaring-man) towards St. Helena, taking it very easy—only sending aloft the studding-sails on the foremast and foretopmasts, and at night jogging along under easy sail in that direction: it being our intention to make a short stay at that rock-bound isle for letters, and then to crack on everything for home.

On arriving within a few degrees of the world-renowned prison-rock of the great Conqueror, sail was reduced, and the ship luffed to the wind. The moon being on the change, our captain, anxious to get one more sperm whale, determined to let no means within his power remain unemployed for that purpose.

This halt in our homeward course was not received with a very good grace. Except the captain, everybody else aboard our vessel had calculated upon a direct passage homeward. But this was in perfect keeping with his conduct throughout the voyage: at one time assuring us that we would be bound homeward on a certain date, and inducing us to write to that effect by his representations, in which at the time of making them he was perhaps sincere. But he suffered his opinions to be changed by the slightest cause. If he gammoned with a ship, he found in her skipper an adviser, who recommended to him a prolific whaling-ground — one on which, he was told, he could not fail to take five hundred barrels of oil, probably, even altogether fill up. These golden visions he received and credited, (although I cannot but think that it was against his better judgment — for, certainly, if a vacillating, he was not a stupid man,) and away he would go to the promised El Dorado. Thus he exhausted his own as well as the patience of every one else by a fruitless search for sperm whales that had been long ago captured!

Where we were now stopping was the ground on which the barque Monmouth, two years since, captured two hundred barrels of oil; and hence our captain imagined that we would be likely to do the same; but in this there was about as much probability of any success and remuneration at all commensurate to the time and trouble expended, as the Kidd treasure seekers have received for their laborious and chimerical search.

Under such phases of affairs, I have written some half-dozen different times, stating to those whom I addressed that I would certainly be home at the periods that had been severally and distinctly determined on. Some of these letters bore the date of August, 1858; and I do not know but that those who received them may have set down such disparities to wilful misrepresentations, or a sickening anxiety on my part to get home, leading me to believe in an early return, because it was so much the more desirable, and in accordance with my hourly wishes. But such, I can safely say, was not the case; for even now, at the present writing, (January 31st, 1859,) I cannot, neither can any other in the ship except the captain — all assurances to the contrary notwithstanding — set a time, which they can firmly believe themselves will be that at which we shall really start for home. So, I must be absolved from the charge of writing at random; and the blame must rest, where it should: upon the captain's wavering, and his being so easily influenced by others.

31*

CHAPTER XIV.

At daylight, February 1st, we hove in sight of the Isle of St. Helena, the world-renowned prison-rock of Napoleon Bonaparte, the conqueror of Europe. At a distance, this isle looked not unlike other isles, despite its notoriety. As we approached nearer, we found it distinctive in all its features: high, frowning, and almost barren. A strange thing, this, for so low a latitude, within the tropics, where Nature dons her greenest garment, and smiles her sunniest smile: spreading rich and plentiful productions over the earth's surface. On approaching still nearer, we found fortifications erected, which, as far as I am able to judge, make the island impregnable; though what enemy would care to take the trouble and expense of an expedition against so worthless an object, I cannot imagine. After passing this chain of fortifications, Rupert's Valley gradually developed itself to our sight, and ensconced on its narrow bosom we saw the city of Jamestown. From the water this town presents quite a creditable appearance. The buildings being of stone, and many of them of goodly size, give an air of solidity and respectability to it, which I for one did not expect to find. On the right of the town, viewed from the sea, is the far-famed Jacob's Ladder, consisting of I do not know how many steps, hewn out of the solid rock, which affords the only means of ingress and egress to the garrison occupying a fort at the summit of the elevation. There is only a single narrow street laid out in the town — the narrowness of the valley not admitting of any farther expansion. On the sides of the acclivities are stone-walls, built for the purposes of travel. They are wide, and admit of the passage of a vehicle upon them; but a misstep will entail upon the unfortunate wight who should make it certain death, as it would precipitate him into an abyss hundreds of feet in depth. Shortly before our arrival an English seaman on liberty, who had been carousing, was suddenly seized with the whim of drinking his brandy on one of these airy places. In pursuance of this phantasy, he procured a bottle of spirits, and, seating himself on the ledge of the wall, with his feet suspended over the chasm, he was enjoying his brandy and his position to his entire satisfaction. He could not be removed by force, as such a proceeding would be productive of imminent danger to him and his rescuers, and as he was proof against persuasion, his shipmates were constrained to allow him to remain in his perilous position, trusting for his preservation in Providence, who assists the seaman out of so many difficulties and dangers. For a time he did very well, and maintained an upright, and consequently a safe position; but, as the spirits he had imbibed began to operate, his body swayed to and fro, and finally, whilst about to take another drink from his bottle, he lost his balance, and was precipitated down, far down, upon the jagged rocks; from whence his body was taken, mangled almost out of the semblance of humanity.

There is no harbor here — ships anchoring in an open seaway unprotected from the winds; but as, during the greater part of the year, this latitude is only visited by the south-east trade wind, a ship may lay in this exposed position with impunity. Some twenty vessels lay at anchor, three of which flew the stars and stripes; one of these was the Messenger, whose crew was ashore on liberty; another was the ship Thomas Glover, of Boston, bound home in a few days. The third, a barque, whose name I did not learn, was in an extremely leaky condition, and her captain, not wishing to have her condemned here, was offering one hundred dollars bounty, and twenty-five dollars per month for each man who would ship aboard to work her home; but if anything else offers Jack Tar is shy about engaging himself aboard a leaky ship, where the pumps are to be kept constantly going, day and night, and, as her semi-water-logged condition renders her unsafe to carry a press of canvass on, the probability is that a passage in her will be an extended one. Then by the time she would get on our coast, heavy weather might be looked for, and it, united with her leaky condition, would render her anything but a comfortable craft.

The other vessels were English, French, Swedish, and Dutch. Inside of all lay a number of condemned vessels, amongst them was the barque Ann, of Sag Harbor, the same vessel we were in company with whilst engaged in whaling on the coast of New Holland. After we left her she proceeded to Desolation, where, from heavy weather, she received severe damages, and, on arriving at St. Helena, a survey was had upon her and she was condemned. The other condemned vessels lying here are, for the most part, slavers, captured on the coast of Africa by the British squadron.

It not being our intention to make any stay here, without there was sufficient freight for home to make it an inducement for us so to do, we did not anchor, but stood off and on shore on alternate tacks. The captain lowered away, taking with him the men who came aboard without an agreement at Port Louis, for the purpose of shipping them before the American consul. His principal object, however, was to get letters, which we had directed to be sent here in numberless missives written many miles to the westward, and on this account St. Helena has been, for months, the wished-for port. Everybody expecting consecutive letters filling up the void of the last eighteen months, since which time none of us have received news of our families and friends, and, from the many dolorous accounts we have heard of the financial affairs of the country, everyone is interested to know what bearing such a crisis had had upon his connections; hence our anxiety. After many injunctions to send the boat off that night, the captain departed. We patiently waited until sundown, when, no boat approaching, we began to be uneasy. An hour later, we were chafing, almost the whole crew were walking decks in an excited, uneasy manner; and, although they did not curse the old man, they invoked anything but blessings upon his head, innocent though he was. Next morning, when the boat arrived, we found that from some misconception of orders, we should have stood in, when we stood off, shore; and, consequently, the third mate was kept chasing us in his boat from nightfall until three o'clock in the morning, when, giving up the pursuit as hopeless, he went aboard the Messenger, and, with his wearied crew, turned in.

On the letters being brought forth, I found that I had four; one of August, 1855, left here by a ship that had carried it about the ocean for years — the other three were of May, July, and November, 1858; this last was inexpressibly welcome to me, as it brought everything down to a comparatively late date, assuring me of a warm welcome home whenever I did arrive. Of this, however unworthy, I had never doubted; but it is a weakness of our nature to take delight in the rehearsal of pleasant facts. The chief topic of interest, after being assured of the welfare of my connections, and one that astonished and, to some extent, perplexed me, was the birth of a niece, a child of my younger brother. This was the first intelligence I had of his marriage, which, however, was not unexpected; I had looked forward to it as a matter of course; but that he should be blessed with issue ere I returned, never once crossed my mind—though why, I know not. At first, I could scarce believe it; but there it was, in black and white, the plainness of the chirography forbidding a doubt of its authenticity; so there was nothing left for me to do but to sit down and acknowledge myself taken all aback by the intelligence. After a few minutes reflection, I could not but laugh at my stupidity, or inadvertency, in never having made a provision in my mind for such a contingency; however, so wags the world; improbable events are fostered by the imagination, whilst probable ones are allowed, through inattention, to escape notice.

After having thoroughly read over my letters, I had leisure to think of my companions. Some, I could see by the expression of the eyes, and nervous exhilarated step, had received good news from home; others, by their troubled air, displayed their reception of unwelcome tidings; whilst those who had received none, either walked alone with compressed lip and lowering brow, refusing all sympathy, or strove by an affected gayety to laugh off the carelessness of their people in not writing.

As the reception of a letter from home, by the seaman, after a long cruise, exhilarates, and encourages him, developing all the best principles of his nature, so, on the other hand, the least inattention or slight on the part of his friends, depresses him; and, on arriving in port where he has long expected intelligence; on being disappointed he goes ashore and is ready to engage in any dissipation, apologizing to himself for his departure from virtue, by the reflection that nobody cares for him, or else they would take the trouble to write to him. Mark a case in point. One of our crew, a Massachusetts boy nearly approaching to manhood, had, for months, talked and thought of nothing but his news and letters from home at St. Helena. He had, to my knowledge, written some twenty-five letters; heretofore he had received no letters from home, but thought, of course, they had written, and their missives were aboard ships we had not seen. Meantime, he had been at work for months, manufacturing trinkets and other articles from ivory, for the purpose of presenting them to his friends and relatives. On arriving at St. Helena, there was not a word or line from home for him. I never saw a person so depressed; his trinkets were given away or sold, and he asserted it as his firm determination, when he did land in the United States, not to go home.

Mothers who wish to keep their sons in the path of virtue, and sisters who cherish a brother's memory, when far away upon the sea, would do well to bear this fact in mind, and be careful to write, so that at every civilized port the object of their solicitude may receive intelligence from home; this, by a little inquiry at the outset of the voyage, can be easily arranged. It does not make so much difference about the reception of letters at sea, for there but few temptations to the grosser paths of sin are experienced; but when, after a long and arduous cruise, his ship enters port, he feels need of relaxation, and, unless reminded of home and kindred, he easily falls a prey to the wiles of the courtezan and the publican, who are ever on the alert to entrap the unwary and inexperienced.

But it is time that I should return to my original topic—the consideration of the Island of St. Helena and its residents. Not having had opportunity to go ashore myself, I must see it through the eyes of others and describe it from their lips. Here comes the boat's crew; it consists of six, who, although dressed alike and of the same country, vastly differ in sentiment. First, we will ask the less refined of the lot—those two whose reckless, careless air, bespeak them jovial, hearty fellows, ever ready for a lark without thinking of or caring for consequences—

their answer to my inquiry as to what kind of place it was, being characteristic of their class (which is largely represented in the whaling fleet), "That Jamestown is a sailor's paradise." "Why so, my hearty?" "Because there is neither lack of women nor wine."

We will now turn to the next comer; he is a Western man, from Milwaukie, Wisconsin, of Scotch parentage, has been with us all the voyage, and is one of the best and most reliable men in the ship; to a naturally strong mind, he unites an acute perception of men and manners, and, withal, a high moral tone pervades all he says and does.

His statement was, that on going ashore he found a stepping-stone, some twenty feet in width, in front of the town, for the convenience of boats landing; they pulled to it and landed, but the swell continually heaving in, rendered it impossible to moor the boat without certainly calculating on her being stoven; so a couple of the boys, of whom numbers were swarming along ashore, were entrusted with her, and our fellows went on a cruise about the town. He described the town as not unlike other colonial cities, with the usual number of government buildings, and red-coated soldiery standing guard, as if to keep these massive stone heaps from escaping. The inhabitants were of all colors, from black to white, each moving in its particular sphere. The blacks are slaves, captured by British cruisers, and sent here to labor and pay the expenses of their capture. Some months since, a cargo of six hundred of these Africans was landed in Rupert's Valley; they were awarded by the Government a twelvemonths' stay at St. Helena; at the expiration of the year they were to be sent to the British West Indian possessions to be disposed of as apprentices. The other inhabitants of St. Helena are bitterly opposed to the introduction of these creatures into their quiet island, stating that they are indolent and insolent to an extreme degree, and are firmly persuaded that the island is a part of Africa and belongs to them. The inhabitants have petitioned the queen for their removal, but she has declined complying with their request.

D.'s principal object in going ashore was to deliver several letters, which had been handed to him by natives of St. Helena, on board ships in the Indian Ocean. One of the parties he found, and made a mother's heart glad by tidings of the good health of her son; after perusing it, she loaded the bearer of the missive with thanks. Another party, for whom he had a letter, was dead; this was from a son who had not seen home or parents for six years. I heard him speak of his home and his anticipated return; but, alas! he will find a cheerless hearthstone — his parents dead, and none but strangers to yield him sympathy.

These people, or rather those who are natives, are brunettes. A number of the children, who were on our vessel, seemed to be perfectly at home upon the water. Their voices are peculiarly sweet, and we were enlivened by these youngsters singing a number of whaling and naval songs; and the spirit with which they entered into the performance, rendered a prophecy of their future callings in life a matter of certainty and easy augury.

I have before me the St. Helena Almanac for 1858,

which contains much information regarding the island — its trade, and inhabitants. From it I learn that the population numbers five thousand four hundred and ninety souls, and to attend to the health of this population, there is but one doctor of medicine; so here is a fair field for any Yankee disciple of Esculapius who wishes for employment, and does not object to leaving home to find it.

The amount of importation for the year 1856, reached the sum of one hundred and one thousand five hundred and sixty-two pounds, of which one-fourth was through American whaleships engaged in the South Sea fishery; the balance was from all parts of the world. The exports for the same time amounted to twenty-four thousand nine hundred and twenty-five pounds, twenty-two thousand five hundred and eighty-five pounds of which was to the United States. These facts show the importance of the whaling trade to the revenue of the island.

This book also contains information relative to the government-officers, the various churches, the telegraph department, &c., of the island; yet, as we are in a hurry to get homeward, we will not tarry for the consideration of further statistics, but return to our ship.

On the afternoon of the 2d inst., having ran close in to land, we were becalmed and in imminent risk of going ashore; but by lowering the boats and strenuously pulling we managed to get the ship's head pointed seaward. A light breeze springing up, we were soon relieved from our apprehensions. At $6\frac{1}{2}$ o'clock P. M. the captain came off, and immediately the order was given to square away for home. Every one at once turned-to with a will: the yards were manned in a twinkling; studdingsail booms and studdingsail rigging were rigged and rove aloft and alow, until the masts wore, as it were, an entire sheet of canvass from the royal yards to the deck, extending twice or thrice our beam, and assisting to the utmost our expeditious return. But the wind was aft and light, and our ship by no means kept pace with our impatient desires. Yet directly onward she made her way, unmarked by incident, until within a few degrees of the Equator. Here the doldorums (those pests of the homeward-bound!) occasioned a delay which well nigh again exhausted our patience. These doldorums are neither one thing nor the other: they are not positive calms, neither are they gales. For instance, one may wake at sunrise, find a pleasant breeze blowing, the wind fair, sky clear, and not a sign in the horizon on which to base a supposition of change: under this impression he will lounge around, congratulate himself on the ship's progress, and occupy his mind with thoughts of home; but, pausing, he glances to the sails, and finds them flapping from the scarcity of wind; and awakened from his reverie by the cheerless booming of the canvass, he directs his attention to the horizon, and finds haze or clouds in every quarter, portending squalls, either of rain or wind. A minute later, the flapping sail is hard aback, with a contrary wind; torrents of rain are falling; squall follows squall, in rapid succession, each from a different point — and thus they continue, until, having boxed the compass in the course of an hour, the ship returns to her former position, and lazily drags herself along for awhile, when the same scenes re-occur, and so alternate day after day. For ten days were we in irons, (as seamen term our situation,) during the whole of which time we made no more than ten degrees — an average of two and a half miles per hour: a pace that was far too slow to be easily endured by men who had been for forty-four months past looking forward to this passage with such intense interest. No idea of the uneasiness (I can use no better word) of the crew can be formed by a person who has never witnessed a ship's company situated precisely as we were. Every mile — every degree of the course was accurately measured and counted. All who were capable might have been seen, with quadrant in hand, taking the sun's altitude, working up the ship's time, comparing one day's run with another, and guessing what the performance of the next twenty-four hours would be; whilst those not possessed of a quadrant watched with peering eyes for the moment that would reveal the result of the operator's calculations. On turning out, before donning their apparel, the first questions of the watch below, were — how is the wind? how many knots is she going? what is the latitude? what the longitude? — all delivered in a breath. If the answer was, "She is going along some eight or nine knots an hour," the interrogator took a long inspiration, thus evincing his relief and inward satisfaction, and would then say, "Pull, girls, pull!" But if the ship was plunging, and the spars and rigging creaking from the pressure of their snow-white pinions, he would be delighted; and, jumping on deck to assure himself that everything was drawing, he would chuckle forth, in the height of his glee,

"Give it to her, old boy! She is all oak. She knows where she is bound to; so, pack on your tappa — she will bear it!" If some one remarked that she was heeled down very much, and sail was being dragged instead of carried, he was hooted at for a soldier, and sent to the cook to learn seamanship. If the officer of the deck started away or took in any sail, he was maligned for a milksop, and fated to hear lots of grumbling, together with the advice, given to him in an undertone, that he should stay at home, when he got there, and send his big sister to sea to carry sail for him.

To obviate this uneasiness, many plans were resorted to, and the true one was at length hit upon: the infallible one of labor. All hands seemed suddenly transformed into a colony of curiosity-hunters. One would be seen with a box of shells, cleaning them; another with a Madagascar spear, polishing it, so as to be presentable; whilst others had articles of ivory, bone, and wood, and were busily employed in improving their appearance, so as to render them more creditable to the donor. Every man in the ship had more or less of this description of articles; the greater part of which had been constructed aboard from the jaws and teeth of the sperm whales. Our occupation with these things continued not only for hours, but for days, and in some instances whole weeks.

Thus the time glided on, until we found ourselves hurried along by the northeast trades. These delightful winds we encountered when but two degrees to the northward of the line; and during their continuance we had nothing to grumble at, as we had a fair wind and plenty of it. From the testimony of former voyagers, who had run up and down these trades, we expected that we would be favored with their continuance until we should arrive in latitude 23 or 24° north; but in this, like in most of our other pleasant anticipations, we were disappointed. When we reached the fourteenth parallel of north latitude, they had almost ceased; and then, forgetful of their benefits, we grumbled at their scarce more than ephemeral existence. I well remember the expression of one of our crew, delivered with approved bitterness of spirit. The occasion of this was a mid watch at night, when all of the starboard watch were grouped together by the windlass, discussing our experience of the variability of the winds, while destined to some port or other in the course of the voyage. The speaker, having heard the opinions of several others, stepped into the center of the little knot, and, with an emphatic gesture of the hand, said: "Shipmates! it is no use talking: we are fated to meet with nothing but foul winds and head-beat seas until we get home, and then the bad luck that has kept us company for the past forty-four months may leave us. But there is, and has been, a Jonah in the ship the whole voyage, from the time we left New Bedford. The first we saw of it was in the Eliza Carrew's coming in contact with us; next, sperm whaling off New Holland. When bound to Balli we had a head wind; bound to the Australian Bight we had one of the dirtiest of dirty passages. To New Zealand we made a first-rate passage; but, when there, what was our fortune? To get scarce any oil, and lose one of our best men! Then, bound from there to Hobartown, we had the wind smack in our teeth for two weeks, when, with a favorable breeze, we should have performed the run in three or four days. Our ill-success in whaling to the southward, and on our visit to the Abrolhas', is too glaring to need particularization. Our passage to Mauritius was but a drawl, from the lightness of the winds. In doubling the Cape we were Jacksoned a week — at the line the same ill-fortune attended us. Now we have lost the northeast trades a week before we ought to. Add to these our other malexperiences, such as men falling from aloft, boats capsized and stoven, a sperm whale's head lost. And, to crown all, here we are, bound on to the North American coast in the worst month of the year, with an unremunerative voyage. Now, in the name of reason! how any one can expect good luck in the face of this category I cannot understand : as for myself, I cannot." And, with a gloomy shake of the head, the speaker concluded, folded his arms across his breast, and seemed resigned to the hard fate he had depicted for himself. His manner, however, was such as to convince the most casual observer that his was a spirit to combat manfully whatever further misfortunes might befall us, through accident or any other cause. The whole bearing of the man, in fact, showed a perfect confidence in the ability of himself and his shipmates to resist every tide of evil the great Neptune might send. His enumeration of our ill-successes heretofore made his argument almost unanswerable; but still I essayed to administer some consolation by quoting the old adage, "it is always darkest before day," and adding that from the fact of our former misadventures we might reasonably look forward for corresponding good ones in the future. Yet I awakened no sympathetic chord in the bosoms of my auditors. My predecessor had something tangible to base his prediction upon: a something, which, through its familiarity to the minds of all, appealed directly to their hearts; and, although I took the other side, I must confess that I myself was almost convinced there was more probability in his than in my theory. I felt, indeed, that our past crosses were sure prestiges of still more to come.

It may be supposed by some that such a conversation and prediction would have a gloomy effect on the minds of persons with such vivid imaginations as seamen; but, fortunately, (or unfortunately, whichever it may be,) in ninety-nine cases out of a hundred neither good nor evil makes any more lasting impression on their minds than water does upon a duck's back. For the moment, they become absorbed in the topic of that moment; but look at them an instant later, you will see the same careless bearing, and hear the merry jest passed around as gleefully as ever. Verily, there is need of a "sweet little cherub to sit up aloft, and keep up a watch over the life of Jack Tar"; for he will not look out for himself. This very thoughtlessness, however, renders him all the more useful aboard ship. Many times, if he should pause to think of the danger to himself in the performance of a particular duty, his hesitation would bring destruction upon the ship and its inmates. For instance, it is blowing heavily: a topsail is clewed up — the ship will not bear it, and the sail is flapping in a manner which will destroy it in a few minutes, for it is sweeping abaft the yard. (Now this is the only topsail that can be depended upon in case the ship on arriving at the coast should be jammed on a lee-shore: for then nothing could be saved except by its proper management and use.) Jack knows that under precisely these circumstances hundreds of seamen have been torn from the foot-rope while in the line of their duty, and hurled into the sea, when the fury of the elements precluded the possibility of an attempt to save them. Perchance in his last ship such an accident occurred: mayhap his messmate was swept from the same yardarm he himself was on. But he does not stop to think of all this: he springs into the rigging, climbs to the yard, gets a foothold, and (at every step forced to throw the sail over his head) arrives at the earing, when his task becomes comparatively easy. Little by little he gathers up, passing his gasket, and securing the sail, until all is snugly lashed along the yard in such a manner that the wind has no effect upon it. His task now done, he descends to the deck, as if nothing more than the most ordinary occupation had been his; and he is ready and willing to go aloft again, if necessity demands it.

It is ever thus at sea. The seaman's life, day by day, hour by hour, is exposed to peril, now in one form, now in another: from the heavy sea sweeping the ship, the unruly canvas, the defective spar. The wheel may throw and maim him, a stranded rope precipitate him to the deck; or, in laying out of a tempestuous night upon the jib or flying-jib boom he may miss his footing: he falls into the sea, the ship passes over him!—Jack has furled his last sail, and dies far from home and friends, without a tombstone to mark his resting-place: his body at the mercy of the wave, whilst his spirit, we hope, ascends to a better and happier state of existence, where he anchors in a bright haven of peace, in vivid contrast with his life on earth, or rather on the sea.

God help the sailor! is the prayer of all who wish him well. And God does help him, or else his would indeed be a comfortless existence. The Creator gives him a merry heart, and a brave one too. The former enables him to meet cheerfully the many discomforts incident to his profession, whilst the latter prevents him from perceiving danger and destruction in every blast that sweeps the ocean: together, they incite him to hope almost against hope, and continue his exertions in the storm, until absolute destruction overwhelms him. Who ever heard of a seaman's giving up in despair, even when the merest thread of hope only remained? None. No, they are manly to the last; and they always have at least the proud satisfaction of having performed their duty, even though their exertions were all in vain. The pleasant poetess, Miss Eliza Cook, has done them but justice, when she says,

"The dark-blue jacket that enfolds the sailor's manly breast
Bears more of real honor than the star and ermine vest.
The tithe of folly in his head may wake the landsman's mirth
But Nature proudly owns him as her child of sterling worth."

Some persons ashore may think that I have allowed my feelings to carry me away, and that in writing of a class of men, endeared to me by association and a participation in the vicissitudes of their everyday life, I have fallen into a rhapsody, or employed rodomontade; whilst not a few readers will think that I have merely blown my own horn. Yet I will appeal for corroboration of all I have written to those who have seen Jack Tar on his proper element: whether, on the sea, he does not display some of the noblest traits of humanity — not merely physical excellencies, but high moral qualities? Whether he is not there the most patient and courageous of human beings? Whether he does not sing the same in storm or calm, and unflinchingly meet all hardships with a cheerful spirit? I feel assured that all who have thus seen him will attest to his good qualities. Ashore he is not the same creature. The only apology I can offer for his excesses here is, that such are naturally prompted by the liberation of his buoyant spirit, — with a hardy frame and hot blood — from a long confinement and abstinence aboard ship. It is from sheer wantonness that he exults in the commission of his thousand-and-one frivolities; but which seldom leads him into the perpetration of any criminal act.

But, let us take a sober second view of this matter, and see whether Jack's follies — crimes, too, if you please — are altogether of his own immoral brewing. Of course there can be no question of this, if we use the cold-blooded formal argument of the self-sufficient man, which is, that inasmuch as he, like all the rest of mankind, is a free agent, his shortcomings and misdeeds must necessarily be voluntary, and therefore he alone should be held responsible for them. But, I would ask, does not society in a measure assist in his demoralization? Are not its respectable avenues closed to the foremast hand? Fathers and mothers of families, do you, in your philanthropic moods, extend to the seaman the same warm welcome into your families as you do to the landsman? Does he, landing in a strange port, find those who take him into the society of the virtuous, and thus place before him the opportunity of passing his hours rationally, and so endeavor to prevent his becoming the victim of irksome idleness, in whose train there usually is such an execrable brood of ills? No!—I can answer from experience — you do not. In your stead, out of consideration for his hard earnings, the harlot and the publican meet him at every landing, and with Judas-like greetings prevail on him to his destruction.

"Nobody cares for me!" one will hear from at least one-half the inmates of every forecastle, and in the greater proportion of such cases it is really too true. If the seaman has no immediate relatives, he finds those whom he meets ashore solicitous to make his acquaintance only for the sake of their own profit. To be sure, Seamen's Homes, Bethels, and Aid Societies, have done much, very much. God forbid! that I should say a word that could be construed into a disparagement of the efforts of these noble and benevolent institutions. But there is something more than these needed to reclaim the outcast seaman for society, and teach him truly that he has a character to maintain, as well as an abiding interest in the commonwealth. In fact, to effect a permanent amelioration of his condition, he must in his youth be educated and disciplined with a view to his profession, become accustomed to revere the ties and restraints of home and society, and be fully imbued with the principles of national citizenship.

In this humane work, the influence of the gentler sex is vitally essential. The time has long gone by when the seaman (the American seaman in particular) was a rude, uncouth being — half fish, half man: apparelled in a blue jacket and tarpaulin hat; his cheek pouched out with a great chew of tobacco; his walk a swagger, and his language redolent of oaths and tar. Such is a picture of Jack that has been drawn (from time immemorial) by too many authors, whose very particularizing, however, discloses to the initiated their ignorance of the subject. Your true sailor, from the general stigma that attaches to his class ashore, rather inclines to conceal, than make an unnecessary display of his calling. I have now been afloat almost four years; in one place or another, met with at least ten thousand seamen, principally belonging to our mercantile and whaling marine; and, although closely observing their habits, manners, and peculiarities, I never saw the original of the false picture above presented — a familiar one, it is true, to the readers of the yellow-covered nautical romances of the day. So, ladies, you need not fear, that, in urging you to extend a cordial greeting to Jack, I desire to favor the introduction of a boorish clown into your refined circles. But I will leave that to your own fair judgments. Compare him with the landsman: ten to one, you will place them on an equality; and, if you have a sparkling of romance in your character, you will give the Tar the preference.

To your parents, dear ladies, I would particularly address myself, and say to them: it is your duty (I speak plainly) to hasten this important matter, by which a noble class of your fellow-men may be so greatly benefitted, both here and hereafter. Do not fear, that by the introduction of the sailor into your families, you would nurse an adder, who would take advantage of your courtesy, and either corrupt your daughters, or entice your sons from home into his own perilous pursuit. His high appreciation and admiration of virtue will secure for the female portion of your family a degree of respect and attention from him, that would be looked upon by the young bucks of the present day with wonder and contempt; whilst his plain matter-of-fact and common-sense descriptions of the sea and its perils, hardships and pleasures, would divest the subject of the glowing imagery with which it is clothed by the fertile fancy of your youthful son, and thus enable him to see it in its true light. If the latter should then, however, still be anxious to barter the comforts and luxuries of home for the discomforts and privations of the sea, let him go! He was cut out for a sailor, and will sooner or later arrive at eminence in the profession of his well-advised choice.

But how, (methinks I hear you ask,) and by what means, is this good work to be accomplished? It is quite easy, says another I imagine, to see and describe the need of such a proceeding; but how is it to be done? My answer is: I have accomplished what I originally intended, namely, to indicate the great good to be done by such a movement. It would be presumption, on the part of so young a man as myself, to point out the means by which it may be effected. Older and wiser heads are now engaged in this good work: men of much experience and pure, active Christianity. But, if these should fail, or wish my views, I will not hesitate to furnish my opinions and plans at some future day, and with great pleasure respectfully submit them to their consideration.

CHAPTER XV.

But I have digressed long enough. I now return to the old Pacific and her inmates, as she was when we crossed the line, or a few degrees to the southward of it; at which time we lost sight of the Magellan clouds. Shortly after this the glorious Southern Cross disappeared from our view. These two constellations had been for years our landmarks in the heavens, (pardon the incompatibility of the expression,) and had become so familiar that at night the horizon seemed to us incomplete without them; but still we hailed their retirement from our view with delight, for it was an earnest of home. For several nights afterward we strained our eyes and patience in unavailing search for the North Star. At last it was sighted by a close observer. It was hailed by a general shout, that made the welkin ring; and hearts warmed as day after day in our passage north we opened still farther the glories of the northern sky; our own, with its fleecy scud and resplendent tints, shedding refulgence on our free and happy land.

And now, as we progressed day by day, it may be wondered, what were the plans of our crew for the future: all having gained little else than experience, and that not being a disposable commodity at our place of destination. But, kind people! do not think that any one of us felt poverty-stricken, or dependent on other than his own exertions for support. A more self-reliable set of men never drew breath than those who were now around me. One and all felt perfectly able to maintain themselves respectably, if health were vouchsafed to them by the Creator; and all had their plans. The first we will consider is that of the Massachusetts men — they forming by far the largest class. Although they mooted a hundred different channels in which they would direct their energies, there was a strong under-current pervading the whole, which bespoke whaling as their chief point, though many declared this their dernier resort, only to be engaged in by them from extreme necessity. Some of them thought that the whaling business was becoming too poor to follow, and declared their intention of emigrating to Oregon or Kansas, in quest of gold, should the accounts from those regions continue to hold out the same favorable inducements they had already done.

The second class whom we shall consider is, that formed of prodigal sons — a proportionably numerous one. Most of this class had left home with a desire to see the world, and a hope of returning with both pockets full of money, to astonish the "old folks at home," and, if necessary, to be expended for their comfort. Their bright anticipations not having been fulfilled, they were ashamed to go home; and, although we may doubt the wisdom of such a course, there is an honorable pride attaching to it, that cannot fail to command respect. Most of them had companions to whom they were attached during the voyage, and they determined that they would embark together to some foreign port or other (those of the Mediterranean were the most popular) for four or six months, when they would be sure of their monthly wages; and should they carry out their resolves, they might then return to their homes. This plan sounds foolish, and was foolish. No doubt they would be welcome to their relatives, with or without money; but I must confess that in the face of the warmest letters, and in the full assurance and conviction of the heartiest welcome, I myself felt a reluctance in returning, without something of moment to show, as a remuneration for almost four years of exile.

The last class (very few in number) is, those who had no homes — children of the sea. These did not take the same warm interest in a return to the States as we did; or, rather, it is a different interest — a mere sensual feeling: a desire to have a good spree, and be off again. They had no settled plan, but were ready, as soon as their money or credit became exhausted, to go here or there, as the caprice of the moment or the prospect of gain might lead them. Poor fellows! theirs was a hard prospective, and they felt it; for, when those, who were so blessed, gathered around each other, and talked of a reunion with parents, brothers, and sisters, they would walk moodily and alone, or strive by a reckless air to show their contempt for the comforts of home — but it was in vain. These now expected to follow the sea for their bread, just as the farmer does his plough. In the absence of good examples ashore, they had nothing to give them a strong bias to remain there; they considered the ocean as the granary from which their daily provision must be procured. God direct them wherever they may go, and in whatever they may do!—that they may avoid the snares spread for them by the designing at every step of the paths they must follow.

On the evening of March 17th we entered and crossed the Gulf Stream. Our near approach to it had been indicated days before by the appearance of the Gulf weed. This weed is inhabited by multifarious marine animals. On being scooped up and placed in a bucket of water, its tiny residents were to be seen swimming and plying about with the intensest activity: crabs, lobsters, various kinds of fish, and the meduca, together with many others that are nondescripts.

On arriving at the Stream we dipped up a bucketful of its water from alongside, and found it quite warm. A short time afterwards we repeated the experiment, and found a variation in the temperature. Thus, at intervals of fifteen minutes throughout our passage across it, we tested the water to the best of our ability; and although our thermometer could not be fully depended upon, yet the result was still decided enough to make me a convert to Professor Bache's theory: that, the Gulf Stream is a series of belts of water, varying in temperature, instead of a body of water of uninterrupted equivalent warmth.

On the following day we experienced one of those southeast gales, attended by fog, which are so common to the American coast in the month of March. As long as we felt satisfied that we had an offing, things went pretty well, and we rejoiced at the way the ship was making before the gale; although, in the absence of sun, moon, and stars, we had nothing by which to ascertain our whereabouts. At noon we spoke the brig Pilotfish, of Boston, and found that by her reckoning we were fifty miles farther to the westward than what our chronometer gave it; however, we felt pretty well satisfied as to our own correctness until night, when we shortened sail, (which throughout the day we had carried to the extent of the vessel's ability,) and luffed to the wind, hove the lead, and sounded with the deep-sea line. At the same time the gale increased to a hurricane, and, as we could not see a ship's length ahead, we were compelled, sorely against our inclinations, to heave the ship to for the night.

At 3 o'clock A. M. the next morning we all at once felt a change in the atmosphere, and, on inquiring the cause, found that the wind had hauled to the westward. A few minutes afterward the fleecy scud drove rapidly to the leeward, and the wind from the southwest bore down on us with extreme violence. But not too violent for us. Oh, no! It was hailed with delight. It was fair and strong; and, although we could show only close-reefed topsails and foresail to it, we bowled away, with it on our quarter, at the rate of twelve knots an hour. As we gradually neared the land we saw a number of small coasting-crafts laying-to, with the water sweeping over them — they not venturing to run in such weather. Of these we spoke several, and ascertained from them the bearings of Montauk Point. We found now that our chronometer was indeed wrong, and that had we depended upon it we would most likely have been by this time high and dry on some part of our own coast. This variation of the chronometer was very strange to us. During the whole voyage we had found it perfectly trustworthy; and, of course, after so long an acquaintance with its exactness, we had learned to place implicit confidence in it. At St. Helena it was correct, and so also off Cape St. Roque only three weeks before. But the present was precisely the case with it on the last voyage, when Captain James Allen commanded the ship. Then, likewise, there had not been a mile's variation in it until he had crossed the Gulf Stream, homeward-bound, when an error of fifty miles was discovered — a pilot-boat giving him his true whereabouts. Now, the question is, what was the cause of this singular variation? Was it the Gulf Stream, or what was it? Here is a question for the savans, and should they solve it, I will be happy to hear of their explanation.

CHAPTER XVI.

AFTER speaking these coasting crafts, our course was still onward and homeward. At noon we saw land; it was greeted with three as hearty cheers as ever swelled American throats. All was bustle and excitement, and naught but the discipline of a well-regulated ship kept our enthusiasm within bounds. The watch below, wearied with exertion, caught the gladsome cry, and, leaping from their berths, hurried on deck as they were, and, without hesitating at the coldness of the weather, sprang, half nude, into the rigging, to catch a sight of their native land. One, more enthusiastic than the rest, made the foretop a rostrum, and, hatless and shoeless, with his shirt flying in the wind, he repeated in a loud voice, intelligible above the shrieking of the gale, the beautiful lines of Sir Walter Scott:

"Lives there a man with soul so dead,
  Who never to himself hath said—
  This is my own, my native land;
Whose heart has ne'er within him burn'd,
  As home his footsteps he has turn'd
  From wandering on a foreign strand.
If such there be, go mark him well,
For him no minstrels' raptures swell;
Proud though his title, high his name,
Boundless his wealth as wish could claim,
  Despite his power and his pelf,
This wretch, concentered all in self,

> Living, shall forfeit fair renown,
> And doubly dying shall go down
> To the vile dust from whence he sprung—
> Unwept, unhonored, and unsung."

Reader, have you ever read these lines before? Of course you have; so had I before I went to sea; and then with me, as it must have been with you, they had made my heart beat quicker, and my eye flash with indignation at the recreant who could unmoved return to his native shore. But it is impossible to describe our appreciation of the beautiful text at such a moment as it was now presented to us; and in the exuberance of our spirits we could have hugged the author to our breasts and pronounced him sailor in feeling if not in practice. A change, however, soon came over the spirit of our dreams; the yards were squared, and, consequently, as we brought the wind aft, we were enabled to show more canvas to the favoring gale, and in this outlet we found a vent for our highly wrought feelings: reefs were shaken out, gaskets cast off in a twinkling, and the yards and sails were mastheaded, as if by magic, to the music of the merriest homeward bound song in our category, although our fingers and other extremities were benumbed with the cold. We were in hopes of getting in this night, but still we had our misgivings; as, even should we come into close proximity with Montauk Point, the weather was so boisterous that we had little hopes a pilot would venture out upon such a night. So, feeling that should we be necessitated to remain out another night, we would need rest, our watch went below to seek consolation in Nature's great restorer — sleep; but in vain, slumber came not to our anxious eyes, although wooed by every means in our power. We rolled our eyes, we counted indefinite units, but all to no purpose; the one idea preoccupied all our thoughts and forbade the intrusion of Morpheus on its domain. At 2 o'clock a light-house was seen, which, at first, was called Montauk light, but the land around it not agreeing with that in the vicinity of Montauk, after some deliberation, it was pronounced Fire Island light. This was a damper on all our spirits and dissipated our air castles, which had been built with the provision of going ashore within twenty-four hours; and long faces and dolorous sighs were the attendants upon this decision. After a few minutes of painful uncertainty, some one, whose memory was more retentive, called to mind the fact of having seen in a newspaper a notice of the erection of a new light between Fire Island and Montauk light. This view of the subject was immediately endorsed by all hands, and a corresponding buoyancy pervaded all; but as landmark after landmark was passed, and still Montauk was not to be seen, we gave up all hopes of seeing New Bedford that night, and were fearful that that much wished for occasion might not occur for a fortnight or more; as these southerly winds are not persistent, and no one knows how soon they may leave him and be followed by a north-easter, which, at this season of the year, lasts for weeks, and forbids all entrance into our destined harbor. But just at nightfall, one, who had voluntarily perched himself on the loftiest lookout on the fore royal mast, sung out, "Light ho!" and we soon found that at last we had sighted the veritable Montauk Point and light-house. This was cheering; but no pilot was to be seen, and our only resort was to shorten sail, heave the ship to, and hang on as closely as possible to the windward, so as to have no difficulty in beating up at the approach of daylight. To this end we clewed up and furled our light sails, reefed and furled the courses, clewed down and close-reefed the topsails— and bitter work we had of it. The weather, although not intensely cold to one accustomed to it, to our tropical sensibilities was frigid; and as, during the day, we had been enveloped by fog, our canvas was damp and heavy, and not to be handled in a moment; so that it was a task of time, patience, exposure, and danger, to reduce the old ship's canvas to a spread commensurate to the violence of the gale which now blew from west-north-west. In reviewing my whole stock of sea experience, comprising over three years of actual life upon the broad bosoms of four out of the five oceans of the globe, I can call to memory no time at which I felt more depressed than during the continuance of this night; not so much from the heaviness of the gale, for I had weathered scores that were much heavier; not from the short, breaking, combing sea, which, from being on soundings and in shallow water, made it but a plaything in the heavy gust, and rendered it trebly unpleasant, breaking upon and against the ship, keeping her continually wet and uncomfortable; but this too was a matter of course to me — I had had my jacket wet a hundred, ay, a thousand times, with the salted spray of old ocean; nor was it from a sense of danger from any or all of these combinations; but the wind gradually, yet steadily, hauling to the northward, occasioned a dead weight; its remaining in its present quarter, west-north-west, being our only hope of getting in; and to be lying here within a few miles, almost in sight, of home, without power to pursue our voyage thither, was a probation by no means gratifying. I strove to shake off the feeling, calling to my aid all the resources of manhood; but in vain. I then attempted to gain some consolation from the old gray-headed seaman, who had for years followed the coast in all its windings from Newfoundland to Florida; but he, like me, was under the thrall of the same vague and undefinable depression, and instead of administering consolation, went off into a narration of how, time after time, he had made the same light with a southerly wind, hove the ship to through the night, anticipating a run in during the next morning, but at dawn the wind came out at north-east with hail and snow, and for weeks nothing could be done but to lay to and sweat it out. This was adding gall to wormwood, and the old fellow, perceiving my lugubriousness, slapped me on the back, and said, "Cheer up, my hearty! we have weathered many a gale together, and, please God, we will make port to-morrow, when we can laugh at our forebodings of to-night." In this state of mental inquietude, at 11 o'clock at night I went below, and with a prayer that the wind should favor us at dawn, I threw myself in my berth, hoping to rid myself of the solicitude in sleep, but fruitlessly; it was a mere repetition of the afternoon's performance. I rolled, tumbled, and almost worried myself into a fever; several times I caught a moment's nap, only to be visited by visions in which the voices of home were calling me, and the outstretched arms of loved ones, prompted by affection, were extended towards me to welcome the wanderer home. But in vain did I struggle to reach them, some invisible agency held me back despite my frantic efforts, and with the sweat profusely dropping from my reeking brow, parched tongue and straining eyeballs, I would awake to find it but a dream.

Thus passed the weary hours until 3 o'clock, when on the calling of the watch I turned out, and took the helm. My attention, of course, was directed first to the wind. My forebodings were too truly realized. There it was, from the northwest; and, with gloomy resolution, I resigned myself to the decree. Our officer of the deck, scarcely a whit behind me, came to the binnacle for the same purpose. From his anxious and careworn face I could see that he had experienced no refreshment in sleep. Sympathizing with him, I forebore remark; but, after satisfying himself, he turned to me, with a countenance on every line of which was written mental torture, and in a tone that expressed his feelings, he said, "There depart all our bright anticipations — God help me to bear the disappointment!" — and then proceeded moodily to walk the quarter-deck. Again he came, and related to me that on two former occasions, in this same delectable month of March, he had been served in precisely the same way, and wound up by saying, "I shall worry no more! I am now satisfied that we will not get in before the first of April; and so we may as well grin and bear it"

Unable to control my own thoughts, I perforce allowed them to run fancy free, and whilst so engaged paid but little attention to the compass: intuitively easing the helm when the vessel pitched from the surging of the waves so as to endanger the spars, and occasionally when warned by the flapping of the sails raising the wheel to keep her off from the wind a trifle; until at length an unusually heavy sea, breaking over the ship and drenching the decks, awoke me from my reverie.

Day had now began to dawn, and casually I glanced at the compass. Could I be assured that the direction in which the magnetic needle pointed was correct, or was it a mere phantasy of my overwrought brain! I rubbed my eyes, and looked again. Could it be possible, or was I in a lethargy, deceiving myself into a belief in the reality of a wished-for fact! I shook myself, and stamped my feet, now grown cold from inaction. Satisfied at length that I was in the perfect possession of all my faculties, I ventured to glance again at the needle, and then I received the fullest evidence that I was not deceived. I called the second mate to me. He at first could scarce credit it—but, there it was! The wind had hauled two points, and now was west-north-west, and we had a prospect of delivery from all our somber soliloquies. Hurrah! The captain was now called (he having gone below for sleep— the two preceding nights he had been upon deck until utterly worn out). He came up skeptical, but was soon a convert. "We cannot show much sail," said he, "but we will venture a little more. Shake a reef out of each topsail. Loose the foresail." (I had now been relieved from the wheel.) Still she did not go fast enough. "Loosen the jib and spanker." No sooner said, than done. I sprang upon the bowsprit and out upon the jib-boom, skinning my hands fearfully, and receiving a severe blow upon the head from the jibsheet-block; both, at any other time, sufficient to make me groan with pain; but now they passed almost unnoticed. Without faltering, I cast the gasket off. The jib was foul. I had to lay out, and to overhaul the hoops. It was done. The jib gradually rose to its proper position. The sheet was then hauled aft by the strength of the entire crew; but still it was not sufficient. A powerful tackle was now attached to it, and with the aid of numerous arms (the captain, cook, and every one else assisting) it was brought flat enough, and thus secured. Arriving on deck, the clotted blood called my attention to my lacerated hands; but it was no time to complain. Half-a-dozen were so wounded. Our skins being dry, parched, and benumbed, the least contact with any hard material produced an abrasion; which, however, no one noticed: for the spanker was to be set, more reefs shaken out, and the staysails loosened.

And, hurrah again! there came the pilot-boat. Now was the time: we could not lose a minute. "Loosen topgallant-sails and royals!" (We dared not set them; but should the wind have moderated, we would have lost no time in casting off gaskets.) A few minutes more, and the pilot-boat was alongside. "Is there a New-Bedford pilot in the boat?" was our hail. "Aye, aye!" came booming across the water. "Send down a boat, with a barrel of pork and a tub of tow-line, and he will board you." This was soon effected. The pilot entered the boat, now half full of water; but her crew knew how to manage her. He was soon aboard the ship, and without further delay took the command of her.

Captain Sherman's vocation has gone — his responsibility is over: the ship is now in American waters, with an American pilot aboard, who gives his orders to the ever-willing crew. He is obeyed with alacrity, as long as he makes sail; but no one wants to take any in — neither does he. He is a perfectly competent man, and fortunately a driver. "Where are your studding-sails? Pack them on whilst we have a chance. Never mind a few yards of canvass, or a whole sail. Give them to her. Let her have all she can spread: the wind may not hold half an hour."

There she goes! — now she is moving! Block Island is passed. There, off the beam, frowns Point Judith. Now for Cuttyhunk light. "Go along, old ship! — cleave the waters, as never you did before. Soon you, as well as we, will be at rest."

Nobly did the old barque answer our appeal. She appeared endowed with life — and, on she goes! The Cuttyhunk light is passed; Clarke's Point opens to our view, and some of the crew, who reside in the rural districts, see familiar landmarks. "There I live," you hear from one. "There is the church-steeple — there, the sawmill — there, the almshouse."

"Hurrah!" — now we near the city. There are new buildings, erected since we left here. There is a new lighthouse. There is Fair Haven. There is the shipping at the docks. And now we are closing-in with Clarke's Point. The wind is hauling — well, who cares — who cares now? We are perfectly independent of the clerk of the weather. But we can go only a few ship's lengths farther: that is near enough — we are only three miles from New Bedford.

"Now, then, round in on your weather-braces. Start away tacks and sheets. Clew up everything. Haul down your jibs and staysails. Start away your halyards, and let your yards come down by the run. Let the spanker remain till she comes to the wind. Hard down the helm. Square the main yard. Brail up the spanker — one minute more. Let go the anchor." The heavy cable runs out unimpeded, and once more we have a firm hold on American bottom!

Our next duty is to furl the sails, and then our engagement is ended: then we are free to do as we please; then we are released from all discipline, except that enjoined by self-respect; then we once more become members of society; then we will discard the blue shirt of the sailor, and in the midst of long anticipated comforts forget our manifold hardships and dangers; then we will take the preliminary steps toward meeting friends and relatives, and in the joy of the moment we are repaid for much that we have undergone of toil and exposure.

Our job aloft was an arduous one, having carried such a press of sail up the bay and river, and then when a ship is at anchor she always swings head to wind — consequently her sails are pressed aft by the breeze, and it is only by considerable tugging and straining that they are drawn up to the yard. However, this, like many other unpleasant duties, could not last for ever. By dint of hauling and tugging, we accomplished it, and descended to the deck, with the gratifying consciousness that we should have no more of it to do for this voyage at least, whatever the future may have in store for us.

Whilst aloft on the maintopsail yard, from which I had a good view of the bay and the ocean beyond, I asked myself whether I should be content ashore, or whether it was decreed that I should form one of that great body of uneasy spirits who gain their livelihood by toil upon the ocean. All my chequered life for the previous four years passed in array before me, with its ills and its pleasantries; and, although the former overbalanced the latter, I could not, without a sigh of regret, bid farewell to old ocean.

On getting on deck, all hands were busily employed packing and securing chests, donning their best suits, and making all necessary preparations for leaving the ship. This leaving the ship was by no means a pleasant operation. Her sturdy sides had so long afforded us protection from the storm and wave, that she was endeared to us by a thousand ties. Every spar and rope in her were as familiar to us as household words, and each object begat some pleasant reminiscence; but we were too busy reflecting on dearer objects to allow the old barque's memory to make us sad — so we continued our preparations in silence, scarce a word being spoken, each heart being too full for utterance.

Fifteen minutes after a boat came alongside, which is technically known as the shark's boat. In it were the proprietors and agents of all the outfitting firms of the city, black and white, Portuguese, Germans, Irish, French, &c., each intent on getting a customer from amongst our vessel's crew. They jumped aboard, and endeavored by passing the bottle around (with which they always go provided, knowing that the sailor is much more easily gulled when half seas over), to get as many to go with them to their places of business as possible; at the same time they readily give their aid in packing and lashing their customer's chests, assiduously waiting upon him, and not allowing him to get out of their sight for a moment — fearful of losing him. After some little chaffering our chests and selves were all aboard the boat and were rapidly approaching the city. A large concourse of spectators had assembled on the wharves, comprising the runners of all the most miserable and nefarious houses of the town. The captain of the boat, anxious to disappoint them, ran to another wharf, to which these harpies speedily conveyed themselves. As soon as we had landed, each man went with his outfitter, or rather infitter, in order to be thoroughly renovated in appearance and pocket. Although we landed on Sunday, we had no difficulty in obtaining clothing, these outfitters being provided for all such contingencies. After enjoying a thorough wash, and getting into an entire suit of long togs, or landsmen's wearing garments, but little was left of the semblance of sailors to us, except the rolling gait and embrowned countenances. Our next trip was to the barber's, where all superfluous hair was removed from heads and faces, and a thorough scrubbing operation gone through with; which, on viewing ourselves in the glass, gave us a pretty good opinion of our personal qualifications, and we started for a walk. The first things, of course, that attracted our attention, were the hoops in female dresses; we had heard marvellous stories of the rotundity of a fashionably dressed lady, but had never seen one. One of my informants having told me six months before, whilst we were cruising off the Island of Madagascar, that it was not unusual for a lady to wear hoops thirty feet in circumference. In the occupation of mind attendant upon getting ashore, I had totally forgotten the existence of hoops, but was astonished at the corpulence of every woman I met, and I thought, no, I won't tell you what I thought; but you must imagine yourself in the same position, and then what would you think? As yet I had not passed close to a lady with hoops, but in turning the corner of a street I came in contact with one, and in my endeavors to escape from my embarrassing position, I made no allowance for the rolling motion acquired aboard ship, and only made matters worse. In a few minutes, however, I managed to get clear, though not without getting into the lady's arms, or she in mine, I do not now remember which; during said contact I was convinced that the large size of the ladies was a work of art and not of nature. This called my wandering memory back to the descriptions of hoops that I had heard, and henceforth the solution of the mystery was easy.

Having made such a poor attempt on my first promenade, I returned to the house, situated on Union Street (I preferred a private house to a hotel), where also were several other of my shipmates; and in talking of old times we whiled away the hours, nor thought them irksome. When evening came and we sat down to supper at the well-spread board, enlivened by the genial and handsome face of our worthy landlady, we began to realize what comforts and pleasures we had been deprived of by our three years' jaunt; instead of sitting down on a rude chest, with tin pan and pot before one, and a sheath-knife to carve out the salt junk that formed the greater part of our repast, here were the various viands arranged in a clean and neat manner, inviting the hungry and the gourmand to partake of them. After supper we smoked our cigars, and, tired with the exercise of the day, retired early, and enjoyed a night of refreshing slumber, uninterrupted by the hoarse cry of "Starbowlines, ahoy!" "Eight Bells!" or the still less welcome one of "All hands turn out and take in sail." Then, again, each was comfortably ensconced between clean sheets, on feather beds, totally distinctive in all their relations from our own straw mattrasses, packed down by three years use, and well-worn, dusky-looking blankets. All was comfort, and we appreciated it as only men can who for years have been deprived of the many little et ceteras that make life bearable.

The succeeding morning I proceeded to the telegraph office and telegraphed home, receiving an answer that satisfied my fullest longings. All my immediate family were alive and well; but such was not the case with some of my less fortunate shipmates — several had lost fathers, one a mother, others a sister or brother; in fact, there were few but had to weep for a near and dear one gone, whom in the fullness of their wishes they had hoped would have been the first to welcome them home.

My shipmates, I said before, looked different from what they did aboard ship; but some of them were exceptions to this rule. Several had nothing coming to them, and could get neither clothing nor money; pretty hard, was it not, after over three years hard work at sea for one employer, to land without the wherewithal to purchase a meal's victuals.

There is a dark side to the whaling service, and I shall endeavor to place it before the community in its true character, and I hope that it may discourage those young men from embarking in it who think that money can be saved on a whaling voyage, because there is so little opportunity to spend it.

In the first place, when a green hand engages to perform a voyage, he knows nothing at all about what clothing he requires. The shark, perhaps, tells him that the ship, being bound to the Indian Ocean, there is no necessity for him providing woolen clothing, and palms off upon him an assortment of blue dungaree raiment, precisely like the summer suits of the population our city supports at the Blockley almshouse. One of these suits will last him about a week; but as he gets into high southern latitudes he finds that he requires woolen clothing, and goes to the slop-chest, imagining that he can get what he wants at a reasonable price. If he inquires how much such an article is valued at, the captain will tell him that he does not know; but, nevertheless, he must have the clothes, and therefore takes them, and thus his account goes on increasing during the voyage. Just before the ship returns home, his bill is handed to him by the captain, and what is his dismay to discover that he is indebted to the owners of the slop-chest, one hundred dollars, or more, independent of the outfitter's bill. He finds a woolen shirt is charged to him at the extortionate price of three dollars and a half; pumps, worth fifty cents a pair, at a dollar and a half; the commonest kind of rawhide boots, five dollars a pair; a frieze jacket, seven dollars; thread, six cents a skein; and suspenders, such as could be bought anywhere else for five cents a pair, aboard ship are sold for half a dollar. These prices are not exaggerated, I copy them from my ship's bill.

Beside these extortions an additional twenty-five per cent is charged on all money advanced in foreign ports by the captain to the crew; six per cent. interest per annum is our legal rate, and I for one should not grumble at paying for cash advanced at that rate; but some of our money we only received seven months previous to our arrival home, and I cannot but think that a charge of twenty-five per cent. for the use of money a trifle over six months, is exorbitant and dishonest. Still there are Shylocks in the world who would absorb the last dollar of earnings from the sailor, after years of exposure to wind and weather have rightfully earned for him his scanty wages.

I have not yet finished with the specifications of these overcharges. The ship is not at home yet, and we only know what the bill aboard ship amounts to; the recipient of it, although he is astounded at its amount, adds it and the amount of his outfitter's bill together, and consoles himself with the thought that he has forty or fifty dollars still due him; and thus persuaded, on the arrival of the ship he goes ashore, confident of being able to pay his board for a week or two, and have enough remaining to secure him a passage home, he goes up to the owners and asks for a small sum of money for present wants. They refuse him, saying that nothing is coming to him. He demands a settlement. On obtaining it, in the first place he finds that twenty-five per cent. interest has been charged on his outfitting bill, next he finds a charge varying from ten to fifteen dollars for loading and discharging the ship. In many cases, three per cent. for insurance is packed on, and with these additional items the poor fellow is brought in debt and knows not what to do. Then the agent claps him on the shoulder and tells him to cheer up, as another ship will be ready to sail in a few days, and, if he will sign his name upon her articles, money and clothing will be advanced to him. Destitute and hopeless, down goes his name, and a few weeks afterward he is at sea again, bound on another three or four years' voyage.

The average number of barrels of oil taken by sperm whalers, during a four years' voyage, is twelve hundred; if the ship carries four boats, a green hand's lay is the two hundredth part; this will give him six barrels of oil, worth about forty-five dollars a barrel, amounting to two hundred and seventy dollars. The ship's and outfitter's bills will amount to at least two hundred and twenty dollars, leaving a residue of fifty dollars or about a dollar a month over and above personal expenses.

Even if the ship should get full of oil and return home in two years, which, by the way, would be a miracle now-a-days, one of her crew cannot, at the most, make more than half as much as the day-laborer ashore.

These are facts, and are palpable enough to deter any and all who wish to go whaling for the purpose of making or saving money; but there is another class who think whaling must be the most delightful of all pursuits from its pleasant adventures, its perils, and the facilities offered by it for seeing foreign lands. This is all extremely visionary, as any one who has ever made such a voyage will tell you. All its adventures, and all its perils are matter of fact, stern realities; for instance, you lower away in the boat, get alongside of a whale, the boat is stoven and you are obliged to remain in the water for an hour or two, until you are almost frozen; or if you are in warm latitudes, with the pleasant reflection that at any minute a shark may come along and snap off one of your limbs, how much pleasure would such an adventure yield you? It would do to tell after you got home, to be sure; and whilst you are telling it, ten chances to one, you will be more fully reminded of it by a twinge of rheumatism, the sowing of the seeds of which dates back to the very day of your adventure. No; there is no fun in going on a whaling voyage; nobody goes a second time but those who are compelled to; they see no adventure in it—it is the mere perilling of life and limb to fill ship owners' coffers.

Then, again, if you go for adventure's sake, it does not exempt you from other and more disagreeable duties that your sense of manliness will revolt at. Go and look at the scavengers at work in the streets of your native city, and ask yourself how you would like to participate in their employment. But there is no such work aboard ship, some one says. I know better; and so does any other sailor who ever was in a ship where pigs were kept, or where the captain had a dog. Yes! he knows it, for he has had a thorough acquaintance with such duty; and so will any one else who is foolish enough to go to sea before the mast, as a green hand.

Now I think I have presented the subject in its true light, and I will conclude by advising all young men who can gain a livelihood ashore, to stay at home. I have been through the mill, and am satisfied to remain; and in reviewing my whole stock of sea adventures and incidents, I must say the most pleasant of all is getting home safe, with a chest full of curiosities, displaying them to appreciating friends, and spinning yarns descriptive of them. Trusting that all my readers may arrive as safe at their journey's end, whether in a voyage to sea or in the voyage of life, I will bid them adieu; also hoping that, in the perusal of this book, they have whiled away their hours pleasantly, and gleaned some little information concerning the whale and his pursuers.

THE END.

www.ingramcontent.com/pod-product-compliance
Lightning Source LLC
Chambersburg PA
CBHW022114290426
44112CB00008B/668